CIVIL SERVICE IN EARLY SUNG CHINA━━━━960-1067

with particular emphasis on the development of

controlled sponsorship to foster administrative

responsibility ━━━━━━━━━━━━━━━━━━━━━━━

E. A. KRACKE, JR.

University of Chicago

HARVARD UNIVERSITY PRESS
Cambridge, Massachusetts

Distributed in Great Britain by
Oxford University Press
London

Library of Congress Catalog Card Number 52–5399
Printed in the United States of America

To my Father and Mother
with loving appreciation

PREFACE

A translator of Cicero's *De Officiis* in 1699 introduced his work by observing

TIS hard, me thinks, that a Man cannot Publish a Book, but he must presently give the World a Reason for't; when yet there's not One Book of Twenty that will bear a Reason; not One Man of a Hundred, perhaps, that is able to Give One; nor One Reason of a Thousand (when they are given) that was the True Reason of Doing it. The True Reason (I say) For there's a great Difference, many times, betwixt a Good Reason, for the doing of a thing, and the True Reason why the thing was done. The Service of God is a very Good Reason for a Man's going to Church; and yet the meeting of a Mistress There, may, perchance, be the True Reason of his Going.

The distinction retains its validity, however difficult it may be to apply. In the present instance, the true reason that first led me to delve in Sung official documents, and urged the writing of this book to completion was, I think, the hope of gaining and communicating an insight into the activity of minds distant from ours in time and tradition, yet sometimes curiously modern in their outlook and in the problems they faced. Sung statesmen were the intellectual elite of a great civilization; in dealing with the problems of civil service they were facing questions superlatively vital to them; the solutions they reached inspired European thinkers, after many generations, when in the eighteenth-century the Occident confronted similar problems.

There are several *good* reasons for undertaking a study of the early Sung civil service, and for presenting the results in this book, that are at least equally pertinent. To those interested in the history of government, on the one hand, China has a special interest as an early and outstanding example of the managerial state in practice; some of China's contributions to civil service techniques have already attracted attention. For those who would analyze China's political tradition, past or present, on the other hand, an understanding of the Chinese civil service system, the key feature of the Chinese state, is essential. The civil service can be studied to special advantage in the first century of the Sung, during which it maintained unusual freedom from interference by the irresponsible usurpers of power that have so often brought ruin to other dynasties. Enjoying high prestige in a time of Confucian revival, the bureaucratic system reached substantial maturity and achieved a stability that rendered the Sung uniquely long-lived among the major Chinese dynasties.

The system of controlled sponsorship, to which the greater part of this book is devoted, was a principal feature of Sung civil service administration, and played an important role in earlier and later periods also. Its use in China has apparently remained unique among world political institutions. Yet no occidental writer on Chinese institutions has, so far as I can discover, ever devoted more than a page or so to it, or even that much except in reference to the Manchu dynasty. Even in China historians seem never to have undertaken a serious study of the system in any period, although Dr. HU Shih some years ago drew attention to its potentialities for application to contemporary Chinese administration.

I have ended this study at the enthronement of the sixth emperor, Shen-tsung, in 1067. That year in many ways marks a turning point in Sung history. The time of greatest prosperity was past, and national difficulties were already mounting in intensity. Two years later WANG An-shih was to win a dominant position in the government and introduce sweeping policy changes, which inaugurated the period of more acrid party strife. As one aspect of the new policy, WANG's followers carried through a governmental reorganization that entailed a thoroughgoing revision of governmental forms and terminology, though most of the basic institutions were in reality preserved. The sponsorship system, its evolution now largely complete, was to pass through some years of disfavor. The first five reigns, therefore, form in the history of Sung institutions a period clearly separated from the reigns that succeeded them.

The institutions of the early Sung invite study not only because of their historic interest, but also through the richness of the source materials that remain. We owe this good fortune partly to the widespread use of printing that began in the tenth century, partly to the literary fecundity of Sung politicians, and partly to the intensified activities and historical tastes of official and private compilers. Apart from the encyclopedias, historical memoranda, and collected papers of officials, which first abound in the Sung, the canonical history of the Sung is more than three times the size of the T'ang history, and the surviving collection of selected Sung documents has more than eight times as much material as the analogous T'ang work, for a similar span of years.

The abundance of sources for the study of Sung institutions is an embarrassment as well as a boon. Even apart from sponsorship, only a few limited aspects of the civil service system have received careful and thorough study by Chinese or foreign students, and it is necessary for the most part to turn directly and unguided to the sources, an experience made less agreeable by the serious deficiencies of the canonical *Sung History*.

A general survey of the Sung civil service organization and practices even as limited as that given in chapters three to five of this book would have been impossible without the aid of the several studies that do illuminate parts of the field. These are listed in the bibliography, but it is appropriate to stress here my special indebtedness to three scholars whose guidance has been particularly invaluable.

The monumental translations of Professor Robert DES ROTOURS have helped constantly in the understanding of Sung offices and practices by showing the T'ang predecessors from which they evolved. The admirable studies of Professor NIEH Ch'ung-ch'i have illuminated problems of administrative geography, the decree examinations, and the system of local public services. Professor CH'ÜAN Han-sheng's brilliant work has revealed many of the economic factors intimately connected with civil service administration. For most of the matters treated in these three chapters, however, it has been necessary to rely on the primary sources. While I have made every effort to confine my statements to safe ground, this necessary caution has obliged me to skirt or omit altogether many topics of interest and importance. I should have preferred to avoid treating even thus briefly aspects of Sung government and civil service that require so much fuller exploration than I have yet undertaken, but I have felt an obligation to furnish the reader with at least a preliminary outline, to help in understanding the subjects discussed in the latter chapters of the book, and to open the way for other students who may probe more deeply into some of the questions here raised.

The chapters on sponsorship are based primarily on the collection of materials on that subject in the *Selected Documents of the Sung* (*SHY:*HC,27 and 28), the most comprehensive and complete extant source. In interpreting the texts to be found in this source, I have compared them whenever possible with variant versions preserved in other sources. The accounts to be found in MA Tuan-lin (*TK*) and the canonical *Sung History* (*SS*) have been fully checked, and helped to fill certain lacunae in the *Selected Documents*. The scattered references to sponsorship in other Sung sources—annals (particularly *HCP*), historical memoranda, collected papers of individual authors, encyclopedias—have furnished a great deal of additional information, but the physical bulk of these sources and the methods of their arrangement have made it impossible to explore them exhaustively in the time at my disposal. Future researches will no doubt help to clarify uncertainties and amplify or modify at many points the interpretations here offered. They may in particular illuminate with further instances the operation of the system in individual cases. But I believe that the materials here utilized contain with little doubt by far the greater part of the extant evidence, and enable us with some confidence to reconstruct the picture of controlled sponsorship in its major outlines.

In choosing translations for Chinese official titles and other terminology, I have tried as far as possible to satisfy the requirements of several sometimes conflicting criteria. The primary consideration has been to suggest the actual function of an official, office, operation, or expression. At the same time, I have tried to preserve distinctions made in Chinese between terms similar in meaning. When it was not for some reason inexpedient, translations already in use for the Sung or other periods have been followed. Finally, I have tried to give a literal rendering of the Chinese terms whenever it could be done without violating the other criteria. Passages quoted from Chinese sources are given in my own translation, which may differ in some degree from renderings by others to which reference is made in the notes. The need to make clear certain particular points conveyed by the Chinese text has also led once or twice to slightly differing translations of the same passage at different places in the book. The pronunciations of Chinese words are given in the Giles-Wade system, as slightly modified in the usage of the Harvard-Yenching Index Series. Thus *yi* and *yüeh* are used rather than *i* and *yo*.

In the rendering of Chinese dates, the years are numbered according to the years of the European calendar to which they roughly correspond, but the months and days are given according to the Chinese calendar. Because of this, an event placed in a given year may sometimes actually fall, by the European calendar, in the year following. Thus the proclamation dated 998, 12th month, 23rd day would have appeared, by European counting, on 13 January 999.

To assist in identifying the relative rank indicated by a Chinese titular office, titles are in certain cases accompanied by Roman capital letters, which refer to the groups of titles so designated in Appendix B.

It will be noted that in referring to the more important documents cited as sources for the Sung sponsorship system, each document is indicated by a text number, corresponding to its place in the list of texts following Chapter XII. Exact page references for the Chinese sources are to be found in that list.

For any merit this book may possess, I must thank first of all the many friends whose ideas I have unconsciously pillaged, as well as the smaller number to whom my debt is a conscious one. That this book could be written at all I owe in the first instance to the unwearying generosity of Professor NIEH Ch'ung-ch'i, who during many hours and weeks in Peiping, with no consideration other than the wish to aid a fellow student, opened to me unstintingly his knowledge of and insight into Sung institutions at an early stage of my research, more than a dozen years ago, and made it possible to surmount in a year barriers that but for his guidance might not have been passed without a decade of laborious groping.

From the time when research on this subject was first undertaken, I have on various occasions had the good fortune of discussing problems relating to its content and presentation with interested scholars, who have afforded help and advice. Among those who have rendered such kindnesses are the late Professor Henri MASPERO, Professors Serge ELISSÉEFF, F. W. CLEAVES, J. K. FAIRBANK, J. R. HIGHTOWER, YANG Lien-sheng, Dr. C. S. GARDNER, Dr. CH'IU K'ai-ming, Dr. K. A. WITTFOGEL, Mr. TSIEN Tsuen-hsuin, Professors Derk Bodde, E. H. Pritchard, Teng Ssu-yü, William Hung, Dr. Hu Shih, Professor Robert des Rotours, Dr. Étienne Balázs, Professor L. C. Goodrich, and Professor Ch'üan Han-sheng. For their aid I am most grateful. My debt is especially great to Professor H. G. Creel, who has read the entire manuscript, offered many thoughtful criticisms, and come to my succor in manifold ways throughout the long process of writing and revision. Mrs. H. G. Creel, Dr. C. O. Hucker, and my sister, Virginia Kracke, have kindly read much of the manuscript and given many helpful suggestions. Professor E. O. Reischauer has at different times aided me invaluably in connection with problems both of preparing the manuscript and of publication. To Miss June Work I am indebted for a helping hand in many things, but especially in the preparation of the index.

The publication of this study in its present format has been made possible by the generous assistance of the Harvard-Yenching Institute. The technical advice and interested coöperation given by the Harvard University Press have contributed much both to hasten the publication of the volume and to enhance its usability.

Finally, my wife has devoted to this book long hours in ways that I cannot begin to recount, and without which it could not have been completed.

The faults and shortcomings of the book, I need scarcely add, are mine alone.

E. A. Kracke, Jr.

University of Chicago,
11 March 1952

Note to the Second Printing

No extensive changes have been made in the second printing. Knowledge of Sung institutions has progressed substantially during the past sixteen years, offering a temptation to expand the text or to recast its expressions in a number of places. Such additions would make a new book, and the temptation has been resisted. I have, however, made several changes where errors of fact or typography have been discovered and call for correction.

E. A. K.

20 January 1968

CONTENTS

ment through protection; miscellaneous methods of recruitment; recommendation; local examination; as a reward for services or contributions.

TABLES

CIVIL SERVICE IN EARLY SUNG CHINA

I

ADMINISTRATIVE RESPONSIBILITY IN THE CONFUCIAN STATE

As ancient Greece and mediaeval England created many of the most vital traditions of representative government, so Confucian China evolved much that has entered the common heritage of personnel administration in the modern state. China early developed techniques to promote the recruitment and advancement of governmental employees on the basis of ability, and to minimize the role of political patronage. It pioneered also in applying techniques to maintain honesty, discipline, and initiative—in other words administrative responsibility—among government personnel. This book is a study of such techniques at the time when they first attained substantially their modern form; and coincidentally at a time when Chinese civilization as a whole was assuming the outlines that were to remain generally characteristic until the nineteenth century.

The manner of treating this subject has been motivated particularly by a wish to understand better the objectives guiding Chinese personnel policy at this formative time, and their relation to the methods then devised. The broader outlines of the problem are sketched in the earlier chapters of the book. As the sources for this subject are rather voluminous, and since only a few aspects of it have as yet received the detailed study they require, it has seemed desirable to select for closer observation a more limited segment of the problem, which may in some degree help to exemplify and illuminate the whole. The segment selected for this purpose is the policy of promotion through controlled sponsorship.[1] Several considerations recommended the choice: the special importance this technique assumed in the civil service at the time, its apparent pe-

[1] *Pao jen* 保任.

culiarity to China, and the fact that it has received very little consideration in previous studies of Chinese political institutions. In its simplest essentials, this technique consisted in granting special promotions within the service on the recommendation of a superior officer, who thereafter was legally answerable for the quality and the acts of his protégé. Systematized and elaborated, the technique was found suitable for use on a large scale to meet widely varied situations and became a regular practice in Chinese personnel administration.

The conditions which prompted early Chinese experimentation in civil service methods are more easily appreciated when we compare them with similar motivating influences in Europe. There the development of considered, impersonal, and standardized procedures for handling an administrative staff seems to have come relatively late. Even imperial Rome, with its vast territories and its preoccupation with administrative methods, seems to have recruited and promoted officials largely on the basis of custom and the personal judgment of superiors.[2] The emerging royal bureaucracies of later mediaeval Europe were recruited largely through nominations by a few officers, who exercised such nomination as a hereditary prerogative, or through purchase, or through the favor of the king's ministers.[3] Only in the increasingly centralized states of the sixteenth century and later do we find the beginning of a more methodical personnel administration. As the rivalry between states became more intense, the rulers realized the vital need to ensure greater responsibility in their administrative staff.[4] The expanding personnel and growing functional specialization made supervision more difficult. Since even the most energetic autocrat had in some degree to see through the eyes of the lower bureaucracy, it was essential that every official place his imagination, initiative, and energy at the disposal of the state, and make its interests his own. He had to be honest. He had to be mentally able and professionally qualified. Only a planned policy and practice of personnel administration could hope to gain these ends.

New methods appeared which would meet the need. Ordinances of 1498 and 1561 seem to have required some kind of professional ex-

---

[2] Cf. MATTINGLY, *ICSR*, esp. pp. 49, 54–55, 64, 66, 71–72, 85–86, 96–97, 119.

[3] Cf. TOUT, *ECS*, pp. 12–16; FRIEDRICH, *CGD*, pp. 38–39.

[4] Cf. FRIEDRICH, *CGD*, 40–42.

amination in the selection of councilors of French Parlements.[5] Alert rulers soon provided other means to increase the efficiency of their administrative personnel—the more careful definition of jurisdictions and procedures, more detailed recording of official decisions and transactions of every kind, and provision for the untrammeled expression of opinion by the individual public servant.[6] By the eighteenth century, impelled by the growth of the larger states and the continued expansion of governmental responsibilities, the evolution of bureaucratic tendencies had progressed far.[7] The new techniques may have owed much to the example of previous Chinese experimentation, although the exact degree of indebtedness has not yet been fully explored.[8]

When we turn to China, we find that the need for better methods of personnel administration had become clear some centuries earlier than in the West. The prompting impulses came partly from the nature of the Chinese state, and partly from the physical obstacles faced by the Chinese administrator. They owed much directly to principles formulated by Confucius. By the seventh century of our era, the competition of rival dynasties, the pressure of necessity, and a millennium of persistent persuasion by political thinkers, chiefly Confucian, had nearly completed the patterns of the Confucian state. The Emperor, theoretically a semiabsolute monarch, in practice usually restricted his actions to arbitration between the frequently dissenting factions of the administrative hierarchy. The enforcement of consistent policies, once determined, presented a major problem. Administrative officials often opposed and obstructed the prevailing policy. When strict control was relaxed, the Chinese

[5] Cf. ANTY, *Concours*, p. 12.

[6] Cf. FRIEDRICH, *CGD, loc. cit.*

[7] In this development Prussia seems to have occupied a leading place. Cf. FINER, *Theory and Practice*, especially pp. 731–734; DORN, Prussian Bureaucracy.

[8] The direct influence of Chinese example on the development of British civil service examinations in the nineteenth century, via the Indian Civil Service, has been clearly shown. Cf. TENG, Chinese Influence; CHANG, Reform. A study of possible Chinese influences on the eighteenth-century Prussian system might also yield interesting results. The introduction of the ever-normal-granary idea by Frederick William I early in the eighteenth century suggests the influence of Chinese ideas possibly derived through Leibnitz, and the accompanying development of civil service procedures strengthens the suggestion. The measures are described in *Civil Service Abroad*, pp. 171–173. We may look forward to more light on this subject as a result of the current research of Professor Donald F. LACH.

officialdom was no freer than others from tendencies toward self-seeking, graft, and nepotism.

Geographic factors added to the problem. As early as the second century B.C., the central bureaucracy governed an area comparable in size to the Roman Empire, intersected by formidable mountain barriers, and lacking convenient sea communications such as those the Mediterranean afforded. The control and maintenance of the system of rivers and canals, which in part took the place of Roman seas and roads, constituted in itself an administrative problem. The Han rulers of the second century B.C. had only with difficulty suppressed a centrifugal feudalism, and for some centuries any slackening of the central control brought either the threat of a feudal revival or the establishment of autonomous regimes by local military leaders.[9] While Rome was declining in the West, and rival empires rose from its parts, China also split into separate and competing dominions.

The way to disunion had been prepared by administrative corruption in the later Han; administrative reform was to prepare the way for reunification. Useful precedents were at hand. The development of fixed civil service procedures had already made rapid strides under the early Han. The Confucian dictum that office should go to men of proven merit and ability was to some extent incorporated in these procedures. They provided for some use of written examinations, regular merit ratings and a schedule of salaries varying with official ranks.[10] The task of improving the bureaucracy was undertaken once more by the partly foreign but rapidly Sinicized rulers of North China, and it paid them well. While Charlemagne was later to attempt the reunion of Europe in vain, the Sui Emperor Yang Chien in 589 successfully reëstablished, and his T'ang successors preserved, a single Chinese state which (except for times of foreign domination and a brief interval of schism) was to unite

[9] Interesting examples of the tendency toward feudal revival after the Han are described by YANG, Chin Economy, pp. 115–117.

[10] Examinations for the men recommended have their beginnings at least as early as 165 B.C., when the Emperor Hsiao-wên set questions for written answer by the men recommended for office. (Cf. DUBS, History, vol. I, p. 259.) By the reign of Hsiao-wu (141–87 B.C.) this had become a regular practice, and the candidates were ranked in sequence according to the merit of their answers. (Cf. Shih Chi, III, 555.) For schedule of salaries, see HHHY, ch. 37. For merit ratings, see DUBS, History, vol. II, p. 317.

the Chinese nation until modern times.[11] China's ability to overcome her centrifugal tendencies more successfully than post-Roman
Europe is partly explainable by her isolation, her cultural homogeneity, and perhaps the economic advantages of large-scale irrigation planning. But it certainly owed much to the development of
a more systematized personnel administration, which was comparatively effective in maintaining the responsibility of the individual administrator to the interests of the state.

The lesson was remembered by succeeding T'ang rulers, and the
development of personnel techniques continued. Within a century
after the reunification of 589, the system of competitive civil service examinations—foreshadowed in limited practice some centuries
before—had begun to assume the important role which it was to
play, with minor interruptions, throughout the remaining centuries
of the Chinese Empire. The Censorate, which also grew from earlier
institutions, was developed as an organ to detect and protect against
administrative misconduct. At the same time there were formulated
systematic methods of promotion on the basis of elaborated merit
ratings and written examinations, which also were to remain as
permanent features of the Chinese civil service administration.[12]
We must not assume, of course, that the merit system at this time or
later achieved the complete exclusion of patronage. The impressive
fact is that Chinese statesmen seriously attempted to set up a real
merit system, and their efforts attained, at times for extended
periods, a large measure of success.

Sweeping economic and social changes were to occur, however,
before China emerged as the mature society which flourished until
the beginning of the twentieth century. Those changes had already
begun in the seventh century, and much of their impact was felt
before the Sung house came to the throne in 960.[13] During the century that followed, the political and administrative organization
inherited from the T'ang was forced to cope with problems far more
complex than those it had been designed to meet. The system, on the

[11] On the precarious unification achieved by the Sui rulers see BINGHAM, *Founding*.

[12] The expansion of the examination system in the later seventh century seems
paradoxically to have owed much to the efforts of the Empress Wu, who sought in
this way to build up a following and overthrow the T'ang house. Cf. *TTCCSS*, pp.
10–15. For details on the T'ang government structure and system of civil service recruitment and promotion, see ROTOURS, *Fonctionnaires* and *Examens*.

[13] For the economic revolution of the later T'ang period, see BALÁZS, Beiträge.

whole, stood the test, and under the stress of necessity evolved most of the basic administrative features that would henceforth characterize the mature Confucian state. The Censorate reached the peak of its political influence. Recruitment examinations assumed a much greater importance both quantitatively and qualitatively. Sponsorship was elaborated and elevated to a major role in personnel administration.

Just as examinations and merit rating procedures grew slowly from older Confucian doctrine, sponsorship also had its roots in the past. The two elements which were combined in sponsorship— recommendation for public office and the recommender's responsibility for the character of his protégé—go far back in Chinese history. We find recommendation pictured in semilegendary accounts describing the middle Chou dynasty, and statements of Confucius, about the early fifth century B.C., clearly favor the principle.[14] The informal practice of recommendation in filling offices is of course common to the most primitive and the most modern types of government. It may be an accepted and open procedure, or it may take the form of concealed wire-pulling. In China, however, it assumed a different aspect. From the earliest clearly historical times, recommendation was not merely sanctioned as an open practice; the recommendation of worthy and able men became at least a moral obligation, possibly reinforced by penalties for its neglect. By the early second century B.C., if not earlier, recommendation had assumed institutional form. Able men were regularly presented to the central government by the local authorities, and were regularly classified,

[14] References to the practice of recommendation by Confucius are probably the earliest of clear validity. It seems to be indicated in an answer to CHUNG Kung, who asked how to know men of talent and virtue: "Raise to office those [of virtue and talent] whom you know. As to those you know not, will others then neglect them?" (*Lun-yü*, XIII, 2). It seems more certainly indicated in the reproof of TS'ANG Wên-chung for his failure to obtain the appointment of CHAN Huo (Liu-hsia Hui) as a fellow official, although he knew of his worth (*Lun-yü*, XV, 13). The *Kuo yü* (Ch'i yü, 6, 7a), in describing the administration of Ch'i under the influence of KUAN Chung (in the seventh century B.C.), depicts recommendation in a rather advanced form. The prince ordains that his officials recommend all men of scholarship, wisdom, virtue, bravery, or athletic prowess known to them, and sets penalties for the concealing of worth. But the *Kuo yü*, while probably written before 213 B.C., seems to be a work written long after the period here described. (Cf. KARLGREN, *The Authenticity;* CH'I, Ch'un-ch'iu, 67.) Its testimony gives us certainty only that recommendation was known when the account was written. I am indebted to Professor H. G. CREEL for the references to LIU-HSIA Hui and the *Kuo yü*.

before receiving office, by written examination. In this way the system of recommendation became the parent of the examination system.[15]

The time at which a legal responsibility became associated with recommendation is less easily determined. The open and formal nature of the act of recommendation in itself served to place the credit or blame for a recommendation on the recommender. This responsibility may have been transformed, by the Han dynasty, into a legal guaranty.[16] Such guaranty clearly existed in the T'ang. The T'ang recommendation system, however, was not a direct continuation from the Han recommendations, which had been transformed, by increasing emphasis on the accompanying examination, into a system of special examinations for promotion. Recommendation in the T'ang appeared under a new terminology. Proclamations of the ninth century began to regulate its use, and from 833 we have a detailed statement concerning the enforcement of guaranty.[17] These were the forerunners of the Sung system. The older T'ang system of promotions had probably become too elaborate for use in the chaos which now overspread the Empire. Sponsorship offered a relatively effective way of filling the gap. From the later T'ang through the tenth century we have increasing evidence of its importance as a method of promotion, until it emerged about 1000 as a new system. Thereafter it was to recur as a feature of the Chinese civil service, under differing forms and with varying importance, until the beginning of the twentieth century.[18]

[15] Recommendation is found in 196 B.C., soon after the establishment of the Han (cf. DUBS, *History*, I, 130–132), and occurs at fairly regular intervals thereafter.

[16] TUNG Chung-shu had suggested rewards for the sponsors of good officials and punishments for those who proved corrupt. These provisions seem to have been incorporated in a proclamation quoted in the *Han kuan yi*, 1, 7a–b. An advocate of guaranteed recommendation in the T'ang dynasty (about 690) interprets the Han practice as amounting ·to a permanent guaranty of the candidate by the sponsor (*HTS*, 112,6b–8a). This interpretation was in turn quoted by Sung writers (*YH*,117,3a).

[17] See *THY*,78,23a to 79,14b. The order of 833 (*TK*,37,34a) contains surprisingly detailed regulations for the punishment of sponsors whose protégés misbehave. These provide graded sentences according to the amount of dishonesty involved, ranging from a reduction in official standing to the quasi-banishment of a small charge far from the capital. See also *TT*,18,13a–14a; *TC*,58,35b–40a; 59,37a–38a, etc.

[18] *WTHY*,4,12a–13b, supplies examples of 927, 954 or 955, 957, and 958, which are very similar to the earliest Sung examples. The Manchu practice of sponsorship, outlined in HSIEH, *Government,* 103–104, shows a general resemblance to the mature Sung system, but a seeming decline in effectiveness and importance.

II

FORCES THAT SHAPED THE SUNG STATE

To understand the rapid development of civil service practices during the first century of the Sung dynasty and the forms they then assumed, we need to have in mind the conditions under which the new forms evolved and the problems with which they were forced to cope.

It was in most ways a time of change. China was in transition: economically, socially, politically, and intellectually. The developments in all these realms were so interconnected and interactive that it would be difficult to assign entire primacy to any one of them. Commerce was expanding; urban centers were growing; the new use of printing made literature more widely available; the literate groups were larger; more men competed for governmental employment and power. Confucian philosophy, triumphant after nearly a millennium of eclipse by the popularity of Taoism and Buddhism, was creating a new mode of speculation. The influence of the professional civil servant as a whole was more widely felt.

Sung China was separated from the epoch of T'ang unity by nearly two centuries of political and military chaos. But it still represented in most ways a continuation of the T'ang civilization. Most of the processes of Sung change found their beginnings in the T'ang. Many trends of development had continued through the period of political disunity. Sung achievements grew from T'ang experience and often fulfilled the promise of T'ang ideas or experiments. But if the Sung continued the T'ang civilization, it was a later stage of that civilization, sobered by the political and military disasters of the later T'ang, less ebullient, more analytical in spirit.

Sung life itself passed through three clear phases during the century following the dynasty's founding. The period of unification and political consolidation, with its wars against the Chinese states of the South and the encroaching foreign peoples of the North, lasted nearly a half century after the new house was proclaimed in 960. With the Peace of Shan-yüan which in 1004 ended fighting on the northern border, there began a time of tranquil development which lasted until a new military invasion, this time from the northwest, reached serious proportions in 1038. This war and its aftermath inaugurated a period of new and increasingly serious difficulties. Coincidentally, the generation which then began was to be singularly endowed with great men, both in its political and in its cultural activities.[1]

1. The Military Problem

When in 960 the successful commander CHAO K'uang-yin assumed the Northern Chinese throne at K'ai-feng, and founded the Sung dynasty, the military task he set himself was at the least audacious.[2] Five dynasties had ruled North China during little more than a half century. Some had existed only by sufferance of their menacing northerly neighbors, the Khitan, who had already annexed lands just within the Great Wall and now supported a rival dynasty in Shansi, not two hundred miles from K'ai-feng. Several of the rulers had been non-Chinese, and one at least had not learned the art of reading.[3] South China was ruled by prosperous states independent in fact, and sometimes in name; the youngest of these had outlived three houses in the North, and some of them had seen the fall of all five. Yet the new ruler—posthumously known as T'ai-tsu—set about to recover both North and South and re-establish the dominion of the T'ang.

He could count among his assets an internal administration strengthened by the preceding house, an army hardened by its constant struggles, able commanders, and above all his own supremacy as a strategist and his discerning selection and use of his generals. Making the fullest use of these advantages, T'ai-tsu in a decade and a half eliminated all challenge of Sung authority in the South, and

[1] See Appendix A for the emperors of this century and their reign dates.

[2] CHAO was enthroned by his officers soon after leaving the capital on an expedition against the Khitan. The extent to which he coöperated in the scheme is not clear. The need for a strong ruler at the time, and the minority of the reigning Emperor were factors in his elevation. Cf. HCP,1,1a–4a.

[3] We are told that a special post of academician was created under the Latter T'ang dynasty because of the illiteracy not only of the ruler, but of his chief minister as well. Cf. HCLY,25,6a.

prepared the way for his successor to eliminate four years later the rival state in Shansi.[4]

It might have seemed, to a contemporary, that the military glory lost for two centuries would now return, and China win back all the dominions once held by the T'ang. But the Sung nation was not martial in its bent as the T'ang had once been. The brother and successor of T'ai-tsu, T'ai-tsung, lacked the military abilities of his predecessor, and the pace of reconquest soon slackened under his leadership; a disastrous rout by the Khitan in 986 ended the immediate hope of regaining the alienated lands within the great wall. (It was in fact to be nearly four centuries before these lands were recovered.) Desultory fighting against the Khitan continued with occasional success during the next two decades. The Chinese were able to win and hold fortified positions. The skill of the Khitan in guerrilla tactics, however, made victories indecisive. The Peace of Shan-yüan in 1004, which at last brought an end to the profitless situation, was no doubt welcome to both sides. The northern border was to remain accepted by both nations until less judicious counsels prevailed in the following century.[5]

The tranquillity of the succeeding generation was broken only by occasional border skirmishes, especially with the truculent Tangut in the northwest. These tribesmen in 1038 began to expand their power and organize their conquests as a new state. Held in check at first, in the years 1040 and 1041 they were able to defeat several Sung armies and place the nation in a critical situation. Several factors had weakened the military machine left by T'ai-tsu. Fear of the warlordism which had destroyed the T'ang led the Sung govern-

[4] A show of force brought the small state of Ching-nan (or Southern P'ing: in Western Hupeh) to submission in 963. The states of Shu (in Szechuan), Southern Han (in Kwangtung and Kwangsi), and Southern T'ang (in Kiangsi, southern Fukien, and the southern bank of the lower Yangtse) were subjugated by arms respectively in 965, 971, and 975. The princes of Wu' and Yüeh (in Chekiang) made no resistance and relinquished their administrative autonomy voluntarily in 978 to T'ai-tsung. That ruler subjugated the Northern Han (in Shansi) in 979.

[5] Although the Sung had at the time suffered severe reverses, and were willing to appease the Khitan by the payment of a regular subsidy, they resisted the Khitan demand for the cession of territory. The relationship established between the Sung and Khitan rulers was one of formal equality. Cf. FRANKE, Geschichte, IV, 138–145; WITTFOGEL-FENG, 585–586, 354–355; SHY:FYi, 23a–38a; NCC:SLCP,3–4.

The Khitan retained the borderlands including modern Peiping and Ta-t'ung. Western Kansu, Eastern Turkestan, and Annam also remained outside the Sung domain.

ment to divide and circumscribe the military authority jealously, hampering operations in time of war. The lack of border grazing lands had from the first limited the supply of cavalry horses, which China was forced to acquire to a large extent from border tribes in exchange for tea and other commodities. Years of peace had softened the regular troops, and the nation as a whole had little enthusiasm for war. To match the martial spirit of the tribesmen, Chinese leaders relied heavily on their superiority in weapons: Chinese technicians had already developed explosive projectiles and what appears to have been a kind of hand grenade.[6] New forces of militia were raised in huge numbers; the men under arms at the end of the war were more than triple in numbers the armies with which T'ai-tsu had won his victories.[7] The Tangut were overcome; but the cost was heavy. The Khitan were barely prevented from profiting by the Sung embarrassment to gain new territory.[8] Tribal uprisings in the South and rebellions of disaffected Sung troops continued for some years, and the uneasy peace of the northern and northwestern borders during the following decades was a cause of constant disquiet. The heavy burden of armament cost was added to those of wartime destruction and economic dislocation, as a heritage for the succeeding generation.

2. The Economic Problem

The economic problems that developed during the century after 960 were complex. The more obvious and immediate phenomena often obscured slower and more lasting changes that took place beneath the surface. While the economy recovered from the effects of pre-Sung disorder, flourished in time of peace, and fell prey once

[6] Cf. GOODRICH-FENG, Firearms, 114–115. Some such weapons had been developed as early as 1000. By 1044, explosive projectiles weighing twelve catties, and explosive sticks of bamboo, iron, and gunpowder were in use. From this time the progress in the use of explosives was rapid.

[7] Cf. *KMPY*,1040–1041,*passim*. The total under arms, 378,000 at the end at T'ai-tsu's reign, had passed 900,000 under Chen-tsung and reached 1,259,000 after 1041. (Cf. *SS*,187,8a.)

[8] The diplomacy of Fu Pi was largely instrumental in averting the Khitan danger. The subsidy, however, was increased. Cf. *SHY*:FYi,2,12b–15b; *KMPY*,1042,*passim*; WITTFOGEL-FENG, 589; 357–358; FRANKE, *Geschichte*, IV, 161–162. An annual subsidy was also included in the settlement made with the Tangut. Cf. *KMPY*,1044/12; *SS*, 485,20a. Much of the credit for preventing a more serious outcome belongs to the able commander TI Ch'ing. For the size of the subsidies, see below, Note 22.

more to accumulating maladjustments and the burden of new war, the process of commercialization and regional specialization went forward continuously. The process had begun in the seventh and eighth centuries, and would by the twelfth and thirteenth bring China substantially to her economy of modern times. During the eleventh the change was already far toward its completion. The economic unit had become national rather than local. Great urban centers had risen in many parts of the country, supported by trade and crafts. A money economy was restricting the role of the old transactions in kind.

North China and the mountainous southwest had grown increasingly reliant on the rice produced in the rich Yangtse delta and in the smaller fertile areas of Szechwan, Hunan, and Kiangsi.[9] In return for the required cereal imports, the less fertile parts of the Empire supplied locally produced commodities such as salt, metals, sea fish, and tea; or the specialties for which the local craftsmen might be famed; or such services as banking, transportation, or providing a depot for foreign and interregional trade.[10] The interchange of commodities was encouraged by the development of transportation facilities, which had progressed far even in the T'ang, and by the development of currency. Paper money came into wide use, especially for transactions between places somewhat removed, where the copper coinage was inconveniently cumbersome. But the main unit of currency was still the pierced copper piece, or "cash," which was issued in larger and smaller sizes. Strings of a thousand large coins served as the unit for larger transactions. By the end

[9] CHS:NSTM,404.

[10] The regional balance of trade in the Northern Sung does not seem to have received special study as yet. That in the Southern Sung has been treated by CH'ÜAN Han-sheng. The rice surplus areas in South China at this time seem to have been Ssu-ch'uan, Hu-nan, Chiang-hsi, the Yangtse delta, and the Pearl River region. Salt was exported from the Huai River region (Liang-Huai), coastal Chekiang (Che-tung), and Fukien. Coastal Chekiang and Fukien depended on their mining, foreign trade, and crafts. Tea was exported from the Huai region and Fukien. Che-tung also specialized in fish, and Liang-Huai in textiles. While farming remained the occupation of the great majority of the population, and food deficit areas still produced an important part of their food supply, the economy of this time was distinguished by the fact that commerce was now concerned not only with luxury items for a few centers of wealth, but also with commodities of large-scale general use in all parts of the country. Dr. CH'ÜAN believes that the picture, except for certain local exceptions, substantially resembled the situation in China of today. Cf. CHS:NSTM,429.

of the tenth century, the copper money minted annually reached some two and a half times what it had been in the middle of the eighth, and by the middle of the eleventh some three million strings were minted a year—nearly ten times that of three centuries before.[11] To avoid the possibility of inflation, on the other hand, the amount of paper currency in circulation was limited after about 1032 to a total value of a little over a million and a quarter strings.[12]

K'ai-feng, the capital, and other centers of arts, crafts, and business grew to great size and importance.[13] K'ai-feng prefecture and some others must by mid-century have numbered a million or more inhabitants.[14] The growth of commerce was also illustrated graphically by the increase of the state revenues, and by the rapidly expanding place which money income assumed. While cash receipts had represented only 3.9 per cent of the total state income at the height of the T'ang prosperity, in 749, the proportion rose by 1065 to no less than 51.6 per cent.[15]

[11] Cf. CHS:SJYHP,216.

[12] Cf. CARTER, *Printing*, 72.

[13] During the Northern Sung, K'ai-feng became an important industrial center, manufacturing for export as well as local consumption. Its products included textiles, printing, ink, metal work, and porcelain. (Much of the evidence, however, comes from later in the eleventh century.) Szechwan was famous for textiles and printing, and Hangchow surpassed in the latter. Cf. CHS:PLHY,203–5, etc. The transshipment, banking, and shipbuilding activities, which in the T'ang had centered at Yang-chou, in the Sung were divided by Chen-chou and other neighboring places, while the copper industry went to Ch'ang-sha and elsewhere. Cf. CHS:YCCC,170–174.

[14] About 1075, K'ai-feng had 235,599 households; Hang-chou 202,806; Fu-chou 211,552; Ch'üan-chou 201,406; Ch'ang-sha 357,824; and there were a number more of this order. Cf. *YFCY,passim*. On the relation between households and total population, see Note 20 below. Except for K'ai-feng, the cities of this size were generally in the Yangtse watershed or on the southeast coast.

[15] The cash proportion had risen by 1021 to 17.6 per cent; by 1049 to 30.9 per cent. Most of the change took place in less than fifty years. A comparison of individual items is also instructive. The total annual revenue in 1021 was three times that of 749, but the amount of grain received through the eleventh century did not differ markedly from the 749 figure. Collections in the form of silk declined steadily and steeply. The amount of cash receipts, however, rose from some 2 million strings in 749 to over 26 million in 1021. While the total revenue gradually declined after 1021, the cash income continued to increase to nearly 37 million in the period 1056–1063, and still more thereafter. Cf. CHS:SJYHP,202–204. Another new factor was the important place assumed in the state income by precious metals, not evident in the T'ang. While they were not minted, both gold and silver appear to have circulated to some extent as a means of payment. Cf. CHS:SJYHP,217–218.

With the growth of trade, the social place of the trader changed also. Wealthy merchants became an important element in the life of the cities, mingling freely in the elite circles of the Imperial family and the bureaucracy.[16]

Agricultural Problems

The commercial development did not, however, go so far as to displace farming as the source of livelihood for the great majority of the people, as well as a major source of state revenue. The condition of farming was the barometer of national economic soundness, and in periods of difficulty became the first preoccupation of the government. Like other economic activities, farming too was moving toward specialization of crops in given areas. But unlike commerce and the crafts, the techniques and organization of farming had changed little during the several preceding centuries. Most farm lands were privately owned. Some were farmed by their owners, in person or with hired hands; some were rented to tenants; some were farmed by a combination of these methods. A smaller share of the land belonged to the state, which rented it to the tillers.[17]

Agricultural problems were among the first that T'ai-tsu faced in repairing the economic ravages of the preceding century and more. The exactions of war and the war lords had been heavy; the land had suffered as well as the farmer; many farms were deserted. The state undertook a program of inducing the unemployed to rehabilitate the waste lands. Implements and seed were distributed without charge, temporary tax exemptions granted, some taxes abolished and others reduced, and agricultural advice made available.[18]

The situation responded to these measures, and a period of general prosperity ensued during the earlier part of the eleventh century. But there were always economic maladjustments; the government was never entirely relieved of the problem of the marginal farmer. This problem assumed graver dimensions after 1040; the impact of the Tangut war no doubt accelerated the development of tendencies, already inherent in the economy, toward the shrinkage of the median

[16] Cf. CHS:SYSY,205–206.

[17] While crops in North China were relatively diversified, the concentration on rice in the fertile areas of the South made the latter very vulnerable to droughts, a situation which the government tried to alter through education. Cf. SYCC,101.

[18] Cf. KMPY,961/1,962/1,962/12,1013/7, and passim.

land holding. While the manifestations of these tendencies are chronicled in some detail, the priority and relative importance of their causes are not clear. The number of farmers and the traditionally equal division of inheritance reduced the average land holding to inadequacy. The small farmer, pressed to meet his daily expenses and tax bills, was apt to overwork and exhaust his soil, so that it was scarcely able to feed his family, let alone supply a surplus for urban needs. The demand for loans in times of need being great, the interest rates were prohibitive. In addition to the heavy tax burden, the small farmer might no doubt suffer inequities in tax collection as well. When pressure became too great, he might lose or abandon his farm, and if he could not rent good land or sell his services, he and his family became dependent on state relief. The larger farmer, on the other hand, had a margin of security which enabled him to conserve the soil productivity, and produce a surplus for the city market. He could more easily weather bad times and might even increase his holdings.[19]

These tendencies were chronic. But the steady growth of population made their pressure ever greater: the registered population of 997 more than doubled by 1014, and tripled by 1063.[20] The Tangut war in turn added to the difficulty through the increase of the tax burden, the conscription of able-bodied males for militia service, and military devastation in the border areas. Poor crop years gave to many the coup de grâce.

[19] Unless he became responsible for local public services. See Chapter III, Note 114.

[20] The population of T'ang China in 755 was given as 9,619,254 households. By 997, only 4,514,257 were reported for an area similar in size; this may represent a somewhat incomplete census. By 1014 the figure was 9,055,729, and by 1063, 12,462,311. It was to reach 20,882,258 by 1110. (Sources differ in detail. Cf. CHS:SJYHP,215–216, LCP,3,20a; SS,85,1a–2b; NCC:TLCKY,I,6,10; HCP,passim.) It is hard to estimate the total populations represented by these figures. The report for 755 is 52,880,488 persons, and other dynasties also give a general ratio of five persons per household. The Sung census figures, however, regularly give an unbelievable ratio of only a little over two persons per household. Modern explanations variously attribute this to (a) failure to report all persons in household, to escape head taxes; (b) omission of women and children from the tabulation; (c) the fictitious subdivision of households to profit by more favorable tax brackets; (d) exaggerated report of numbers of households by local officials, to obtain rewards. Cf. MI:TS; HK:SK. The latter argues that the explanation is a combination of (a) and (c). On this basis, the actual 1063 population was perhaps somewhat less than the 62,000,000, which the household numbers would imply.

The government resorted to the old remedies of resettlement, tax remission, and relief. Beyond these, land was resurveyed, and tax rates graded according to the relative soil productivity. Irrigation and drainage works were carried on to an extent which gave the northern Sung an average of yearly projects seemingly trebling that of any former dynasty.[21] These measures, however, could not eliminate the causes of the trouble, and later Sung centuries were to inherit it.

Fiscal Problems

This economic situation made increasing difficulties in the administration of governmental finance, from the middle of the eleventh century, when expenditures began to draw ahead of income. To the expenses of relief and agricultural reconstruction programs were added those of war and military preparedness. Demobilization after the Tangut war was inhibited alike by the continued threat of invasion and the problem of reëmploying the veterans in civilian occupations. The Khitan and Tangut appeasement payments, while probably less significant than sometimes painted, added to the burden.[22] More serious was the steady expansion of the government payroll.[23] Increasingly stringent economies were able to keep the budget at a figure little higher than that in the prosperous days of Chen-tsung's later reign (an amount several times what the first two

[21] Cf. *TK*,4,24b; *KMPY*,1040–1067,*passim;* CCT,35. The greater fullness of data for later periods, however, probably exaggerates in some degree the apparent rise in water control activity after the T'ang. The interest in irrigation during the middle eleventh century is illustrated by SHAN O (1031–1110), who devoted himself to a study of the problem and wrote a book on it. Cf. *SSYi*,23,9a–b; *SKTM*,69,2a. Another successful specialist in water control at the time was SUNG Ch'ang-yen. Cf. *SS*,291,11a.

[22] Under the Peace of Shan-yüan the annual subsidy to the Khitan was set at 100,000 oz. (liang) of silver and 200,000 pieces of silk. To these were added in 1042 another 100,000 oz. of silver and 100,000 pieces of silk. (Cf. FRANKE, *Geschichte*, IV, 143; 162; WITTFOGEL-FENG, 354–355; 357–358.) The Tangut were given from 1044 a total of 255,000 units of silver, tea, and thin and variegated silk. (Cf. *KMPY*,1044/12; *SS*,485,20a.) These total an annual expenditure of 755,000 units by 1044. While these units were all in theory worth a string of cash each, the prices of silk and silver varied, being sometimes less than one, or (rarely) as much as two or three strings. (Cf. MASPERO *J.As.*, 212 (1928), 171–172; CHS:SJYHP,219–220.) A generous estimate of the total annual cost would scarcely exceed 2,000,000 strings, well under 2 per cent of the budget. Compare the total budgets given below.

[23] See below, Table 3.

rulers had had at their disposal).[24] But the lavish income of 1021 was no longer available. While the curtailed budget of 1048 left a safe surplus, the following year's income barely met expenditures, and the further reduced revenues of 1065 fell short by over fifteen million strings.[25] This seems to have represented especially a decline in the collections from rural areas. Had it not been for the increasing share of the tax burden borne by the urban population, the difficulty might well have been still greater.[26]

These economic problems affected the civil service administration in several ways. The need to gain control of funds misappropriated by local agencies was one motive for centralizing the appointment of local officials early in the dynasty. The administrative problems of an urbanized economy naturally increased the tasks of government, and the ample revenues of the early eleventh century permitted the civil service to grow rapidly. The fiscal difficulties of the mid-century, on the other hand, inhibited the improvement of the service through adequate pay and prospect of promotion at the very time that they

[24] Expenditures about 997 were still apparently within the receipts of 22,245,800 strings. About 1021 they reached no less than 126,775,200 strings. In 1048, expenses seem actually to have been reduced to 111,780,000, but the following year they rose to 126,251,964, and in 1065 to 131,864,452. Cf. *SS*,179,3a–b; 6b; 8a; HK:*TRD*, 291. An Office of Economy (*Sheng-chien Ssu* 省減司) was established in 1058 to coöperate with the Finance Commission in eliminating unnecessary items from the budget (*KMPY*,1058/11).

[25] The rise and decline of income are illustrated by the following years:

c.997:	22,245,800	1048:	122,190,000
1003:	60,260,000	1049:	126,251,964
1007:	63,730,000	1065:	116,138,405
c.1021:	150,850,100	(Cf. *SS* and HK:*TRD, loc. cit.*)	

[26] The collections from commerce taxes rose from an annual 4 million strings in 995–998 to over 12 million in 1021, and 22 million in the period 1041–1049; then fell to 7 or 8 million during the rest of our period. The income from the salt, wine, and tea monopolies rose from over 11 million in 997 to over 45 million around the period 1041–1048, and 50 million in 1076. While the monopolies affected the farmer, they affected the urbanite as well, and probably more severely. This was specially true of the wine monopoly, whose income rose from some 2¼ million in 995–998 to over 12 million in 1021, 17 million in 1045, and declined to 12 million again in later years. Both moonshining and heavy consumption would be more easily detected by the revenue officer in the city. Receipts in the form of grain declined from some 30 million bushels (tan) in 1021 to some 27 million in 1056–1063. For a discussion of the problems involved, see CHS:SJYHP. The above data are drawn from pages 202–204 and 207–213 of that article. See also Note 15 above for the rise in money revenue.

called for greater governmental efficiency. They raise, too, the question whether the civil service could have met the challenge more successfully had greater attention been given to professional specialization. These problems will be considered further in the following chapters.

3. Cultural Developments

Meanwhile, other developments also were to have their influence on the character of the civil service personnel. The educated group had no doubt been slowly expanding before the tenth century. But the rapid development and new applications of the art of printing, which came during the early Sung and the years immediately preceding it, certainly played an important part in stimulating that expansion. The rapid growth in the scope and quantity of printing in the early Sung hastened the spread of education among those for whom books were previously too costly. In addition to Buddhist texts, two editions of the Confucian classics had appeared almost simultaneously at the middle of the tenth century.[27] By the beginning of the eleventh, official activity had added to the books in print such diverse items as the *Historical Records* of Ssu-ma Ch'ien and several other histories, an encyclopedia (the *T'ai-p'ing kuang-chi*), the chief dictionary of classical Chinese (the *Shuo wen*), a local history, an additional voluminous classical commentary. During the first half of the eleventh century the progress continued still faster, and the printing done by governmental agencies at the capital was supplemented by official publications in the prefectures and by private printers, one of whom at this time developed movable type. Belles-lettres were published along with more serious works, and along with literature of respectable age both official and private printers published the writing of active contemporaries.[28]

Facilities for formal education were also expanding. During the earlier Sung, advanced education was provided almost entirely by private academies, some of which were endowed with extensive buildings and revenue-producing lands by wealthy individuals.[29] The

[27] CARTER, *Printing,* 52.

[28] Cf. *op. cit,* 56–57; 160–161; *SLCH*,3,1a–1b; 5a; 7b; 18a–b.

[29] E.g. the White Deer Grotto Academy (*Pai-lu-tung Shu-yüan* 白鹿洞書院), the most famous school of the time, which had been endowed by the Southern T'ang prince with several hundred acres of good land, and in 977 "regularly num-

government had merely provided limited educational facilities at the capital for children of officials. During the eleventh century, however—particularly after 1030—the state undertook the responsibility of supplying schools for private citizens as well, at the capital, and in all the prefectures and more important subprefectures. While the implementation of this measure seems to have progressed rather slowly, it must have meant from the beginning a considerable widening of educational opportunity.[30]

The mood of the time was scholarly. The remains of antiquity which now and then came to light, once commonly treated as curiosities, omens, or magic things, were now systematically studied and classified.[31] The generation which flourished in the mid-eleventh century was unique. Historians living in 1050 left works which in quality, scale, and number could scarcely be matched by any earlier generation, though the following century was to achieve still more.[32] Some of the poets of this time rank very high in Chinese literature.[33] But, except in a few poetic forms, they had not won the fame of the greatest T'ang poets; the literary genius of the time was in its prose, and there it reached the first rank. The Sung contributed six great masters to the movement for a reformed and simplified prose, and all were living in this generation.[34] The study and practice of painting

---

bered [its students] by thousand and hundred" (*TK*,46,12b; *JCSP*,III,5,3b). Or the Ying-t'ien-fu Academy, built and maintained at private expense (*SHY*:CJ,2,2a).

[30] *SS*,167,26a; *YH*,112,25b. T'ai-tsung had shown an interest in local education by donating books to the private academies; in 1006 and 1009 the government showed a more active interest by granting official rank to certain local teachers. Cf. *SHY*:CJ,2, 2a–b.

[31] A bronze found and presented to Chen-tsung in 1000 was made the subject of a scholarly report. Illustrated catalogues of ancient objects appeared about 1051 and in 1063, the latter printed. Cf. JK:CCSC,661; 679–80.

[32] The official histories written at this time and covering the early Sung are not preserved. But we have the *Hsin T'ang-shu* of Ou-yang Hsiu, Sung Ch'i, and others; Ssu-ma Kuang's *Tzu-chih t'ung-chien;* the works of Sung Min-ch'iu; and many valuable memoranda.

[33] E.g. Su Shih, Ou-yang Hsiu, Liu Yung, who were to remain outstanding Sung poets.

[34] The six prose masters were Ou-yang Hsiu, Tseng Kung, Wang An-shih, Su Hsün, and the latter's two sons, Su Shih and Su Che. The eight recognized T'ang and Sung masters of the *ku-wen* movement were these and the two T'ang pioneers, Han Yü and Liu Tsung-yüan. The great Sung art historian Kuo Jo-hsü lived at this time (see Soper, *Experiences*), and Su Shih was one of China's great calligraphers. The

and calligraphy too were enjoying an especially flourishing period.

Under the Sung rulers Confucianism occupied a place of influence in some ways still greater than that which it had enjoyed eight centuries earlier, before the era of Buddhist supremacy. The reinvigoration of Confucian thought had been heralded in the ninth century; in the middle of the eleventh, five outstanding pioneers created the basic patterns of Neo-Confucian thought, which were to be harmonized and systematized by CHU Hsi a century later.[35] At this stage, Neo-Confucian speculation was still free from the dogmatic formulation which was to confine it in after centuries. While the explanation of the universe these thinkers offered need not concern us here, one aspect of their thought is significant: their philosophic egalitarianism. Nature revealed its laws to the disciplined mind. While the ancients had pointed out the way to truth, the fullest knowledge was only to be reached by each individual through the perfecting of his own understanding. The teacher could only assist in the task; potentially, at least, all men were equal in wisdom.

A factor of particular significance for our present purpose is the leadership which the professional civil servant now assumed in all these fields of scholarly and cultural activity. In the writing of history and philosophy, the composition of fine prose, and even poetry, the most notable figures were with perhaps three exceptions not only active but prominent in government.[36] Even the art critic and the painter often engaged in minor governmental activities quite unrelated to the arts, and there was scarcely a perceptible line separating the professional artist holding a governmental post from the official who painted as a pastime. Culture was in many ways shaped by the outlook of the civil servant; but the halls of government were equally permeated with the attitudes of scholarship and philosophy. While this condition had also characterized other periods of Chinese history, the extent it now reached was unique. For better or for worse,

landscapist KUO Hsi and the great painter of bamboo WEN T'ung were also of this generation.

[35] The five were SHAO Yung, CHOU Tun-yi, CHANG Tsai, CH'ENG Hao, and CH'ENG Yi. All were born between 1011 and 1033. Cf. BRUCE, *Masters,* pp. 17–55; FUNG-BODDE, Rise, esp. p. 100.

[36] The philosopher SHAO Yung declined office and lived in poverty rather as a recluse. His friendship was, however, cultivated by influential officials. SU Hsün failed to pass the doctoral examinations, and received a governmental post only late in life. LIU Yung received his doctoral degree, but did not achieve success as an official.

the practices of government were molded by scholarly attitudes and Confucian political theories in a way scarcely matched earlier or later.

4. The Political Outlook

But while the contemporary Neo-Confucian metaphysicians had helped win political prestige for Confucianism, they had added comparatively little to the political doctrines of their school. The basic teachings were still those of Confucius and his disciples, largely in the form and interpretation given them by Mencius some thirteen centuries earlier. The Confucian classics became a fundamental part of the state constitution, with a force which neither the Emperor nor his subjects could venture to deny, even though they might on occasion follow other teachings privately. This function of the classics was not formally stated in the legal codes; it was accepted as an assumption so basic that it required no statement. The state undertook the responsibility of establishing the correct versions of the classical texts; their teachings tempered the clauses of the laws and the way in which they were applied.

Some of the practical effects of this exaltation of the Confucian influence will be discussed in the next chapter. Here, however, we may note several significant attitudes to which Confucianism gave currency.

One was an acceptance of the conditional nature of Imperial authority. The classics taught that the Imperial throne had been granted by Heaven, which might withdraw its gift from an unworthy occupant. The displeasure of Heaven might be shown in several ways: by omens and portents, by natural disasters, by the existence of political disorder. The common people were ultimately the judges of Heaven's pleasure. As they had been its agents in granting the throne, so they might be its agents in withdrawing it.[37] In the killing of the tyrannical ruler Chou, no assassination had been committed; the one who struck him down had as Heaven's agent executed a varlet.[38] Heaven saw and heard with the eyes and ears of the people.[39]

[37] Cf. Mencius, V,A,5: "The people were content with it; this was the people giving it. Heaven gave it, men gave it. Therefore it is said: an Emperor cannot give the Empire to anyone." Cf. also I,B,10; II,A,3; 5; for statements of Confucius, see CREEL, *Confucius*, chapter X.

[38] Cf. Mencius, I,B,8.

[39] Mencius, V,A,5.

Another aspect of the Confucian teaching was the comparative stress on personal relationships. In comparison with our Western political concepts, obligations were determined less by abstract institutions and rules, and more by personal ties and personal character. The state was symbolized in the personal relationship of the Emperor to Heaven, the source of his authority, and to the people of the state, his children, to whom he owed care in exchange for their fidelity and help. The sanctions of the state rested on the virtues of the Emperors of the reigning family; when these virtues no longer existed, that state came to an end, and a new state would be created by a new family. The official owed his obligations not to a political abstraction but to the Emperor, whom he aided and admonished, and to the people in his charge, whom he was to cherish as his junior kindred.[40] In the light of this relationship, it seems quite natural that frank criticism of a ruler's policies was not regarded as a right, but as a duty of an official. Such criticism not only served the people—it prolonged the life of the dynasty. It was like the frank opinion which a son owed to his parent.[41] Beyond this, however, the individual merits of an official might properly grant him equality in prestige with the ruler, and as a specialist in government he was in matters of his craft the ruler's master, not his disciple! [42] The official should hold his position only on the basis of demonstrated merit, moral as well as intellectual.[43] But if a man was qualified, it was his duty to accept office.[44]

This obligation to accept office had further implications; it helps to explain why the abilities of the time were so preponderantly channeled into the civil service. In earlier times, when Neo-Taoism and Buddhism claimed an important following among the educated, it was possible without suffering disapprobation to live a life of retirement from worldly affairs, and for some the Buddhist and

[40] This relationship appeared in the terminology used. Referring to himself in the Emperor's presence, the official called himself "your servant" (ch'en 臣). The general officials in direct contact with the people were "those who treated the people as their kindred" (ch'in-min 親民), and their duty was to "cherish the people" (tzu min 字民).

[41] Cf. Hsiao ching, 15.

[42] Mencius, II,B,2; II,A,7; I,B,9.

[43] See below, Chapter IV, note 77.

[44] Mencius, III,B,3.

Taoist hierarchy offered a satisfactory career for the ambitious. This was now no longer so. Nor did business activity compete in attractiveness with the governmental career. The merchant might gain wealth and even access to elite social circles; but commercial activity still lacked full Confucian approval, and could never satisfy completely the ambition for prestige.

The personal relationship of the government to the governed expressed itself in the scope of governmental responsibility, which embraced all aspects of popular welfare—spiritual development, economic sufficiency, and military security. We have seen that in practice the state was already concerned with education and agriculture: it was believed that the ancient sage-kings had provided schools, and Confucianism recognized that without economic security the average man, uneducated, could not be expected to maintain moral stability.[45]

This broad governmental responsibility might have implied the need for social and intellectual regimentation, had it not been for the Confucian emphasis on example as the most effective and desirable method of persuasion. Men were essentially good. Given the proper example, laws were not needed; without such example, they were inadequate.[46] A noted scholar-recluse of the early Sung, brought to court and pressed for his views on administration and defense problems, refused to give any advice beyond that of love for the people, which would work its slow transformation.[47] With respect to central administration, this outlook, while it acknowledged state responsibility for basic services such as public works, emphasized governmental economy and light taxation rather than highly organized regulative activity.[48] On the local level, it called for flexibility on the part of the administrative official. This followed not only from the personal concept of government, but from the scope of responsibilities and the reliance on example rather than law. An official, properly chosen for ability and character, could best fulfill his obligations if he were free to adapt his methods to the character of the people and the circumstances which he met. (This precept was

[45] Mencius, II,A,7.

[46] *Lun yü,* XIII,6; 11.

[47] *SS,*457,8a. The hermit was CH'UNG Fang. Cf. also SOPER, *Experiences,* 91–92 and note 682.

[48] Cf. *Lun yü,* XIII,21.

reinforced in practice by the vast territorial extent of the Empire and the difficulty of communications, which made it natural to delegate to private persons and groups such functions as the latter could assume.)

These facts must not lead us to exaggerate the personal and unregulated character of Chinese administration.[49] Long before Sung times, the ideal had collided with two intractable facts: the evolution of a more complex society and economy, and the practical difficulty of ensuring uniform ability and altruism in a large civil service. The first compelled the state to assume ever-expanding functions, and the second compelled Confucians to reconcile their ideals with the need for a detailed body of regulations that restricted an official's acts. The compromise was made, but it remained an uneasy balance of essentially conflicting standards.

5. The Character of the Emperors

The character of the Sung government unquestionably owed much to the personalities and standards of the Sung rulers, and above all to the founder, T'ai-tsu, who bequeathed a pattern of conduct to his successors. When at the age of thirty-two he received the throne, his experience had been chiefly military. His military abilities we have already noted; his qualities as a civil administrator were to be no less remarkable. He was a man of great energy, physical as well as intellectual, skillful and daring as a horseman and an archer. Even as Emperor he led his armies personally in battle. When necessary he could be a merciless disciplinarian. Yet he demonstrated a breadth of perspective which moderated his discipline with patience and flexibility. He had little taste for show or luxury; his palace was modest in comparison with the grand structures of the T'ang, and at the end of his life he rejected the proffered title of "Unifier and Pacifier" because the northern lands were not yet completely recovered. He understood the popular point of view and sympathized with it. He lectured his commanders on protection of the civilian population, and avoided bloodshed whenever possible. He conformed to Confucian teachings with apparent sincerity. With his civil officials, if he was at times impatient, he was also accessible and open to advice; with some of his old advisers he was on terms of intimacy and affection,

[49] For an extreme and idealized view of the personal character of Sung government, see FRANKE, *Geschichte*, IV,352.

seeking their opinions and taking in good part criticisms that were occasionally sharp.[50]

T'ai-tsu's vigor he could not transmit to his successors. But his Confucianism, his example of deference to his ministers, and his less prodigal way of living began a tradition which influenced all the Chao line. It may be argued that these things were a part of the spirit of the time, and rulers could not afford to flout contemporary standards. Yet it is conceivable that a military leader of equal ability but less amenable to Confucian ideas might have won the throne. Perhaps unlettered, more authoritarian in temperament, less scrupulous, such a man might have founded a tradition that would have stifled in some degree the potential trend. The lasting influence of T'ai-tsu's character can certainly not be discounted.

T'ai-tsung, the brother and successor of T'ai-tsu, was not at all his equal: not so capable in handling men, and inclined to suspicion, he was both less daring and less humane. Yet he continued the same general policies, the same thrift, and in a time of abating crisis he showed his respect for learning by patronizing such scholarly projects as literary encyclopedias and a national geographic survey.[51] The third Emperor, Chen-tsung, a son of T'ai-tsung, had good intentions and gave promise of ability at the time of his accession. A tendency toward mental instability, however, led to definite unbalance in his later years. Prompted by a minister both cynical and Taoist, he participated in ridiculous frauds to demonstrate Heaven's approval of his government, including a Heaven-sent document which was received with great fanfare.[52] But his reign saw surprisingly solid

[50] CML,58–62; 67; HCLY,1,1a–b; HCP,17,3a–b; LPC,2,15a. A writer two generations after T'ai-tsu's time tells a characteristic story about him. Once bothered by an importunate official on trivial business at the end of an arduous day, and exasperated by the man's persistence, T'ai-tsu struck the man with his staff and dislodged two teeth. When the man placed the teeth carefully in the breast of his gown, the ruler asked sardonically if the man planned to sue him. "I cannot sue Your Majesty," was the reply; "I shall forward these teeth to the Bureau of History." For this courage in delivering a deserved and appropriate reproof, T'ai-tsu commended and rewarded him (HCP,1,26b).

[51] CML,66–67; TENG-BIGGERSTAFF, 92; 149; PELLIOT, BEFEO,II,338–339. T'ai-tsung is reported to have worn his clothes until threadbare; a throne canopy about to be discarded he had redyed for flags and pennants (LPC,2,15a). He rejected a proposal to extend the palace because it would have disturbed the dwellings of K'ai-feng citizens (SHY:FYü,1,11b–12a).

[52] Cf. HCP,66,1a; KMPY,1008/1.

accomplishment through the influence of able councilors such as K'ou Chun and WANG Tan; under them the Council of State assumed the larger role in government that it would hold thenceforth.

The son of Chen-tsung, posthumously known as Jen-tsung, inherited the throne when not yet quite twelve, and during the first years of his reign was guided by a regency. In youth somewhat irresponsible, in his later years he showed serious concern for national and popular welfare. But to the end his policies were in most matters suggested by his councilors. The last Emperor of the period we are considering, Ying-tsung, a cousin of Jen-tsung once removed, died after a reign of less than four years, during which the same councilors were in power. Thus, reign by reign, circumstance and the ruler's character combined to promote a tendency already inherent in Confucian thought: the restraint of the ruler's exercised authority and the enhancement of the civil servant's power and prestige.

6. The Need for a Pragmatic Policy

Political circumstance and the state of cultural and economic development combined to stimulate a continual process of change and development in governmental organization and policies and in civil service practices. But the fluidity was especially notable during the period before the Peace of Shan-yüan in 1004. Flexibility was above all imperative during the unification of Chinese territories before 979. Most Chinese dynasties have required soon after their foundation a reinvigoration of old political forms and an administrative reorganization. But the Sung problem went far beyond this. The Sung unity was constructed in a few years from the fragments of an Empire whose last traces of cohesion had disappeared more than half a century earlier. The new government was to be built from the ground up. An experimental approach was unavoidable.

The breakdown of the central authority after the middle of the T'ang had been accompanied by the abandonment of orderly procedures for appointment to office. Local administrative authority tended to become in practice hereditary. Subordinate posts were bestowed without regard for proper qualifications, at the whim of an immediate superior, and the central control over local administration was tenuous in the extreme. These conditions existed even in the administrations of the northern dynasties which nominally inherited the remnants of T'ang authority. The last of these northern dynasties, the Later Chou, had begun the task of revamping the government and retrieving the usurped powers, but the task was far from completed. Now it was necessary to expand rapidly the partly renovated governmental structure in order to control effectively the newly acquired southern regions. Both in North and South, discretion suggested that the change of real control be made with the least possible offense to the existing body of officials, whose aid was necessary during the military phase of reunification. The requirements of tact and the unfinished reorganization alike favored the use of temporarily improvised offices, procedures, and agencies, supplementing but not clearly distinguished in function from the previously existing governmental structure. Because of the inefficiency which had permeated many of the traditional government offices, new offices were created to handle vital functions. Officials were temporarily relieved of their nominal duties and assigned to man the new offices in the capital or to undertake special functions elsewhere, until it came about that a very large proportion of the officials were occupied in fact with duties other than those to which they were nominally appointed. The nominal duty thus neglected might be temporarily discharged by a lesser official or a man from still another office. The vacancies created in many offices remained unfilled; left with skeleton staffs, such offices carried out only a few formal duties, while their real functions passed to new bureaus. As this condition was gradually regularized, it grew into the dual system of commissions and titular offices, which will be described later.

By 1004, nevertheless, the administrative structure had settled into a pattern that was to remain with little basic change until a fundamental reorganization was undertaken in 1080. The system of personnel recruitment had also assumed what were to be its general outlines, though much detail remained to be worked out during the following half century. The procedures for promotion and allocation of duties, however, were during that time to undergo still more important development.

III

THE STRUCTURE OF CIVIL GOVERNMENT

The government of China during the first century of the Sung belonged to the general type that we may call the Confucian state, although it incorporated elements that were non-Confucian. The basic structure of administration was in fact derived from forms created by Legalist thinkers some twelve centuries before, and to these forms a trace of the Legalist spirit had clung.

This spirit was in many ways the antithesis of the Confucian. It proposed as its ultimate good the advantage of the ruler and as its ethos unquestioning obedience to authority. The Confucian state, therefore, has at all times represented a combination of frequently conflicting forces, ideals, and inherited practices, which struck a new and distinctive balance in each period of Chinese history. The balance that existed in the later tenth and earlier eleventh century was outstanding for the great weight then placed on the Confucian side of the scale.[1]

1. The Role of the Emperor

The political ideals of early Sung Neo-Confucianism have been sketched in the preceding chapter. These ideals joined with political accident to restrict the ruler in the arbitrary exercise of his authority. The first Sung Emperor seems to have been a sincere Confucian, and despite his forcefulness and direct rule, generally conformed his conduct to the Confucian pattern, accepting criticism, and showing deference to his officials and to popular opinion. Partly for this reason, and partly through the care of the leading officials, his successors also were carefully trained in the Confucian way.[2] The

[1] This chapter sketches the more important and lasting elements of the organizational pattern before 1067. Many deviations and temporary variations are necessarily omitted. Only offices actually carrying out governmental functions are here treated.

[2] The power exercised by officials in this way is interestingly illustrated in the

concern with public welfare and opinion which they thus acquired was reinforced by the natural concern of the Emperors for the future security of their house; despite present popularity, a period of serious misrule could always be interpreted as manifest loss of the Mandate of Heaven, and so encourage a revolutionary movement. To the history-minded Confucian ruler, moreover, the reputation Confucian historians might give him if he violated the accepted code was not a slight consideration. Finally, a further practical thought limited the ruler's actions: he could not afford to act in a way that would antagonize the bulk of the officialdom, on whom his power depended.

The combined effect of these pressures on the Emperors led them to act, when selecting, changing, and sometimes overruling their councilors of state, for the furtherance of Confucian governmental policies; and to follow the classical admonitions in accepting criticism of their acts. This criticism might come from any of three sources. It might come from any subject who wished to offer advice or voice a grievance.[3] More often, it might come from any governmental official, either on occasions when an Emperor specially called for such criticism or when an official felt that it was needed.[4] Or it might come from the organs specially constituted for such criticism, the Bureau of Policy Criticism or the Censorate.

The characters of the Emperors themselves, neither forceful nor especially able after the founder, also contributed to restrict the scope of their actions. As a result (in varying degree according to the ruler), the chief responsibility for normal administration fell to the Council of State. All important measures were issued in the name of the Emperor, however, and usually received his formal approval.[5] Since he was accessible to the censors, policy criticism officials, and others who might object to the policies pursued by the Council, the

---

influence of the Chief Councilor WANG Tan on the education of the future Jen-tsung, discouraging his concentration on literary studies in favor of ethical training (*WCWKYS*,1b).

[3] See, for instance, the example of CH'UNG Fang mentioned in the previous chapter, Note 47.

[4] See in *KMPY* the recurrent requests by emperors for "straight speaking" 直言 often following some inauspicious or unfavorable happening. The "Myriad Word Memorial" of WANG An-shih exemplifies the voluntarily submitted criticism.

[5] A trusted councilor might act in the Emperor's name without even obtaining formal approval. Cf. *SS*,282,13a.

Emperor also filled an indispensable role as the moderator and final arbiter of divergent opinions.

The first five Sung rulers appear to have played this role for the most part conscientiously. Their success was modified, however, not only by their varying ability, but also by other factors which at times interfered with the operation of the system. Most serious were those that might interfere with the vital channels of information on which the ruler was completely reliant. If one of several opposing groups within the government could pack the Council of State with its adherents, and from there capture the Censorate and Bureau of Policy Criticism, appoint its leading opponents to posts away from the capital, and keep others from access to the Imperial ear, the ruler was in fact (perhaps unconsciously) a prisoner. Eunuchs and members of the Imperial family or personal entourage had been instrumental in achieving such coups in other dynasties; with the corruption and fall of the T'ang house vividly in mind, the early Sung rulers and their officials were sufficiently alert to the danger from that direction to avoid it. But dangerously influential alignments among the officials themselves were less easily perceived and less successfully avoided. The implications of this vulnerable point for personnel administration we shall consider in later chapters.

2. The Primary Policy Organs

Measures requiring the Imperial approval were formulated by the Council of State. They were drafted with the advice and technical assistance of the Bureau of Academicians, and subject to criticism through the Censorate, Bureau of Policy Criticism, and other information and rectification organs.

The Council of State

This council consisted during this period of a variable number of councilors [6] of different grades. The chief councilors [7] most often numbered two, though sometimes only one and sometimes as many as three. They were at the same time the heads of the Secretariat-Chancellery. The assisting councilors [8] were divided between civil and military. The assisting civil councilors [9] were at the same time the assistants of the chief councilors in the Secretariat-Chancellery.

[6] Tsai-chih 宰執.   [8] Chih-cheng 執政.
[7] Tsai-hsiang 宰相.   [9] Fu-hsiang 副相.

TABLE 1

THE SUNG CENTRAL GOVERNMENT

960–1080

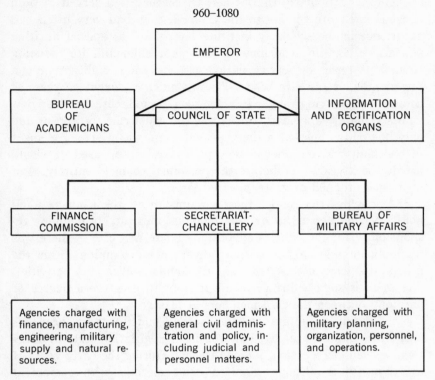

They varied from one to three. The assisting military councilors, who held varying titles, were the chief officials of the Bureau of Military Affairs, and numbered usually from two to four. The total number of councilors of all kinds might vary from as few as five to as many as nine.[10]

[10] The term *tsai-hsiang* (or *cheng-hsiang* 正相) was used informally in place of the proper title, *t'ung chung-shu men-hsia p'ing chang shih* 同中書門下平章事 , which may be rendered as "first privy councilors." Similarly, the proper title of their civil assistants was *ts'an-chih cheng-shih* 參知政事 , or "second privy councilors." First established in 964, they did not become regular members of the Council until 973; from the last years of T'ai-tsung, their privileges were increased until there was little to distinguish their powers from those of the chief councilors. The assisting military councilors are named below. The chief councilors, according to their number, divided between them the headships of the three institutes (see below, Note 102; *TK*,49,11a; *SS*,161,7b–9b).

The chief councilors were usually drawn from among those who had already served for some time as civil or military assisting councilors, particularly the former. Often they had served in both capacities. Before coming to the Council, they had very often had experience in the scholarly institutes, and later as special drafting officials or Han-lin academicians. Both for chief and for assisting councilors, terms of service varied greatly: they might be only a few months, or (as with WANG Tan) as much as seventeen years as councilor of varying ranks. In a ten-year period, three or four new names generally appeared. But it was the usual rule to drop or add only one or two men at a time, so that there was a strong element of continuity. Even when a new policy trend appeared, it would usually be a year or so before the personnel changed entirely. And men once dropped often reappeared later.[11]

It is obvious that under these circumstances, the Council could not very well act as an ever-harmonious unit, accepting joint responsibility for the policies advocated. There was often—there was no doubt intended to be—a sharp divergence of opinion within the group. But carried to extremes, this could handicap its activities, and there is some evidence of an attempt to preserve a degree of harmony between the civil members at least.[12]

The kind of business transacted by the Council was homogeneous only in its importance. It might consist of legislation, executive action, or even, on occasion, judicial review. During the early years of the dynasty, the Emperors often dealt directly with competent agencies such as the Bureau of Military Affairs or the Finance Commission, without informing even the chief councilors; but later most proposals and actions passed through the Council, which might even take final action in the ruler's name.[13]

The Bureau of Academicians [14]

This bureau was staffed by officials distinguished as scholars, commonly given the title of Han-lin academician.[15] Those of special

---

[11] Cf. *SS*,210–211,*passim*.

[12] *SS*,211,8b; 9a. Such harmony between civil and military members was, it seems, felt to be less necessary.

[13] Cf. CH'IEN Mu, Hsiang-ch'üan, and above.

[14] *Hsüeh-shih Yüan* 學士院.

[15] *Han-lin hsüeh-shih* 翰林學士.

distinction might be accorded the title of Han-lin academician for the transmission of directives,[16] while others might be assigned to the function without the formal title, as Bureau auxiliaries.[17] The titles of Han-lin reader- or lecturer-in-waiting [18] were also accorded at times. In addition to their duties of drafting, research, and advice for the Emperor and Council of State, they might also be assigned to other commissions while retaining their Han-lin titles, as we shall see below.[19]

The Information and Rectification Functions

These were divided among several agencies in addition to the Censorate and Bureau of Policy Criticism. Between them, and with intentional overlapping of functions, they were to keep the Emperors and central authorities informed on local conditions and the functioning of the government throughout the Empire, provide a channel for complaints and suggestions from all sources, criticize policy suggestions, and cause reconsideration where it seemed desirable. The institutional expression of the information and rectification functions, and the protection afforded those performing the functions, formed the closest Chinese parallel to the constitutional separation of powers.

In the matured system there were three public attention agencies whereby citizens and officials could call governmental notice to complaints and suggestions which they felt had not been properly heeded by the normal administrative authorities. These agencies were the Public Attention Message Bureau,[20] the Public Attention

---

[16] *Han-lin hsüeh-shih ch'eng-chih* 承旨.

[17] *Chih-yüan* 直院.

[18] *Han-lin shih-tu, shih-chiang hsüeh-shih* 侍讀侍講學士.

[19] *TK*,54,4b; *SS*,162,15a. This organ must not be confused with the *Han-lin Yüan* 翰林院 (Han-lin [Artisans'] Bureau), although at the beginning of the dynasty it was occasionally referred to by that name! (Cf. *SLYYP*,7,1b; *SHY:CK*,36,75a.) The title of Han-lin academician is also to be distinguished from similar titles that were conferred on councilors of state or other high officials as a mark of honor: e.g. senior academician of the Kuan-wen hall (*Kuan-wen tien ta-hsüeh-shih* 觀文殿大學士), or academician of the Tzu-cheng hall (*Tzu-cheng tien* 資政殿 *ta-hsüeh-shih*), etc. The Bureau of Academicians (known also as the Imperial special consultants or *nei-chih* 內制), together with the special drafting officials of the Secretariat or *chih-chih-kao* 知制誥 (known also as the Departmental special consultants or the *wai* 外 *-chih*) constituted the two kinds of special consultants (*liang* 兩 *-chih*).

[20] *Teng-wen Chien Yüan* 登聞檢院.

Drum Bureau,[21] and the Message Handling Bureau.[22] All maintained offices at the capital open to the public, and by their triplication were meant to ensure a fair hearing to a complainant who might receive insufficient attention at one of them. They transmitted to the central authorities not only matters of individual concern, but messages concerning matters of state.[23]

A Document Reviewing Office [24] existed from 993. Staffed by officials of high standing, its duty was to review the measures issued by the central government before their final promulgation. It scrutinized the documents it received not only to detect errors of form, but to pass on matters of substance as well. If an action seemed unwise or unjust, the Office would return it for reconsideration.[25]

In the preoccupation with urgent administrative tasks during the earlier part of the dynasty, officials seem to have been assigned to the duties of policy criticism only rather irregularly. In 1017 it was decreed that there should be a staff of six policy-criticism officials,[26] but the Bureau of Policy Criticism [27] does not seem to have become established on a regular basis until the following reign, when its members came to attend the Imperial audiences daily and took a more active part in policy discussions.[28]

[21] *Teng-wen Ku Yüan* 鼓院.

[22] *Li Chien Yüan* 理檢院.

[23] The first two agencies mentioned existed from 1007, and the third from 1029. At the beginning of the dynasty there was but a single agency, called the *Kuei yüan* 匭院 . This was in 984 renamed the *Teng-wen yüan* 登聞院;subordinate to it there was a Drum Office (*Ku ssu* 鼓司), which was the forerunner of the Public Attention Drum Bureau. A *Li chien yüan* had been established in 991, but seems to have been abolished in 995 or soon after. When reëstablished in 1029, it was placed under the administration of an executive censor (*SHY:CK*,3,62a–67b; *SS*,161,16b).

[24] *Feng-po Ssu* 封駁司.

[25] This function had been in the T'ang, and was again later in the Sung, that of the reviewing policy advisers (*chi shih chung* 給事中). For a short time in 993, officials were appointed to "coadminister the affairs of the reviewing policy advisers," but the title was changed later the same year. (This date, given in *HCP*, is verified by other circumstances; *SHY* and *TK* by error say "ninth year" for "ninth month".) The Office was at first under the jurisdiction of the Document Transmission Office; from 1001 it came under that of the Chancellery, but in 1059 returned to its former status (*SHY:CK*,2,42a; *TK*,50,17b; *KMPY*,993/6; 993/8; *HCP*,34,7b; *KMPY*,1059/4).

[26] *Chien-kuan* 諫官.

[27] *Chien Yüan* 諫院.

[28] Titular policy criticism officials might be appointed to the duties their titles implied. (For titular offices, see Chapter V.) These were especially the right and left

The Censorate [29] also was rather slow in developing, and during the first two reigns its duties were largely carried out by specially delegated investigators [30] or investigating auxiliaries.[31] Beginning with Chen-tsung's reign, however, the organization began to realize in practice the theoretical structure it had inherited from the T'ang. This was headed by an executive censor.[32] Second in responsibility was the censor of miscellaneous affairs.[33] Under these, the Censorate was divided into three sections: the Bureau of General Affairs,[34] the Palace Bureau,[35] and the Bureau of Administration,[36] staffed respectively by the general, palace, and investigating censors.[37] In 1045, policy censors [38] also were added to the number, formalizing the censorial participation in policy criticism which was an important Sung innovation in the system.[39]

It is noteworthy that the information and rectification organs of this period stressed very strongly their function of watching over

policy critics (*ssu-chien* 司諫, before 988 called *pu-ch'üeh* 補闕), and the right and left policy monitors (*cheng-yen* 正言, before 988, *shih-yi* 拾遺). Other officials appointed to the work were called administrators of the Bureau (*chih Chien-yüan* 知諫院). In 1032 they were assigned a building of their own, and in 1043 four men of prominence were appointed to the Bureau, including Ou-yang Hsiu (*TK*,50, 23b–24a; *SS*,161,12b; *SHY*:CK,50a–53b; *KMPY*,1017/2; 1031/7; 1032/7; 1043/3; 1043/8).

[29] *Yü-shih T'ai* 御史臺.

[30] *T'ui-k'an* 推勘.

[31] *T'ui-chih* 推直.

[32] *Yü-shih chung-ch'eng* 中丞.
Or an official with another titular office discharging the duties of that post (*TK*,53, 4a–b). The office of censor-in-chief remained titular only.

[33] *Shih-yü-shih chih-tsa-shih* 侍御史知雜事.

[34] *T'ai Yüan* 臺院.

[35] *Tien Yüan* 殿院.

[36] *Ch'a Yüan* 察院.

[37] *Shih-yü-shih, tien-chung shih-yü-shih, chien-ch'a yü-shih* 殿中侍御史，監察御史.
The three bureau scheme was inherited from the T'ang censorate. The first designation of a titular censor to carry out censorial functions is said to have been in 974 (*TK*,53,4b). The movement to return all titular censors to their proper duties is found in 1001/3 (*KMPY*), and was carried out actively during the following decade (*SHY*:CK,17,5a–b). In addition to the executive censor, that of miscellaneous affairs, and the investigating auxiliaries, there were to be six censors of lower rank.

[38] *Yen-shih yü-shih* 言事御史.

[39] *TK*,53,20a; *KMPY*,1045/1.

the policies of the central government, and directed their efforts much less toward the policing of detailed administrative activities, which was left largely to other hands. The lesson of the T'ang decay and dismemberment had made the statesmen of the time concerned above all with the integrity of the central power and with the institutional checks which seemed to protect it. The Censorate was destined, later in the Sung, to develop elaborate procedures for checking on the day-to-day operations of all the central governmental agencies; in later dynasties this system covered the whole empire.[40] In the early Sung this apparatus seems still almost wholly lacking. (Had it existed, it might indeed have proved an invaluable asset.) But in the realm of policy the information and rectification organs were more effective; under Jen-tsung and Ying-tsung they made their power felt to an extent perhaps unparalleled in any other period of similar duration.

This power was by no means exercised without opposition, particularly from some councilors of state who resented any encroachment on the Council's authority. This opposition may explain why no head of the Censorate at this time bore the high-ranking title of Censor-in-Chief.[41] It may also explain the desire of some councilors to divert censors and policy-criticism officials from their accustomed duties by giving them special charges outside their normal field.[42] Despite such opposition, however, the censors and policy-criticism officials succeeded in establishing a fair degree of independence from the Council and other organs. The prestige which their title carried was reinforced by a conviction that censors should be men of unusual attainments; the executive censors were not infrequently former councilors of state.[43] Their appointment was removed from the exclusive jurisdiction of the Council.[44] Within the Censorate also there was some protection of the individual censor's independence of

[40] The development of censorial machinery through the dynasties, especially the Ming, has been interestingly described in a study by Dr. Charles O. HUCKER on the fifteenth-century Ming Censorate, as yet unpublished. A briefer outline is to be found in KYH:*CKYSCT*.

[41] *Yü-shih ta-fu* 大夫.
TK,53,8b.

[42] *KMPY*,1019/4.

[43] Cf. *SHY:*CK,3,50b; 17,5a; *SLYYP*,7,1b.

[44] See Chapter X. They seem to have enjoyed also some protection of tenure; cf. *KMPY*,1017/2; *SHY:*CK,17,5b; *JCSP*,IV,11,13b.

action: after 1022, censors were directed to make their accusations and criticisms without prior consultation with their administrative superiors.[45] Those who furnished the censors with information and complaints were likewise protected by the rule permitting censors to keep secret the sources of their information. (In this connection, it should be noted that a censor's complaint normally led to a further investigation of the situation in question before action was taken.) [46] The censors' remarkable immunity from reprisals in this period was vouched for by Su Shih, who claimed that although before the Sung some hundred censors had died for their frankness, during the century from the founding of the Sung to his own time not a single criticism had been punished.[47]

This protection emboldened the censors and criticism officials to make free use of their powers. Their criticisms, said Su, ". . . disregarded position. If their words touched on the Imperial person, the Son of Heaven's composure was disturbed; if the matter concerned the halls of government, chief councilors behaved with humility." [48] Through the action of these public gadflies, not a few officials lost posts in the Council, or were prevented from obtaining them: a more concrete, if less eloquent example of censorial influence.[49]

3. The Division of Administrative Authority

As we have seen, the distinction between the legislative and policy-making functions on the one hand, and the administrative function on the other, was not absolute, but only a matter of emphasis. As the organs just described were concerned with administration as well as policy, so the organs now to be considered were responsible

[45] This rule was established by the Executive Censor Liu Yün (*SS*,305,10a–b; *HCP*,99,9a; *KMPY*,1022/11).

[46] *JCSP*,IV,13a.

[47] *STPCC*, tsou-yi,1,23b. This statement was made in a memorial submitted to Shen-tsung. A part of it is translated in Lin, *Gay Genius,* 121–122. It is not quite literally true; cf. the case of K'ung Tao-fu (*SS*,297,2b–3b).

[48] *Loc. cit.*

[49] For example, two chief councilors thus lost their posts in 1038, others in 1051, 1053, 1054, 1056. An assisting military councilor lost his post in 1043; in 1047 an intended appointment to chief councilor was changed to that of assisting military councilor (*SS*,211,*passim*). The initiative in these cases was shared by the censors and the policy critics.

for suggesting policies within their individual spheres, as well as with the problems of administration.

The administrative authority was divided broadly into three spheres: economic, military, and ordinary civil administration. This scheme does not seem to have been planned according to any theory, but to have evolved during the later T'ang and thereafter because of immediate need to supervise closely the financial and military operations. The ordinary civil administration and the military administration were headed respectively by the Secretariat-Chancellery [50] and the Bureau of Military Affairs.[51] The chiefs of both, as we have seen, were members of the Council of State, and the two together were known as the "two authorities." [52] The economic administration was entrusted to the Finance Commission,[53] which had a somewhat different and rather ambiguous status. While its heads were often referred to as the "accounting councilors," [54] they had no place in the Council. Satisfactory under the direct control exerted by the first Emperors, this relationship became less workable later, and eventually (in 1070) the economic organization underwent a fundamental reorganization.[55]

The Military Administration

The Bureau of Military Affairs was headed by a varying number of officials whose titles differed from time to time. They might be commissioners of military affairs,[56] or administrators or coadministrators of the Bureau,[57] assistant commissioners of military affairs,[58] or signatory or cosignatory officials of the Bureau.[59] The heads of the Bureau were aided by six auxiliary academicians of the Bureau of Military Affairs,[60] one of whom might on occasion act in the absence of a higher functionary as signatory official. The heads might

[50] *Chung-shu Men-hsia* 中書門下.

[51] *Shu-mi Yüan* 樞密院.

[52] *Liang-fu* 兩府.

[53] *San-ssu* 三司.

[54] *Chi-hsiang* 計相.

[55] The administrative control of the three chief administrative organs was strengthened from 990 by a rule that they should receive for revision all measures within their respective spheres before final promulgation (*KMPY*,990/12).

[56] *Shu-mi shih* 使.

[57] *Chih (t'ung-chih) Shu-mi Yüan shih* 知(同知)樞密院事.

[58] *Shu-mi fu-shih* 副使.

[59] *Ch'ien-shu (t'ung ch'ien-shu) Shu-mi Yüan shih* 簽書(同簽書)樞密院事.

[60] *Shu-mi chih hsüeh-shih* 直學士.

be selected from civil service officials as well as from military. The Bureau planned and directed the national defense, either through its own activities or through the supervision of other military agencies.[61]

The Economic Administration

The organization of the Finance Commission varied during the early years of the dynasty. Its duties were usually divided among three offices: the Office of Salt and Iron,[62] the Office of Funds,[63] and the Office of the Census.[64] At times the three were under a single finance commissioner;[65] at times a separate commissioner was appointed to each. For a while, the authority was divided between two commissioners of accounts[66] on a regional basis, under the supervision of a commissioner of general accounts.[67] From 1003, however, the system became established under which the Commission was headed by a single Commissioner aided by an Assistant Commissioner in Charge of Salt and Iron,[68] another in charge of Funds,[69] and another in charge of the Census.[70] The Salt and Iron Office was

[61] Cf. *SS*,162,1a–4b; 210–211,*passim; HCLY*,25,1a; 27,11b.

[62] *Yen-t'ieh Ssu* 鹽鐵司.

[63] *Tu-chih Ssu* 度支司.

[64] *Hu-pu* 戶部.

[65] *San-ssu shih* 三司使.

[66] *Chi shih*.

[67] *Tsung chi shih* 總計使.

[68] *Yen-t'ieh fu-shih* 副使.

[69] *Tu-chih fu-shih*.

[70] *Hu-pu fu-shih*.

With the growth of the Empire during the latter years of the first Sung Emperor, increasing attention was given to the personnel of the finance administration, and officials of high rank were entrusted with the task of recovering the control of funds from the irresponsible local officials inherited from the Five Dynasties. In the eighth month of 983, three commissioners were appointed to assume the responsibilities of the three offices. In the fifth month of 993 they were replaced by a single commissioner, assisted by six supervisory officials (*p'an-kuan*) and three investigators (*t'ui-kuan*). In the tenth month of the same year, the empire was divided geographically into left and right "accounts" (*chi* 計) under commissioners of the left and right accounts, in the hope of overcoming the disorder occasioned by the increasing arrears in bookkeeping. Shortly thereafter, the two accounts were placed under the supervision of a commissioner of general accounts. In the twelfth month of 994, there was a reversion to the system of three commissioners. The final return to a single commissioner took place in the sixth month of 1003, and lasted without important change until a radical reorganization of the whole financial administration was undertaken in 1069. (See *KMPY*, under the dates indicated.)

generally in charge of the exploitation of natural resources, river communications, supervision of commerce and excises, and the provision of materials for military use. The Office of Funds prepared and balanced the governmental budget, and cared for and distributed the funds and products gathered for State use. The Census Office administered the population census, the collection of taxes (including the wine excise), long-term storage facilities, and certain construction projects. Within each office, these duties were divided among five to eight desks,[71] each responsible for a particular field of activities.[72]

The Finance Commission thus took over practically all the former functions of the Ministry of Finance, leaving the latter only the formal duty of registering and reporting tax receipts.[73] It assumed the task of directing the arsenals, traditionally belonging to the Directorate of Military Supplies.[74] It took from the Directorate of Construction[75] the control of carpentry and soil engineering.[76] It also took over some of the former functions of the Ministry of Works,[77] including the administration of agricultural colonies, forests, and waterways (sharing the two latter after 1058 with the Directorate of Waterways).[78] Its jurisdiction duplicated or superseded in places that of the Court of Agricultural Supervision [79] and the Court of the Imperial Treasury.[80] The former retained, however, the control of the ever-normal granaries.[81] Still other related economic functions were left entirely to other agencies. The prefectural mints, for instance, were under the Directorate of Imperial Workshops.[82] The

[71] An 案.

[72] SS,162,12a.

[73] TK,52,24b. The Ministry (Hu-pu) is not to be confused with the office of the same Chinese title under the Finance Commission.

[74] Chün-ch'i Chien 軍器監.
SS,165,23a; TK,57,22b.

[75] Chiang-tso Chien 將作監.

[76] TK,57,11b; SS,165,21b.

[77] Kung-pu 工部.

[78] TK,52,41b; 25a; SS,165,24b.

[79] Ssu-nung Ssu 司農寺.

[80] T'ai-fu Ssu 太府寺.
SS,165,6a; 9a.

[81] KMPY,1006/1.

[82] Shao-fu Chien 少府監.
TK,57,8b.

Commission provided, nevertheless, a greater measure of centralization in governmental economic activities than had existed under previous dynasties.

The Ordinary Civil Administration

The oversight of governmental administration apart from the military and fiscal realms was, as we have already seen, entrusted to the Secretariat-Chancellery. This organ, combining what in the T'ang had been two independent agencies, now had authority over a rather bewildering number of subordinate offices.[83] Some were ministries, directorates, or courts inherited from the T'ang system; many more were special agencies created to take over special functions; some were independent, some were subordinated one to another. Two groups concern us particularly: those concerned with judicial administration and those concerned with personnel problems.

Judicial administration. The judicial functions were in part performed by special organs and specialized personnel, but many functions were in the hands of general administrative officials, and the threads of judicial administration were tied into the executive line of authority at a number of points. In local administration, as we shall see below, the judicial officials tended to be specialized and nonspecialized on alternate levels. At the capital, the supreme judicial organs were subject to the supervision of the Secretariat-Chancellery and the Council of State, as well as to the scrutiny of the information and rectification organs.

There were three chief agencies at the capital concerned with law in its several aspects: the Bureau of Judicial Investigation,[84] the Ministry of Justice,[85] and the High Court of Justice.[86] Their primary functions were both legislative and judicial. They proposed measures concerning judicial procedure and administration, and amendments

---

[83] Some of the special agencies, such as the Bureau of Judicial Investigation and the Bureau of Administrative Personnel, were created to take over functions originally discharged directly by sections of the Secretariat-Chancellery. This was done partly to reduce the power of that organ, it seems. Cf. *TK*,52,17a; *SCSS*,9,153. In a special relation to that organ stood the Bureau of Drafting Officials (*She-jen Yüan* 舍人院), which drew up state documents, and the special drafting officials (*chih chih-kao* 知制誥). (*SS*,161,19b.)

[84] *Shen-hsing Yüan* 審刑院.

[85] *Hsing-pu* 刑部.

[86] *Ta-li Ssu* 大理寺.

of civil and penal law.[87] They reviewed sentences passed by lower judicial authority throughout the empire, when there were difficulties of legal interpretation or severe penalties involved.[88] In the procedure of review adopted at the end of T'ai-tsung's reign, cases were received by the Bureau of Judicial Investigation, sent from there to the High Court of Justice for an opinion, and back to the Bureau for further review. The opinion of the Bureau was then sent to the Secretariat; if it met approval there, the verdict was then announced. If not, the case received further consideration by the Chief Councilors before the final decision was delivered.[89]

The Censorate and its associated agencies also played an important role in the administration of justice. They provided the natural channel for appeals if an injustice remained undiscovered through the chain of local supervision (discussed below), or if the judicial organs at the capital should err. Certain of the Censorate investigators and investigating auxiliaries were specially responsible for checking on local prosecutions, and seeing that no one was improperly detained under arrest. Censors were spe-

[87] The Sung code of 963 was prepared by a supervisory judge of the High Court of Justice. Since traditional Chinese law applies penal sanctions to civil law relationships, the distinction of civil and penal law is difficult to draw.

[88] From 962, all capital sentences were to be reviewed by the central government before execution (TK,166,31b). This revived a T'ang practice which had lapsed during the Five Dynasties.

[89] The duty of review at first belonged to the Ministry, which in addition to the one or two officials in charge (chu-p'an 主判 kuan) in 990 appointed six (five?) reconsideration officials (hsiang-fu 詳覆 kuan) for the purpose (KMPY,990/5; TK,166,36b; HCLY,25,4a). The High Court soon received the duty of examining cases before they reached the Ministry. This organ was headed by a supervisory judge (p'an ssu shih 判寺事) aided by a provisional lord assistant chief justice (ch'üan shao-ch'ing 權少卿); it was at first staffed by varying numbers of revisory judges (cheng 正), assistant justices (ch'eng 丞), judicial investigators (p'ing-shih 評事); and later men with other titular offices were chosen, called reviewing officials (hsiang-tuan kuan 詳斷官). Six at first, these were later increased to eleven or twelve;. they were assisted by two legal auxiliaries (fa-chih 法直 kuan), or legal examiners, and aides of other kinds (SHY:CK,24,1a; SS,165,1a; HCLY,25,4b). In 991, the Bureau was established to oversee the previous judicial agencies, which were suspected of undue preoccupation with legal technicalities, if not chicanery. It was staffed by an administrator and six deliberating officials (hsiang-yi 詳議 kuan), selected from men with judicial experience (TK,166,37a; SSYT,5,4b–5a; SS,163,29a; 199,13a; KMPY, 991/8). The review by the Ministry, at first preserved, was dropped in 993 (HCP, 34,3b).

cifically charged with inspecting the prisons at the capital for this purpose.[90]

Personnel administration. Matters of personnel administration came in general under the authority of the Secretariat-Chancellery, but that organ delegated most of its functions to other agencies, retaining for itself the right of general supervision and direct jurisdiction in certain cases. The personnel functions were distributed partly according to the class of the civil service in question, and partly according to the kind of activity required of the administrator.

The doctoral examination administrators,[91] officials of high prestige, were specially appointed on each occasion. They were assisted by a corps of examiners and other officials who carried out the details of the examination procedures to be described later, and by a Bureau of Examination Copyists.[92] The Ministry of Rites, once charged with these functions, retained only the administration of candidates' records and other such routine duties, which were entrusted to its Examination Bureau.[93]

Routine details of civil service administration apart from the doctoral examinations were carried out by the Ministry of Personnel.[94] But the more significant functions were removed from its control. The administration of merit rating, the reveiw of past performance for reward or penalty, and the proposal of specific appointments, all were divided among different agencies according to the rank and function of the officials for which they were responsible. The division of responsibility for most groups assumed its characteristic pattern, after a period of experimentation, in 993. From that time, the case reviews and appointments of officials in the executory class were under the jurisdiction of the Bureau of Executory Personnel,[95] nominally an office of the Ministry of Personnel.[96] The lower

---

[90] *TK*,166,36b–37b; *SS*,164,4b; *HCLY*,25,4b; *KMPY*,990/5.

[91] *Chih kung-chü* 知貢舉.

[92] *T'eng-lu Yüan* 謄錄院.

[93] *Kung Yüan* 貢院.

*SHY:*CK,13,1a; 8b; *TK*,52,29b. The Ministry of Rites also administered the rarely given decree examinations, described later.

[94] *Li-pu* 吏部.

*SHY:*CK,8,1a; 10,20a.

[95] *Liu-nei Ch'üan* 流內銓.

[96] For the classes of the civil service, see Chapter V below. The Bureau of Executory Personnel apparently had this responsibility under T'ai-tsu (cf. *LPC*,2,14a). In 992,

administrative class officials were placed under the jurisdiction of the Bureau of Administrative Personnel.[97] Both of these bureaus made use of the reports and merit ratings made by local officials concerning their subordinates.[98]

The higher administrative-class officials remained under the direct jurisdiction of the Secretariat-Chancellery. A special difficulty, however, remained in the case of the civil circuit intendants, who supervised the operations of local government. Since they had no superiors in their local areas, it was difficult to assess their performance. To remedy this, an Office for Case Review of Judicial Intendants,[99] was established in 1036, and in 1049 the system was extended to include the fiscal intendants as well; both were placed under a Circuit Intendants Merit Bureau.[100]

The special importance which men of this time attached to personnel administration is attested not only by the attention given to organizing these several offices, but by the high calibre of the officials selected at different times to head them. Often men of high personal prestige, they frequently were chosen from among the censors or Han-lin academicians.[101]

These agencies were only a few of the many that existed at the capital to carry out the details of governmental operation. The

---

for a short time, and under changing names, a special agency was set up to administer the merit ratings for this class, but in 993 this function reverted to the Bureau of Executory Personnel (*SHY*:CK,59,4b–5a; *HCP*,33,7a–b; 34,4b; *KMPY*,991/int.2; *TK*,39,38b–39a).

[97] *Shen-kuan Yüan* 審官院.

A Bureau of Commissions (*Ch'ai-ch'ien yüan* 差遣院) had been established as early as 981 to supervise the appointment of the lower administrative officials. Some ten years later, a separate Administrative Officials Case Review Bureau (*Mo-k'an ching-ch'ao kuan yüan* 磨勘京朝官院) was apparently established. The early history of these bureaus is somewhat confused, but they were eventually merged and from 993 became the Bureau of Administrative Personnel (*HCP*,22,10b–11a; *TK*,52, 16b–17a; *SHY*:CK, 11,1a–b; 59,4b; *KMPY*,991/2; *SS*,266,10b).

[98] See Chapter V.

[99] *Mo-k'an Chu-lu T'i-tien-hsing-yü Ssu* 磨勘諸路提點刑獄司.

[100] *Chuan-yün-shih Fu T'i-tien-hsing-yü K'o-chi Yüan* 轉運使副提點刑獄課績院.

The titles of both these were at first rather variable. Cf. *SHY*:CK,59,6a–8b; *HCP*, 119,12b; 191,15b; 195,7b; 208,6a–b; *KMPY*,1049/2; 1061/10; *TK*,39,44a.

[101] MA Tuan-lin noted that in this respect the Sung invested personnel administration with more importance than had the men of the T'ang dynasty (*TK*,39,39a).

general term by which they were known, the "hundred offices," originally hyperbolic, ended as a modest understatement.[102]

4. The Organs of Local Administration

The responsibility for local administration throughout the empire was divided primarily on the basis of territorial units. Functional lines of authority cut across territorial divisions to some extent; the growing economic interdependence of the different regions en-

---

[102] Among the agencies devoted to miscellaneous civil administrative activities at the capital, the following few may be noted:

Agencies of transmission:
  Document Forwarding Office (*T'ung-chin Ssu* 通進司)
  Document Transmission Office (*Yin-t'ai Ssu* 銀臺司)
  General Memorial Acceptance Bureau (*Tu Chin-tsòu Yüan* 都進奏院)
  Palace Postern Office (*Ho-men* 閤門)
Agencies concerned with details cf foreign relations:
  Court of Diplomatic Reception (*Hung-lu Ssu* 鴻臚寺)
  Hospitality Commandancy (*K'o-sheng Shih* 客省使)
  Usher Commandancy (*Yin-chin Shih* 引進使)
  Commandancy of General Comity (*Ssu-fang Kuan* 四方館)
  Bureau of Foreign Interchange (*Li-pin Yüan* 禮賓院)
Agencies concerned with educational administration:
  Directorate of Education (*Kuo-tzu Chien* 國子監)
  National University (*T'ai Hsüeh* 太學)
  School of the Four Gates (*Ssu-men Hsüeh* 四門學)
Archives, libraries, and research institutions:
  The "three institutes" (*san kuan* 三館) housed in the Ch'ung-wen Library
    (*Ch'ung-wen Yüan* 崇文院):
      Chao-wen Institute (*Chao-wen Kuan* 昭文館)
      Chi-hsien Library (*Chi-hsien Tien* 集賢殿)
      Institute of History (*Shih Kuan* 史館)
  Imperial Archives (*Pi Ko* 祕閣)
  Imperial Recording Bureau (*Ch'i-chü Yüan* 起居院)
  Directorate of Astronomical Observation (*Ssu-t'ien Chien* 司天監)
Agencies of protocol and state cult:
  Bureau of Protocol (*Li-yi Yüan* 禮儀院)
  Court of Imperial Sacrifices (*T'ai-ch'ang Ssu* 太常寺)
  Bureau of Imperial Sacrificial Ritual (*T'ai-ch'ang Li Yüan* 太常禮院)
  Court of Imperial Banquets (*Kuang-lu Ssu* 光祿寺)
Agencies of Imperial Family administration:
  High Office of Imperial Family Affairs (*Ta Tsung-cheng Ssu* 大宗正司)
  Court of Imperial Family Affairs (*Tsung-cheng Ssu* 宗正寺)
  Imperial Genealogy Establishment (*Yü-tieh So* 玉牒所)
Some of these also had functions outside the fields under which they are here listed.

couraged this tendency. But in the early Sung, as in other periods of Chinese history, functional administrative centralization was discouraged by the need to administer vast areas with a relatively small body of officials and a communication network which, though extensive, was slow.

The basic administrative unit was the subprefecture,[103] the smallest in area and closest in its contacts with the ordinary citizens. Groups of subprefectures were supervised by prefectures, and these in turn by the circuit intendants, who inspected governmental operations over larger regions, and were the most important authorities outside the capital.

The Subprefectures

A subprefecture characteristically consisted of a town, which was the administrative center, and its surrounding country and villages. A larger city might, however, have one or more subprefectures of largely urban character within its limits. During the early years of the dynasty, subprefectures of the largest class had populations in excess of four thousand households, while the smallest might have under five hundred.[104] In general the numbers increased steadily during the period we are considering. If the subprefecture were one of lesser importance, its government would be headed by a subprefect,[105] a middle executory-class official.[106] If more important, it might be headed by a subprefectural administrator[107] drawn from the administrative class, the civil aides, or military officers.[108] The head official was assisted by a staff which, according to the importance of the place, might include an assistant subprefect,[109] a registrar,[110] a sheriff,[111] and a number of clerical officials.[112]

---

[103] *Hsien* 縣.

[104] The average was perhaps around 2,500 or 3,000 households. The number of subprefectures in the Empire passed 1,230 in 980 and does not seem to have varied greatly thereafter, until the loss of the North in 1127. For the population figures, see also previous chapter. (Cf. *SS*,85,1a–2a; NCC:TLCKY,I,6,8–9.) The classification of subprefectures by population is that of 960 (*TK*,63,28a).

[105] *Hsien-ling* 縣令.   [106] For the classes of the civil service, see Chapter V.

[107] *Chih-hsien* 知縣.   [108] *SHY:*CK,48,25a.

[109] *Ch'eng* 丞.   [110] *Chu-pu* 主簿.

[111] *Wei* 尉.

[112] Assistant subprefects were confined at this time to the subprefectures of the capital, where they were appointed beginning in 1026. At first executory-class officials, they

TABLE 2

SUNG LOCAL GOVERNMENT

960–1080

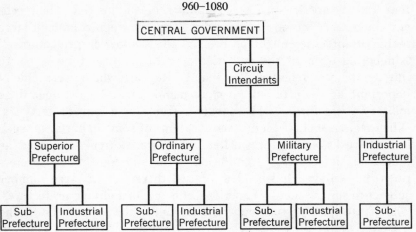

The head of the subprefecture assumed responsibility for the general welfare of the population under his jurisdiction. His duties included not only care for public safety, justice, education, taxation, and the command of a local garrison contingent, but concern with the moral and economic well-being of the community as well: a heavy responsibility to be carried by an official of comparatively low standing in the service. The assistant subprefect and the registrar gave the head general assistance in his duties, while the sheriff was particularly responsible in matters of public order.[113] Many of the duties of local administration in the rural areas were carried out, under the guidance of these officials, by local functionaries who served without pay and who undertook such tasks as tax assessment, police duties, the management of storehouses, local public works, and the settlement of minor litigations.[114]

---

were from 1051 men newly appointed to the administrative class (*SHY*:CK,48,53a). In smaller places the posts of registrar and sheriff might be held by the same man (*SS*,167,28b; *SHY*:CK,11,76a).

[113] *SHY*:CK,48,25a; *CKFC*,42,7b–9b.

[114] From 980 local families were divided into nine groups on the basis of wealth, and the lower five groups exempted from such services. By Jen-tsung's reign the expense devolving on those thus bearing the exclusive burden had become in many cases disastrous, and in 1055 a system of rotation was devised to mitigate it. Under Shen-tsung, the system was replaced by one of paid services. Cf. NCC:SYFS.

The Prefectures

These supervised the subprefectural administration and were of four kinds: superior, ordinary, military, and industrial. Their general importance varied in that order. Regions which contained large or important cities might be designated as superior prefectures.[115] Numbering eight at the end of the tenth century, these grew to thirteen by the reign of Ying-tsung. Regions which were chiefly important as seats of military command might be designated as military prefectures.[116] These varied from forty-four to forty-six. When regions included industrial locations of some importance, such as salt works, mines, or smelters, they were often designated as industrial prefectures.[117] In addition to three or four of such prefectures that enjoyed independent status, there were a large number subject to supervision by superior, ordinary, or military prefectures. The greater part of the country came under the supervision of the ordinary prefectures [118] which varied from 253 to 255.[119] Ordinary, military, and industrial prefectures were further classified according to their relative size and importance, and superior and ordinary prefectures also according to the rank of their military command, since they generally had local troops under their authority.

Each prefecture normally supervised several subprefectures. Large prefectures might have from ten to twenty of these, while military or industrial prefectures might have only one or two. A smaller industrial prefecture, itself supervised by another prefecture, would have none.[120]

The center of prefectural administration was located in a large town or city of the area, whose name was given to the prefecture as

[115] *Fu* 府.
[116] *Chün* 軍.
[117] *Chien* 監.
[118] *Chou* 州.
[119] See NCC:FCCC,53.

[120] These statements summarize the enumerations to be found in YFCY, which notes changes down to about 1075. (See also Table 2.) The prefectures were further classified on the basis of their military commands as:

Regional command (*chieh-tu* 節度)
Regional supervisory (*kuan-ch'a* 觀察)
Regional defense (*fang-yü* 防禦)
Militia command (*t'uan-lien* 團練)
Prefect (*tz'u-shih* 刺史).

a whole. The prefecture was headed by an administrator.[121] In a place of greater importance, he would be assisted by one or two vice-administrators.[122] These officials exercised authority in matters of all kinds, including judicial administration. They were aided by several civil aides,[123] including a staff supervisor,[124] a secretary[125] or general secretary,[126] and a prefectural judge.[127] Under these, the duties were divided among a staff of inspectors: with titles such as executive inspector[128] or general executive inspector,[129] police inspector,[130] judicial inspector,[131] finance inspector,[132] educational inspector,[133] instructor,[134] or teaching assistant.[135] Under these was a corps of clerical and police functionaries and employees of other kinds.

[121] *Chih-fu* (*-chou, -chün, -chien*) 知府(州, 軍, 監).

[122] *T'ung-p'an* 通判.

SS,167,22a; *HCLY*,25,8b. When an Imperial prince headed a superior prefecture, he was called a metropolitan prefect (*yin* 尹), (*SHY*:CK,37,4a). The assistant administrators were first appointed in 963 as a check on prefectural heads of uncertain loyalty. Large prefectures had two, others one, except for those of 10,000 or fewer households which were administered by civil officials (*SHY*:CK,47,2a; 58b; *SS*,167, 24a). FRANKE, *Geschichte*, IV, 362–363, has made a triple confusion between the assistant administrators, the industrial prefectures, and the circuit intendants.

[123] *Mu-chih* 幕職.

[124] *P'an-kuan* 判官.

[125] *Chih-shih* 支使.

[126] *Chang-shu-chi* 掌書記.

[127] *T'ui-kuan* 推官.

A general secretary was similar to a secretary, but of higher standing. *TK*,62,25a–b.

[128] *Lu-shih ts'an-chün* 錄事參軍.

[129] *Ssu-lu* 司錄.

[130] *Ssu-li* (or *ssu-k'ou*) *ts'an-chün* 司理(司寇)參軍.

[131] *Ssu-fa ts'an-chün* 司法參軍.

[132] *Ssu-hu ts'an-chün* 司戶參軍.

[133] *Wen-hsüeh* 文學.

[134] *Chiao-shou* 教授.

[135] *Chu-chiao* 助教.

A full staff of such officials would be found only in a large and important prefecture. In others, the duties would be combined in various ways. The prefectural heads might also have such upper staff (*shang-tso* 上佐) as an associate official (*pieh-chia* 別駕), office chief (*ch'ang-shih* 長史), and assistant office chief (*ssu-ma* 司馬). Cf. *SS*,167,25a–26b; *TK*,62,24a–25b; *TK*,63,22b; 25b; *SHY*:CK,48,1a–2b; *HCLY*,25,1b. A larger metropolis such as K'ai-feng was also subdivided into boroughs (*hsiang* 廂), largely concerned with public order and safety, and with police staffs headed by police supervisors (*chün-hsün p'an-kuan*) and police executives (*kung-shih kan-tang kuan* 公事幹當官). Cf. *TK*,63,5b; *SS*,166,16a–b.

The above were general administrative officials, whose duties were considered to affect the popular welfare. The prefectural heads had under their jurisdiction also certain officials whose activity was concerned exclusively with revenue matters. These service agents [136] were charged with the administration of governmental monopolies or other sources of revenue in the prefecture.[137]

The Circuit Intendants

The circuit intendants [138] acted as deputies of the central government in supervising the administration of the prefectures, which were divided at different times among fifteen to twenty civil circuits.[139] The intendants' function was one of oversight rather than

[136] *Chien-tang kuan* 監當官.

[137] *SS*,167,53b.

[138] *Chien-ssu* 監司.

[139] The circuit division fluctuated greatly during the opening years of the dynasty, but was comparatively stable during the eleventh century. There were 15 in 997, 17 from 1001, 18 from 1029, and 19 from 1051. From 1053 to 1055 there were 20. (The number increased in the later Northern Sung to a high point of 26). Those of about 1054 were:

Ho-pei 河北
Ho-tung 河東
Shensi 陝西 (the Yung-hsing and Ch'in-feng of late Northern Sung).
Ching-tung 京東
Ching-hsi 京西
Ching-chi 京畿 (existed 1053–1055; formed from neighboring circuits)
Huai-nan-tung 淮南東 }
Huai-nan-hsi 淮南西 } single circuit of Huai-nan before 1051
Ching-hu-pei 荊湖北
Ching-hu-nan 荊湖南
Li-chou 利州 }
K'uei-chou 夔州 } forming before 1001 the single circuit of Hsia-hsi 峽西
Yi 益 -chou   (after 1059 Ch'eng-tu 成都)   before 1001 the
Tzu 梓 -chou   (the T'ung-ch'uan of later   single circuit of
Northern Sung)   Hsi-ch'uan 西川
Liang-che 兩浙
Chiang-nan-tung 江南東 }
Chiang-nan-hsi 江南西 } single circuit of Chiang-nan before 1029
Fu-chien 福建
Kuang-nan-tung 廣南東
Kuang-nan-hsi 廣南西

The circuits, literally "roads," were called *tao* until 997/12, thereafter *lu*. Cf. NCC: TLCKY,I,6,9; *SS*,85,2a–b; *CKFC*,47,4b–6a. The locations of these are indicated in HERRMANN, pp. 42–43.

control; the prefectures remained in direct administrative contact with the capital. In this way local administration was provided with a rectification apparatus similar to that of the Censorate in the central government. Intendants were of four kinds: fiscal, judicial, exchange, and military.

The fiscal intendants,[140] while originally charged particularly with supervising financial matters, soon came to have general responsibility for all affairs of civil government within the circuits which they severally headed. They made annual tours of inspection. They were responsible for the appraisal of all local governmental personnel, and at times bore the concurrent title of intendant-inspector.[141] They were generally aided by assistant fiscal intendants [142] and circuit fiscal supervisory officials.[143]

The judicial intendants [144] supervised the judicial and penal administration within their circuits, which were identical with those of the fiscal intendants. First established for a short time in 991 as subordinates of the fiscal intendants, they were reëstablished with a more independent status in 1007. For a time they also held the duty of promoting agricultural development, with the concurrent title of agricultural intendant.[145] The area of the capital, K'ai-feng,

---

[140] *Chuan-yün shih* 轉運使.[141] *An-ch'a shih* 按察使.

[142] *Chuan-yün fu-shih* 副使.

[143] *Chuan-yün p'an-kuan* 判官.

Officials with the duties of local fiscal supervision were appointed under varying titles as early as 972 at least. They were not at first found in all circuits. Under T'ai-tsung they were established everywhere, and the title became fixed and the duties extended. Assistant intendants and supervisory officials are found as early as 972, but they were not always appointed at first. At times a circuit had two cointendants, or two assistant intendants without an intendant. The title of intendant-inspector was held from 1043 to 1046. Fiscal intendants might also be attached to military commands. Cf. *CKFC*,47,4a–5a; *HCP*,13,8b; 9a; 12a; 141,3b; *TK*,61,18b; *KMPY*,1033/12.

[144] *T'i-tien hsing-yü* 提點刑獄.

[145] *Ch'üan-nung shih* 勸農使.

At times they were assisted by military officials with the title of judicial cointendant (*t'ung* 同 *t'i-tien hsing-yü*) or assistant intendant. Agricultural intendants were established in 996 as separate officials, but soon dropped. The title was after 1006 given to fiscal intendants or prefectural administrators. It was held by the judicial intendants 1020–1026.

On the creation of judicial intendants in 991, the prefectures were directed to report to them every ten days concerning imprisonments and unfinished litigations. They were abolished from 1028 to 1033 and from 1064 to 1069. Cf. *TK*,61,26b–30a; *CKFC*,47, 11b–13a; 46,14a; *HCLY*,25,2b–3a.

had a judicial intendant during the time it constituted a circuit; K'ai-feng had in addition a special court of review for local cases, the Office of Judicial Investigation for the Capital [146] established in 1009.[147]

The intendants of exchange [148] and the officials who aided or replaced them formed an extremely vital link in the local administration. The matters which at different times were placed in their hands included several economic problems distinct in nature. Their primary responsibility was to oversee the handling, storage, and transportation of goods and commodities. A specially important aspect of this was the supply of grain to the capital and other important consumption centers from the main centers of production. A second responsibility was supervising the local operation of the state tea, salt, and alum monopolies. A third was the supervision of the local mints.

The jurisdiction of such officials was generally confined to the great bread basket areas: the circuits including the basins and alluvial plains of the Huai, Ch'ien-t'ang, and middle and lower Yangtse Rivers.[149] The transportation problems of the Grand Canal, the difficult stretches of the Yellow River, and certain other waterways also occasioned at times the appointment of special officials in those areas.

Intendants of exchange were appointed as early as 964. At times two or three men shared the responsibility for the combined three to five bread basket circuits; at times the chief authority was vested in one intendant. In 993 an official was associated with the intendants of exchange, to oversee the monopolies, and two years later the transportation and monopoly supervisions were combined. The intendants were assisted by directors-general [150] or assistant intendants,[151] and by supervisory officials.[152] At times these officials functioned without a full intendant above them. The supervision of mints was at times entrusted to a separate mint intendant,[153] at times to the intendants of exchange. One or another of the exchange

---

[146] *Chiu-ch'a Tsai-ching Hsing-yü Ssu* 糾察在京刑獄司.

[147] *CKFC*,47,12b; *TK*,166,40b; *HCLY*,25,3a; *KMPY*,1009/7; *SS*,163,29a. (The last seems to be in error on the date of establishment.)

[148] *Fa-yün shih* 發運使.

[149] These were the circuits of Huai-nan, Chiang-nan, Liang-che, and Ching-hu.

[150] *Tu-chien* 都監.   [152] *P'an-kuan*.

[151] *Fu-shih*.   [153] *T'i-tien chu-ch'ien shih* 提點鑄錢事.

intendant's normal functions was also on occasion entrusted to one or all of the fiscal intendants of the circuits concerned.[154]

The military intendants [155] supervised the armies within their circuits. The military circuits' boundaries did not coincide with those of the civil circuits, and they differed also in number.[156]

In addition to the four kinds of intendants here mentioned, there were others appointed on occasion to meet special situations or cope with emergencies, such as local famines. Together the intendants formed the final link in the chain of authority which bound the local communities in regional groups and connected them with the central government.

[154] When charged with supervision of the monopolies or local mints, the intendant held a concurrent title such as "regulator of the tea, salt, and alum revenues of Huai-nan, Chiang-nan, Liang-che, and the Ching-hu circuits" (*chih-chih Huai-nan Chiang Che Ching-hu ch'a yen fan shui* 制置淮南江浙荆湖茶鹽礬稅); or "intendant of mints." Outside the breadbasket area, we find "intendants of exchange of the Yellow River San-men sector" (*Huang-ho San-men* 黃河三門 *fa-yün shih*), "intendants of exchange of San-men, Pai-po 白波, and the Yellow, Wei 渭, and Pien 汴 Rivers," and so on. There were also other subordinate officials concerned with the administration of land and water transportation. Cf. *SHY*:CK,42,15a–18a; *CKFC*, 47,1a–2a; 6a–b; *TK*,62,3b; *SS*,167,11b.

[155] *Ching-lüeh an-fu shih* 經略安撫使.

[156] Their titles and powers also varied at different times. Cf. *TK*,61,25b–26b; 62, 2b–3a.

IV

THE CIVIL SERVICE AND ITS RECRUITMENT

1. The Character of Early Sung Civil Service Administration

In the search for a more workable administrative structure the willingness to make radical and repeated organizational changes has already been noted. The same willingness to change appears in the early Sung civilian personnel administration. Here also pragmatic tendencies reflected the need to cope quickly with the demands of a rapidly expanding area of control, an inherited local officialdom riddled with corruption and nepotism, and administrative problems more complex than those faced by earlier dynasties.

The early Sung rulers met the need by departing from previous personnel practices in several ways. The numbers recruited into the civil service were greatly expanded by methods which stressed particularly the merit principle. The T'ang system of civil service classification was elaborated to allow greater flexibility. New methods of promotion were devised. They were used at first to move young and able men to important positions more rapidly. Later, as a glut of qualified personnel replaced the earlier shortage, emphasis shifted to distributing promotion more equitably in order to improve the morale of the service.

It would, of course, be an oversimplification to believe that the proponents of new devices always held long-range objectives consciously in mind. Often we have evidence that they did. But not infrequently it seems that the new devices came about almost by accident, incidental to the solution of some immediate and perhaps minor problem. The long range utility of a device commonly appeared only after it had been tried, and the improvised scheme was then shaped into a conscious procedure. In this way the foundation was laid for the more rationalized civil service system which was to appear in the later eleventh century.

2. *The Civil Service and the Other Services*

The civil service was one of four general groups which we may distinguish among the state employees of the early Sung period. It was paralleled by the military service and supplemented by two groups of inferior rank, the clerical service and the irregular status officials.

TABLE 3

DATA ON NUMBERS OF CIVIL AND MILITARY
SERVICE OFFICIALS, 960–1067*

PERIOD	c. 976	997–1022	1023–1032	1034–1038	1038–1040	1046	1049–1053	1064–1067	SOURCES
CIVIL AND MILITARY SERVICES		9,785			15,443		17,200	24,000	a, b, c
CIVIL AND MILITARY COURT OFFICIALS†	200	400	1,000+						a, d
MILITARY SERVICE‡				4,000–		6,000+			a, b
CIVIL SERVICE Court and Capitai Rank†			2,000–			2,700+			a, b
Executory Rank†						10,000		3,300+	a, b

Sources: a: *YH*, 119, 30b–31a.   c: *SS*, 169, 6b–7a.
      b: *TK*, 47, 28a–b and   d: *SCSS*, 9, 139.
        CYTC, I, 12, 14a–15a.

* It is not clear whether these figures refer to the number of qualified officials (not necessarily on active duty), or in some or all cases to the smaller number actually filling functional posts. The numbers seem to agree better with the latter interpretation. *SS, loc. cit.*, describes the total numbers of 997–1022 and of 1038–1040 as those receiving governmental salaries. The rise in numbers of military officials is partly explained by the Tangut war.

† Titular rank, not indicating place of duty. See below, Chapter V.
‡ Including officers only.

The civil service furnished all the most influential officials in the central government except for those especially concerned with military affairs. Beyond this, it supplied men to fill most of those positions in the civil administration which required initiative and the making of decisions. The service performed these functions with a relatively small personnel. In 1046 it seems to have numbered slightly over 12,700 men, and even this represented a considerable increase over its earlier size.[1]

[1] Our data on the numbers of officials in the civil and military services are fragmentary, often very general, contradictory, and sometimes difficult to interpret. The

The military service provided not only officers for the leadership of the Sung armies, but also staffs for the governmental agencies dealing with military administration and for certain offices serving the Emperor and Imperial household. Certain of the posts in the Imperial household services were filled by eunuchs, and in the early years of the dynasty eunuchs occasionally moved from these offices to active military command in the field, where some of them served with distinction.[2] A military official might also hold certain posts in the civil administration, particularly in the local government. He might on occasion be appointed associate judicial intendant of a circuit. He might serve as administrator of a unit of prefectural or subprefectural rank. When he administered a nonmilitary prefecture, care was taken to associate with him a civil official of similar rank to provide civilian administrative experience and to check on his conduct.[3] The suspicion betrayed in this provision reflected the prevailing official attitude in the early Sung, when the usurpations of the war lords in the T'ang and the Five Dynasties were still vividly remembered. While the two services were in theory of equal rank, and the members of both were, properly speaking, "officials," [4] the civil service was generally prized and favored above the military. But it was possible to transfer from either service to the other.

The number of military officers seems in the earlier Sung to have been smaller than that of the civil officials, but it tended to grow more rapidly during the mid-eleventh century. In the period 1023–1032 there were fewer than 4,000 military officers, but by the year 1046 they had passed 6,000.[5]

The third group mentioned above, the clerical service (referred to as "outside the career"),[6] was greatly inferior in status to the civil

---

selected data in Table 3 cannot be accepted as dependable, but might help to form some idea of the size and growth of the services. The sources supplying our data usually give them to illustrate the undesirable expansion of the services. PAo Ch'eng, for example, in 1049 estimated that a total of 5,000 or 6,000 would suffice to staff the existing governmental units (YH,119,30b–31a). We see in such instances a concrete expression of the Confucian stress on economy, and on minimizing governmental activities; but the call for economy had a practical basis as well.

[2] See CTK:SHKTYCS; see also SS, ch. 466 for biographies of such men.

[3] Cf. TK,61,26b–27a; SS,167,24a; text 106.

[4] Kuan 官.

[5] See Note 1.

[6] Liu-wai 流外.

service. It included the subordinate staffs of the various governmental offices, whose work was routine in nature and involved little or no exercise of independent judgment. The number of clerical employees in a given office generally exceeded by far the number of civil service officials.[7]

Finally, we must note the existence of a fourth category of governmental employees, the officials of irregular status.[8] These functionaries never occupied a completely approved place in the scheme of governmental services. During the early part of the dynasty they were a carry-over from the irregularly invested local officials of the previous period, and an effort was made to eliminate them. They were tolerated, however, as emergency appointees in border regions, such as the southern border circuits of Kuang-nan-hsi, when properly appointed officials were unavailable. They were to be recruited from local inhabitants, including sometimes Sinicized aborigines, for short terms of service under strict supervision. After a period of probation they might have their status regularized and become civil servants.[9]

3. The Recruitment of the Civil Service

The General Character of Early Sung Recruitment Policies

Despite the pressing need for officials felt during the opening years of the dynasty, the Sung from the first reacted strongly against the lack of a systematic and centralized personnel control which had characterized the preceding half century or more. Except for the posts in the capital, most officials had come to receive their offices from their immediate local superiors, mostly no doubt on the basis of personal considerations, and certainly according to no standardized procedures.[10] All this was now changed as rapidly as the central government could exert its authority in the local areas. The government at K'ai-feng reserved to itself the powers of appointment; it distinguished the functionaries within the civil service

[7] The poor esteem in which the clerical service was held is reflected in a passage of WANG An-shih's "Ten-thousand-word document" of 1058. See *LCHSWC*,39,12b–13a. Translated somewhat freely in WILLIAMSON, I, 72–73, and more exactly in FRANKE, *Bericht*, pp. 38–39.

[8] *She-kuan* 攝官.

[9] Cf. *SHY:CK*,62,38a–39a etc.; *HCP*,25,8b.

[10] Cf. *SCSS*,9,155–156; *SHY:CK*,48,5a; *HCP*,6,6b.

from those without, and determined uniform methods of civil service recruitment. These fell into three major categories: recruitment through examination, through transfer from other services, and through protection.[11] As we shall see below, it is very difficult to determine the exact relative importance of the three major methods. The examinations far surpassed all others in prestige. Each of the three seems to have accounted for the recruitment of a significant proportion of the total number of officials, but by the end of the century under consideration the number of offices filled by holders of examination degrees may have considerably exceeded the combined total filled by other methods.

Recruitment Examinations [12]

In the search for men adequately qualified for civil administrative tasks, the early Sung government increased the numbers recruited through the regular examinations to several times the highest previous level. But the process did not stop there. The unsuccessful candidates were processed once more through facilitated examinations to yield a further gleaning of potentially useful officials. A sprinkling of specially talented men were taken in through the decree examinations also.

The regular examinations. Passing regular examinations was the favored method of entrance into the service for those who were sufficiently qualified and able and who hoped to achieve a distinguished career in the governmental service. Men so entering were called "regularly submitted names."[13] In the opening reign of the Sung, the number of doctoral degrees given was very restricted, as it had been since the later years of the T'ang. During the fifteen years of the reign, the total number of doctors was only 293, or an annual average a little under twenty.[14] Beginning with the accession of the

[11] The two latter categories also generally included some kind of examination. There were also, as we shall see below, several minor categories of recruitment.

[12] *K'o-chü* 科舉.

[13] *Cheng-tsou-ming* 正奏名.

[14] Numbers of Sung doctoral examination graduates, unless otherwise attributed, are taken from *TK*,32. This is the most complete of the early sources on the subject. Other sources differ on some of the figures, but no comprehensive study of the *TK* list has yet appeared. The distinction between the regular and facilitated examinations at the beginning of the Sung is not a clear one. The number here quoted excludes cases which seem to resemble the facilitated. As noted below, early Sung examinations were given

second Emperor, T'ai-tsung, however, there was a sharp increase. Between 976 and 1019 there were no less than 9,323 doctoral degrees conferred, or an average of nearly 212 per annum. Between 1020 and 1057 there were 8,509, an average of nearly 851 for each of the ten examinations held during that period. This represented a yearly average of nearly 224. The annual average was apparently the highest for a period of such length in the history of the Chinese civil service until 1905.[15] At about 1050, the regular doctoral examinations seem to have recruited enough men to supply roughly half the replacements then necessary to maintain the civil service at its current level.[16]

The increased number recruited through a competitive process was of course extremely significant in its effect on the social com-

---

at irregular intervals. The average per examination would thus be higher than the annual average.

[15] During the period 1106–1124, the doctoral graduates (including the university graduates, who had the same civil service standing) reached an average of nearly 239 men per annum, but numbers declined somewhat thereafter. For the last years of the Sung, no figures are available. The doctoral graduates during the Yüan dynasty, after the examinations were restored, averaged at the highest some 33 men per annum (with one possible exception). Cf *KKK, passim; HTK*,34,53b–56a. During the Ming the per annum average gradually rose from about 50 and at times reached nearly 140. Cf. *MKCKL, passim*. During the Ch'ing, the per annum average as a whole was 118, although during the opening years of the dynasty it reached 185. Cf. HSIEH, *Government*, 184. The large number who passed the examinations in the early Sung, desirable in other respects, nevertheless contributed to the excess of men qualified to hold office. It was proposed, apparently without effect, that the number of doctoral graduates for a single examination be limited in 1052 to 400 in letters and an equal number in other fields combined (*YH*,119,31a). The number accepted after each examination did begin to fall several years later.

[16] This estimate is based on the number of around 12,750·civil servants (see Note 1), and an estimated service career of not quite twenty-seven years for the average individual. The general (not invariable) retirement age in the Sung was seventy. Four hundred ninety-three distinguished men of the Sung period whose age at death was indicated in *YNLHP* would have served until an average age of over sixty-two, if we allow for retirement at seventy. (All ages Chinese style. See Chapter V, Note 24. An element of inaccuracy here is of course the fact that the life expectancy of already prominent men is not exactly the same as that of men just entering the civil service.) Evidence from the later Sung points to an age of over thirty-five for the average doctoral examination graduate (see Note 17). This would indicate an annual need for nearly 480 men, if they were to staff the whole service. The actual yearly average of doctoral degrees was 254 at this period. Not all these, however, were necessarily in active service. Cf. Note 83 below.

position of the service. The importance of the doctoral degree rested, however, not only on the numbers who entered the service under its aegis. Still more important was the part played by these numbers after entering the service. They were a favored group, advancing more rapidly than others in the service and rising to positions of greater influence. Their ages at the attainment of the degree varied greatly—from the late teens to the seventies—but at this period probably approached the average of a little under thirty-six years of age, which we find in the later Sung.[17] Many of the most brilliant men graduated much younger. During the first century of the Sung at least three regular examination graduates, all of whom had won first place in their respective palace examinations, were made councilors of state in less than ten years.[18] Some regular examination graduates achieved the important position of special drafting official in the Secretariat before the age of thirty, and some reached the Council of State before forty.[19] A Sung historian tells us that no official without a doctorate in letters became a censor or policy critic during the century.[20]

During the first century of the Sung, examinations were held at rather irregular intervals. At times they were given annually, at times they were suspended for a year or several years in succession. On several occasions they were given only for residents of a single region of the empire. The number of degrees conferred at a single examination varied greatly; the highest was that of the year 1000, when 1,548 candidates were passed. Gradually, during the eleventh century, a tendency toward greater regularity became perceptible. Examinations were given generally only once in several years, and the number of degrees given varied less. In 1057 it was determined to hold the examinations only in alternate years. In 1065 the rule was amended to provide for one examination every third year; put in force beginning in 1067, this procedure was to remain unchanged (except for extraschedule examinations and interruptions caused by internal disorder or foreign invasion) until the present century.

---

[17] The two lists of successful doctoral candidates preserved from the Sung indicate the age of each candidate. Omitting cases where data were lacking, the average age in 1148 was 35.64; in 1256 it was 35.66. The lists are reproduced in *SYKCSL*.

[18] *CYTC*, I,9,14a–14b.

[19] *Op. cit.*, I,9,8b.

[20] *CYTC*,I,9,11a.

Subject matter of the regular examinations. The fields of specialization permitted in the early Sung doctoral examinations offered a considerable variety of subjects. It was possible to receive the doctorate in letters, law, history, rituals, or classical study. The degree in letters stressed cogent reasoning and skill in composing several kinds of prose and verse, but required also attention to ritual, history, and ethics. The degree in law required, beyond the legal specialties, some work in other subjects. Degrees were given in two fields of history, one covering the four chronicles treating the feudal period and one covering more recent histories. In rituals there were two fields, ancient and modern. Classical degrees were given in three different fields, all of which included the studies of history, poetry, and cosmology, and, according to the field, additional work in classical Chinese grammar, rituals, or ethics.[21]

All these studies were colored, of course, by the traditional approach to the subject matter, which emphasized their political aspects. Among the prescribed history texts were the ancient *Book of Documents,* the *Spring and Autumn Annals,* and their three early commentaries, treating the feudal states of the eighth to the fifth centuries B.C., and the standard histories treating antiquity and the early years of the Christian era. All were studied as lessons in political conduct and its consequences. Poetry was the study of the ancient *Book of Odes,* again stressing the supposed expression of ancient political ideas. Ritual, whether ancient or modern, stressed the proper forms to observe in the conduct of government. Cosmology was studied in the ancient divination manual, the *Book of Changes,* interpreted as a study of the principles governing the functioning of the universe, and including basic moral and political laws. Ethical problems were studied especially in the Confucian *Analects,* with their emphasis on political morality. Classical Chinese was studied through the early dictionary, the *Erh-ya.* Law stressed the study of the current code and its commentaries. Some of these studies, it will be observed, were based on relatively con-

[21] This five-group division of the doctoral fields is based on the nature of their subject matter, as seen from a modern point of view. The Sung writer distinguished only between the doctorate in letters (*chin-shih* 進士) and "the several [other] fields" *chu k'o* 諸科. All the works studied could be considered as classics (*Ching* 經), except for the standard histories, the modern rituals, and the laws. For a list of the fields other than letters, see Note 28.

temporary writings, but the chief emphasis was placed on the study of the older writings as a guide to present conduct. Stress on the classics no doubt promoted a trend toward intellectual conservatism which would later become increasingly conspicuous. But it had the advantage of using a standard body of literature which was most widely available to potential candidates, thus tending to equalize opportunity.

Perhaps even more important to the operation of the examinations than the subject matter was the method by which the knowledge and reasoning powers of the candidates were tested. Here we find a strong divergence between the field of letters and the other fields. In letters, the candidate was required to demonstrate his knowledge of the *Analects* by completing from memory ten test passages [22] to which he was given several words as a clue. In addition, he showed his knowledge of the *Spring and Autumn Annals* or of the *Record of Ritual* by summarizing in writing [23] the meaning of ten passages from those works. But the major emphasis was placed on the writing of compositions by which he might demonstrate his originality and skill in reasoning and expression. He wrote carefully composed papers proposing solutions to five complex problems [24] assigned him, usually based on seeming conflicts in the texts he had studied. In addition, he composed a discussion,[25] a poetic description,[26] and a piece of poetry.[27]

The examinations in history, law, ritual, and classics, on the other hand, called for none of these original compositions. They depended entirely on the memory test passages and written elucidations, which were multiplied in number. And even the elucidations seem to have been rather routine, stressing memory more than originality. Where the field of letters called for ten memory test passages, some other fields called for eighty or one hundred and twenty. Where the field

[22] *T'ieh* 帖.
[23] "Written elucidations" or *mo-yi* 墨義.
[24] *Ts'e* 策.
[25] *Lun* 論.
[26] *Fu* 賦.
[27] *Shih* 詩.

Cf. *SS*,155,2a–b; *TK*,30,11b. Although the details of the requirements fluctuated constantly during the Sung, the sources give no exact date for the situation described in this summary. It was probably early. *TK* substitutes a "miscellaneous composition" (*tsa-wen* 雜文) for the discussion.

of letters called for ten elucidations, the least required for any other field was forty, and two fields required three hundred.[28]

Relative popularity of the fields. Both the memory test passages and the elucidations gave rise to much complaint. It may be significant that in the examination of 973, for which we have data by field, rather comparable numbers received degrees in the general areas of history, classics, and ritual, but within those areas an overwhelming majority chose the fields placing a smaller stress on memory questions.[29]

[28] *Ibid.* The fields other than letters and their requirements were as follows:

Law (*Ming-fa* 明法). 40 written elucidations on the laws and ordinances. Combined with this, additional classics as in the *Mao Odes* field.

History. Field of the *Three Commentaries* (*San chuan* 三傳). 110 written elucidations of passages from the *Tso, Kung-yang,* and *Ku-liang commentaries* on the *Spring and Autumn Annals.*

Field of the *Three Standard Histories* (*San shih* 三史). 300 written elucidations of passages, presumably (as in the T'ang) from the *Shih-chi,* the *Ch'ien Han shu,* and the *Hou Han shu.* (Cf. Rotours, *Examens,* 150–151.)

Rituals. Field of the *Three Rituals* (*San li* 三禮). 90 written elucidations of passages, presumably as in the T'ang from the *Chou li,* the *Yi li,* and the *Li chi.* (Cf. Rotours, *Examens,* 130.)

Field of the *Ritual of 732* (*K'ai-yüan li* 開元禮). 300 written elucidations of passages. This field was changed to that of the Ritual of 973 (*K'ai-pao t'ung-li* 開寶通禮), as soon as the latter ritual was completed. It was compiled under the supervision of Liu Wen-sou, and extended to 200 chapters. It was supplemented by a commentary of 100 chapters, called the *K'ai-pao t'ung-li yi-tsuan* 義纂, submitted by the Han-lin academician Lu Te-hsün. Cf. *TK,*30,15b; *KMPY,* under 993, 4 mo.

Classics. Field of the *Nine Classics* (*Chiu ching* 九經). 120 memory test passages and 60 elucidations.

Field of the *Five Classics* (*Wu ching* 五經). 80 memory test passages and 50 elucidations.

Field of specialization in the *Odes* according to the Mao version (Hsüeh-chiu *Mao Shih* 學究毛詩). 50 elucidations on the *Mao Odes,* 10 on the *Analects,* 10 on the *Erh ya* and the *Book of Filial Piety* combined, and 25 each on the *Book of Changes* and the *Book of Documents.*

[29] Cf. *TK,*30,15b. The trend is clearest in the classics fields, where none passed in the *Nine Classics,* four in the *Five Classics,* and eighteen in the *Mao Odes.* Here there was a choice between memory test passages and elucidations. In other cases, the choice was merely in number of elucidations. In history, three passed the *Three Histories* as against twenty-six in the *Three Commentaries.* In rituals, seven passed in the *Ritual of 732* as against thirty-eight in the *Three Rituals.* To complete the picture, twenty-six took the degree in Letters and five in Law. (It may be noted that these figures differ slightly from those given in *TK,*32. These are confirmed by *KMPY,*

Partly for this reason, perhaps, the increasing numbers taking the degree in letters led to a gradual eclipse of the other fields.[30] This trend was by no means uniform in all regions of the empire. The opportunity for intellectual scintillation afforded by the examination in letters seems to have attracted particularly the men from the region of the capital and from the southeast, as we are told by OU-YANG Hsiu.[31] The men from the north and west, on the other hand, preferred the more solid grounding in history and ethics to be gained through the studies that led to the classical degrees. Dissatisfaction with the imperfections in the method of examination for both the letters degree and other degrees was repeatedly voiced, however, in government circles. As early as 1023 it was proposed to get away from the dull routine of fields other than letters by adding to their examinations a section of problems for solution, but the plan was shelved because of the decreasing interest in such fields.[32] In 1044 the memorization and written "elucidation" questions were for a short time dropped from the prefectural preliminary examinations in favor of problems for solution, discussions, poetry, and poetic descriptions, and elucidation of the "broader meaning" of the texts studied.[33] But the examination officials objected to the use of questions which, precisely because they stimulated greater originality in the candidates, inevitably called for a somewhat subjective evaluation on the part of the examiners. They preferred the safer ground of the traditional compositions, which could be graded objectively, if mechanically, on the basis of set rules. It was not until after 1067 that the movement to stress fresh thought on more practical subjects finally won out.

Administration of the examinations. We must note, before leaving the regular examinations for the doctorate, certain other factors

---

entry for 973, third month, and *HCP*,14,2a.) Other factors beside the question of memorization, such as a preference for the older texts, of course influenced the choice of field, but the consistent tendencies, particularly in the Classics field, cannot be altogether ignored.

[30] Cf. *TK*,32. This trend did not begin at once. The great expansion in the number of doctoral degrees after 976 saw a decrease in the proportion in letters from 59 per cent of the total (under the first Emperor) to somewhat over 32 per cent (976–1019). In the period 1020–1057, however, the degrees in letters rose to 44 per cent of the total, and in 1058–1067 to some 74 per cent.

[31] Cf. *OYWC*,113,9b. This discussion is there dated 1064.

[32] Cf. *SS*,155,9b.

[33] Cf. *KMPY*, under 1044, third month, and 1045, third month; *SS*,155,11b.

which had a bearing on the fairness and objectivity with which the candidates were selected for the civil service. These had to do with the process by which candidates for the final examination were selected, and the impartiality with which both the preliminary and the final examinations were conducted. In the absence of any ballot system by which the views of the population might be expressed and the interests of the whole population safeguarded, the welfare of the nation depended above all upon the quality and interests of the officials chosen to govern. The problem was not merely one of recruiting able and honest officials. The breadth of the social basis of power—the size of the segment of the population whose views would receive effective expression and consideration—depended in a considerable degree upon the extent to which different social and geographic groups were represented in the civil service. Sung Emperors and statesmen have left us sufficient evidence that they were aware of this and tried—many of them at least—to ensure that the examinations would not only exclude the unfit, but keep open the path of opportunity for able men from all parts of the empire, including those who lacked the advantages of wealth or official connection. Much research remains to be done before we can evaluate the success of this effort to create free opportunity, but we can at least note some of the measures and factors which favored or hindered it.

During most of the hundred years we are considering, the doctoral candidates were subjected to three successive competitive examinations: the prefectural examinations [34] or their equivalent, the school examinations; the departmental examinations; [35] and the palace examinations. [36] The competition in the prefectural examinations was intense. Exact figures for the early periods are not available, but by 1066, according to Ou-yang Hsiu, the numbers passed on this level varied from 1 to 10 per cent. The competition was especially keen in the region of the southeast and near the capital, and there the elimination seems to have been highest. [37]

The administration of the prefectural examinations was divided between the prefectural staff supervisors, who examined the candidates in letters, and the executive inspectors, who examined those

[34] *Chieh-shih* 解試.
[35] *Sheng-shih* 省試.
[36] *Tien-shih* 殿試.
[37] *OYWC*,113,10a.

in the other fields. If these officials were not scholastically qualified for the duty, other better qualified officials were designated to act under the staff supervisor's supervision. Any unjust admission or exclusion of a candidate for the examinations was held to be sufficient cause for the dismissal and severe punishment of the official responsible. For candidates who were students in the university or other capital or local schools, the examination was directed by the school head. Those who passed the local examinations were ranked in order of their showing and provided with a certificate which admitted them to the examinations at the capital.[38]

The first examination the candidate underwent at the capital, the departmental, was given under the supervision of specially appointed doctoral examination administrators.[39] Here again the competition was intense. In 992, we are told, while over a thousand men passed the examination at the capital, the qualified candidates exceeded 97,000.[40] Usually, however, it appears that the average number passing was nearer to 10 per cent. Candidates often took the departmental examination a number of times before they succeeded in passing. During the early years of the dynasty, this examination resulted in the conferment of the final doctoral degree. As the result of several instances of personal favor shown to candidates by examination administrators, however, the Emperor T'ai-tsu adopted the practice of reëxamining the candidates personally, and by 975 this practice had evolved into the separate palace examination.[41] This final test thenceforth determined the ultimate placing of the successful candidates, and until 1057 also eliminated some of those who had survived the departmental test.[42] During the early years of the dynasty the systems of ranking were somewhat variable, but from the beginning of the reign of T'ai-tsung, a system of grouping began to develop. According to the system finally evolved, the successful candidates were placed in exact order of achievement, and further divided into five groups.[43] Those in the first two groups were

[38] SS,155,2b; Hsing-t'ung, 9, 2a. An example of prosecution for maladministration of examination in 998 is found in HCP,43,5b.
[39] Chih kung-chü. Cf. Chapter III, Note 91.
[40] KMPY, under 992, third month.
[41] TK,30,16a–b.
[42] TK,31,3a; KMPY,1057/3.
[43] Chia 甲.

considered to have "passed with distinction." [44] Those in the third group were "formally qualified." [45] Those in the fourth and fifth groups were simply "passed." [46] To be listed as the first man in the first group, or "first palace graduate" [47] was an achievement eagerly sought and highly honored.

While the palace examination thus remained a permanent part of the examination system, it was obviously inadequate to ensure impartiality in the selection and grading of candidates. In 992 a Sung official proposed and obtained the revival and extension of a measure which had been tried during the T'ang dynasty for a brief period and for limited purposes—the system of candidates' anonymity (*hu-ming*), or as it was more often called in the Sung, *feng-mi*. [48] This involved the obliteration of the candidate's name on the examination paper and the substitution of an identifying number, so that the examination readers might not be influenced in their judgments by a knowledge of the writer's identity. First used for the palace examinations, the practice was extended in 1007 to the departmental examinations, and in 1033 to the examinations in the prefectures. [49] The remaining possibility that the readers might recognize the handwriting of a candidate was met in 1015 by the establishment of a Bureau of Examination Copyists [50] to reproduce the examination papers in another hand before they were read. [51] Each examination paper was read independently by two examiners; a third examiner received their sealed grades, opened them, verified, and if necessary reconciled them. [52] Little more could be done to safeguard objectivity. Still other precautions were taken to certify the identity of the man taking the examination, and prevent substitu-

---

[44] *Chi-ti* 及第.

[45] *Ch'u-shen* 出身.

[46] *T'ung ch'u-shen* 同出身.

[47] *Pang-shou* (more colloquially *chuang-yüan*) 榜首 (狀 元).

[48] *Hu-ming* (or *feng-mi*) 糊 名 (封 彌).
HCP,33,2a; TK,30,21a; YH,116,20b.

[49] *TK*,30,29b.

[50] *T'eng-lu Yüan.* See Chapter III, Note 92.

[51] *TK*,30,33a.

[52] The whole process was perfected by 1019, when we find it described in connection with a prosecution of two officials who deviated from the prescribed procedure. Cf. *SHY:*CK,64,24a. An interesting glimpse of the system in practice, and an amusing example of overcaution, will be found in Lin, *Gay Genius,* pp. 38–39.

tions. It is, of course, obvious that such devices alone, however multiplied, would fail to ensure an honest conduct of the system in the absence of a will to carry out their spirit. The creation of such devices is interesting especially as evidence of such a will on the part of the government; and it seems that on the whole the half century of effort to stamp out corruption bore fruit during the following years.

Social representation in the examinations. The complaints of Sung reformers toward the middle of the eleventh century turn in a different direction. The high proportion of successful candidates from the regions of the southeast and the capital occasioned proposals by the historian-statesman SSU-MA Kuang, on more than one occasion, that a fixed number of degrees be earmarked for the men of each circuit, set at 10 per cent of the number of qualified candidates from each such area.[53] He quotes figures from the years 1058, 1060, and 1062 which show that although an average of 10 per cent passed the capital examinations, the successful proportion of those from the capital prefectural examinations and from the students at the Directorate of Public Education there ranged between 16 per cent and 25 per cent.[54] The circuits of the north, the far west, and the far south, in contrast, regularly averaged only around 3 per cent, and on occasion fell far lower.[55] Among the reasons for this condition, he cites the partiality of the examiners, themselves often from the capital or southeast, for the polished compositions in which the men from these regions were skilled, and a tendency to disparage the classical studies which were preferred by the men of the north.

The opposite side of the question was upheld by the great writer and statesman, OU-YANG Hsiu.[56] His argument stressed the higher selectivity of the southeastern prefectural examinations as a reason for the greater success of the candidates they qualified. That area, as we know, was distinguished by a high degree of urbanization and

[53] *SMKWC*,30,1a–5b.

[54] A similar imbalance in favor of K'ai-feng is reported to have prevailed in 998. Cf. *TK*,30,24b. SSU-MA's memorial, as now extant, gives no figures for the southeast. SSU-MA Kuang was himself a northerner, from Ho-nan. OU-YANG Hsiu, who defended the status quo, was from Chiang-nan-hsi in the southeast.

[55] Ho-pei circuit in 1062 sent 154 candidates, of whom one only passed. On several occasions circuits sent considerable numbers (Kuang-nan-tung once seventy-seven) without one passing.

[56] See Note 37.

high educational levels. OU-YANG felt that the empire should be considered as a whole, and that conferment of degrees on the sole basis of merit, guaranteed as it was by the system of candidates' anonymity, should be preserved. In the arguments on the two sides we find, beyond an immediate disagreement on disciplines, a more fundamental clash between the principle stressing merit as the primary criterion of recruitment, and that stressing the political need for wider geographic representation within the service. The merit principle, for that time at least, won out.

How did the examinations provide for other aspects of social representation? Here we are on highly speculative ground. Statistics for the first century of the Sung are lacking, and the evidence of individual instances must be inconclusive. If we may assume—and the assumption seems justified—that freedom of opportunity during the early Sung at least equaled that of later Sung centuries, we have at least one good source of light in the examination lists of 1148 and 1256. Here we find that 40 per cent or more of the successful doctoral candidates were sons, grandsons, or great-grandsons of civil servants. This degree of occupational heredity is not surprising when compared with a similar phenomenon in our own professional groups. A clear majority, however, came from families with no history of civil service employment in the paternal line for three previous generations.[57]

From what social groups did these latter men come? We know that they included men from both comparatively prosperous and comparatively indigent families, but the relative proportions are not clear. I think we should not be far wrong if we assumed that few acquired the necessary education without one of two advantages: either birth into a family of moderately comfortable economic standing, or into one which, even if poor, had some literary education.[58] Certain groups were definitely excluded on moral grounds: at the time of the prefectural examinations the local authorities were responsible for an enquiry into the records of the candidates and their families, and considerations ranging from un-

[57] See KRACKE, Family vs. Merit. Further facts concerning the implications of the 1148 and 1256 figures are there discussed.

[58] The term "gentry" is here avoided because it tends to imply a degree of homogeneity, and continuity of family standing, which have not been demonstrated for such a group in this phase of Chinese social evolution.

filial behavior to kinship with one guilty of treasonable conduct were grounds for disqualification.[59] The exact status of merchants and artisans is rather obscure. Considered beyond the pale during the T'ang, they had by the Sung acquired a position of acceptance, perhaps reluctant. They entered the civil service by other means, we know.[60] But there is some evidence that in theory, at least, they remained ineligible to take examinations.[61]

The facilitated examinations. The facilitated examinations, as we have noted above, were essentially a method of reprocessing the candidates who had been eliminated at some stage of the regular examination procedure.[62] All the men eligible for facilitated degrees [63] had passed the prefectural examinations; some of them had passed the departmental examinations as well, only to be eliminated in the final test at the palace. They were required in addition to have attempted the examinations at the capital a number of times. The number of unsuccessful attempts which made a man eligible varied over the years. In 970 it was set at fifteen attempts for the candidates of that year.[64] In 1005, the degree was granted to a number of men who had tried five times.[65] About 1034, the qualifications were elaborated: for candidates in letters who had passed the prefectural examinations, it was necessary to have tried fifteen times and to have reached an age of fifty or more. For similar candidates in other fields it sufficed to have tried six times, but an age of sixty or more was necessary. For candidates in letters who had passed the departmental examination but failed at the palace, three trials were necessary; for those in other fields, five. In the last two categories there was apparently no age qualification. For men who had reached the palace examinations during former reigns (this would mean twelve or more years previously) no number of trials was set.[66]

---

[59] *SS*,155,3a; *TK*,30,12b.

[60] CHS:SYSY,206. The examples there given, however, are slightly later in date.

[61] *SS* and *TK, loc. cit.,* seem to disqualify them, as well as former Buddhist and Taoist priests. But WITTFOGEL, Public Office, 25, suggests on the basis of the passage in *SS* that they were permitted to participate with reservations.

[62] Those who entered in this way were referred to as *t'e-tsou-ming* or "specially submitted names." They were also said to have "qualified in the field of grace" (*en-k'o ch'u-shen* 恩科出身).

[63] *T'e-tsou-ming* 特奏名.

[64] *YH*,118,22a; *TK*,30,14b–15a; *YYY*,1,1a–2a.

[65] *TK*,30,27b; *YYY, loc. cit.*   [66] *TK*,31,2a; *YYY, loc. cit.*

Having thus qualified, the candidates were subjected to a review of the merits of their cases. In the later years of our period, this apparently included an examination in the writing of discussions.[67]

In the opening years of the dynasty, little distinction seems to have been made between the conferring of facilitated degrees and occasions when the Emperor decided to increase the numbers who received regular degrees by adding to the list men who had previously been failed. (The term later applied to facilitated degrees [68] was not used until 1005.) The motives for the practice seem to have been several. The proclamations dealing with it stress the fear of losing men who might be useful to the state, and consideration for the hardships experienced by scholars of slender resources who faced an uphill struggle to enter the civil service. Perhaps it was felt that the perseverance of a man who took a difficult examination six— or fifteen—times and persisted until the age of fifty or sixty might prove a useful asset to the state. If the gamble were unfortunate, he would not burden the payrolls too many decades thereafter. Possibly certain proponents of the practice hoped to favor friends thereby, though the established qualifications allowed little scope for such favor. Very likely the most valid explanation of the system was that offered by the twelfth-century historian WANG Yung; he attributed to it the aim of mollifying ambitious men who, frustrated in the examinations, might turn to the fomentation of rebellion.[69] Available figures on the numbers receiving facilitated degrees are incomplete; it is clear from isolated instances that the numbers were considerable. WANG Yung credits the system with a significant part in padding the numbers in the civil service with men of inferior talent who eclipsed the more able, to the ultimate detriment of government efficiency.[70]

The decree examinations. The decree examinations were not primarily for recruitment, but for promotion within the civil serv-

[67] *SS*,155,17a.   [68] *T'e-tsou-ming.*

[69] *YYY, loc. cit.* Such frustrated aspirants to office have in fact become rebel leaders in other periods.

[70] In 970 (before the great increase in regular degrees) there were 106 facilitated to 8 regular. In 977 there were 184 facilitated to 316 regular. In 1005 there were some 170 facilitated to 817 regular (see Notes 64 to 66). WANG Yung, *YYY, loc. cit.*, adds that in the eleventh century the number of doctors in letters entering office came to be ten times the old numbers, and often up to twenty times; "the multitudes of facilitated degrees were also thus henceforth."

ice. They will be discussed below in that capacity. It should be noted here, however, that in rare instances these examinations were open to men of unusual ability outside the civil service, who by passing them might receive official position. Thus technically it became a possible method of recruitment for a very select few only.[71]

Recruitment through Transfer

Recruitment through transfer was of several kinds. Officials might be transferred from the military service, or from the clerical service, or on occasion from irregular status.

Transfer from the military service differed from the other kinds of transfer because of the theoretically equal rank of the civil and military services. A table of equivalent ranks in the two services was arranged for the purpose of transfer from the military to the civil or vice versa, and transfer of an official to the appropriate rank in the opposite service was accomplished by the issuance of a governmental order.[72]

In contrast with this, transfer from the clerical service was a method of recruiting the lower ranks of the civil service. The different offices of the central government might nominate a set quota of their clerical employees who were considered to be of exceptional ability and merit. The exact procedure differed somewhat according to the office in which the candidate was employed. The candidates were given an examination, simpler than the doctoral, seemingly emphasizing calligraphy or knowledge of the laws. To prevent cheating, it was provided that each candidate should, after writing the examination, recite his answers orally. Those with previous service records of exceptional merit might, however, be excused from this rather humiliating test. On the successful completion of the examination, the candidates were appointed as regular civil service officials.[73] The numbers so recruited were certainly appreciable, but beyond this it is as yet impossible to judge their effect on the composition of the regular civil service.[74]

[71] See below, p. 95.

[72] *HCLY*,28,6b–7a. In this case also examinations were sometimes used. Cf. *HCP*, 73,2b–3a.

[73] *Pu cheng-ming* 補正名.

[74] *SS*,159,16b; *SS*,169,17b–20a; *SHY:*CK,11,56b; 58a–59a; *SHY:*HC,25,18a; *HCP*, 24,2b.

The process by which officials of irregular status might be converted into regular civil service officials seems, as one might expect from the grudging toleration accorded them, to have been governed by no very constant system. Sometimes it seems that their appointment to regular status itself was preceded by a comparatively simple examination. On a number of occasions at least they were given examinations after a designated period of probation. Their cases were judged by the personnel agencies on the basis of their examinations and their previous record of service, and they might then, if approved, be appointed as regular officials of the lowest rank. Through this process the service absorbed a certain number of Chinese border settlers, as well as some Sinicized aborigines, but they must have been too few to affect greatly the composition of the service outside the border areas, where no doubt most of them continued to be assigned.[75]

As a whole, these several methods of recruitment through transfer seem to have offered an opportunity to men who had some native ability but who lacked an education, economic status, or family connection which would make available other ways of entering the service.

Recruitment through Protection

Together with the beginnings of the examination system, the Sung dynasty inherited from the T'ang the practice of recruitment through "protection." [76] This practice extended to certain officials of higher titular office the privilege of nominating for entrance into the civil service one or more of their sons or other family members, and on occasion even dependents not related by blood.

There were certain ways in which this practice could be reconciled with Confucian principles. It served as a kind of social insurance for the dependents of an official, and thus might relieve the financial pressure which often tempted him to swell his stipends by irregular means. In this sense it was advocated by WANG An-shih, and found support in a passage of Mencius.[77] The candidates who

---

[75] *SHY*:CK,62,38a–39b; *HCP*,25,8b.

[76] *Yin-pu* 蔭補.

[77] *LCHSWC*,39,4b. Later in the same memorial, however, WANG criticizes the quality of the men so recruited (12b). Mencius, I,B,5 and 7, refers with approval to the principle of "hereditary emolument" (*shih lu* 世祿) supposedly followed by the

benefited from it might be supposed to have absorbed in their homes a knowledge of governmental problems and a sense of the civil service code of behavior. The privilege of nomination, bestowed as a reward for official achievement, might serve as a stimulus to greater effort.[78] But when all this is said, the practice was still in conflict with the Confucian principle that office should be conferred for merit. The abler Emperors, and statesmen such as FAN Chung-yen and SSU-MA Kuang, regarded it critically, and took steps to limit its exercise. In 963 its potential beneficiaries were limited in number. In 996 their flexible and irregular way of appointment was altered, and they were placed on a level with those with a passing mark in the examination field of concentrated classical study, less favored than the field of letters.[79] In 1009 it was required that "protected" candidates must study at least two years in the Directorate of Public Education and pass an examination given by the supervisors of the directorate and the Bureau of Senior Civil Service Personnel Ratings. After 1040 the exercise of protection was further limited.[80]

Even with these restrictions, the method of protection must have remained a rather easy way of entering the service for those in a position to enjoy it. It is true that this very ease and lack of competition deprived it of prestige, and men ambitious to attain positions of influence in the government continued to enter through the regular examinations even when eligible for protection.[81] But the practice was still unquestionably harmful to the morale of the serv-

---

ancients, and in the latter passage further says that a prince cannot but be careful in causing the churl to rise above the honored. But he also says that men should be employed only when their worth is universally attested by the people as well as by the high officials, and in VI,B,7, he seems clearly to disapprove the giving of office hereditarily to shih (shih wu shih kuan 士無世官) unless the descendants manifest their virtue clearly. The commentary by the Sung philosopher CHU Hsi reconciles the two positions by distinguishing the hereditary bestowal of office from that of pay, and concludes that while the state should educate the sons of officials, those who do not turn out well should be pensioned, not given office. Whether or not this is a correct reading of Mencius, it throws light on the Sung Confucian attitude on the question.

[78] For example, the privilege might, at least in the Southern Sung, be conferred on a first palace graduate (CYTC, chia, 9,14b–15a).

[79] TK,34,25b; KMPY, under 996, fourth month.

[80] TK,34,27b–28b.

[81] See KRACKE, Family vs. Merit, p. 121, for examples from the later Sung.

ice as a whole. Many less ambitious relatives of officials entered the service without the rigorous intellectual discipline and stiff competition necessary to other candidates. The representative social character of the service, furthered in differing degree by the other recruitment methods, was reduced by this. And the numbers permitted to enter in this way further expanded the public payrolls. The numbers recruited through protection during the first century of the Sung—and indeed for later centuries—are far from clear. Our incomplete information on the numbers of the higher officials makes it difficult to estimate the numbers even of those eligible for protection, though we may hope for more light on this point through further study.[82] The fact that the privilege was granted on several occasions to the same "protector," and the extension of the privilege at certain times to officials of the censorate and the three departments as low as the sixth grade, suggest that the numbers eligible may not have been too far below those recruited by examination.[83]

Miscellaneous Methods of Recruitment

In addition to the more important methods of recruitment already described, there were a number of other practices in use for longer or shorter periods. Local officials were occasionally directed to recommend men unusual for character or ability, who for some reason had not availed themselves of the regular examinations. These men were sent to the capital, and tested by examination; if they passed, they received titular offices or doctoral degrees.[84] Occasionally, in border circuits, men who had passed the regular examinations but

[82] The sources cited provide rather detailed data from which the numbers eligible for protection, if not those who actually benefited, might be estimated. Some statistics will be found in WITTFOGEL, *op. cit.*, pp. 29–31, and KRACKE, *op. cit.*, pp. 119–120.

[83] If the numbers actually benefiting by their eligibility approached such proportions, we should seem to have a total number of civil servants considerably exceeding the reported number of official positions. This might be explained by assuming that many, chiefly drawn from those recruited by the less favored methods, remained unassigned to active service.

[84] Such men were apparently guaranteed by the sponsor. The terminology, however, differs from that of sponsorship for promotion. Both terminology and procedure seem to derive rather from the Han practice of sponsorship. The number of candidates was generally limited; in 1059 intendants were to select two or three from each circuit. In 1060, 23 recommended men were assigned one solution problem (*ts'e*) and one discussion (*lun*) as examination; the degree or office given varied according to the examination mark. Cf. *SHY:*HC,34,47b–48b.

failed at the capital were permitted to fill certain posts when properly qualified officials were lacking.[85] Entrance to the civil service might be specially allowed for some service to the state, as in 962 when it was offered as a reward for information on cases of bribery in sponsorship.[86] More frequently, it was granted to those who had voluntarily supplied grain for public relief in a time of famine. This practice, of course, amounted to the sale of office. But it was not allowed to approach the proportions once reached in the Han, and later under the Manchus, when its prevalence seriously damaged the morale of the service. In the early Sung, it seems to have been practiced only in connection with a specific emergency, by special order of the central government, and the contribution seems to be regularly for local relief rather than to supply the central treasury.[87] Entrance by this method, as we shall see, offered much less prospect of advancement than the regular examinations. But even on a restricted scale, it was necessarily prejudicial to the morale of the service. Apart from its avowed intention of encouraging grain donations in time of emergency, it had, however, the merit of broadening the social base of the civil service through the number of merchants thus recruited.[88]

[85] Cf. *SHY:*CK,62,41a. In 1022, doctoral candidates in letters were to have passed the local examinations twice, in other fields three times.

[86] Text 2.

[87] *SHY:*CK,55,29a–37a. This was known as "qualification through contribution" (*chin-na ch'u-shen* 進納出身).

Specific scales were set, indicating the favor to be given according to amount of grain contribution. For the most part the contributors seem to have received honors or offices at the bottom of the rank scale, and for the largest contributions in general, no more than a titular capital office or a degree.

[88] CHS:SYSY,206–207, gives instances of merchants so recruited, from slightly later years.

V

THE UTILIZATION OF CIVIL SERVICE
PERSONNEL

At least four major considerations appear to have had some part in determining the treatment of civil service personnel and the assignment of their duties: morale, efficient use of abilities and knowledges, budgetary considerations, and immediate administrative expediency. Ideally, no doubt, morale should have come first, and there is evidence that it did in fact receive much attention. Measures were adopted or proposed to further the officials' welfare, to enhance their prestige, and to offer hope of advancement in reward for good service. Classification to make better use of abilities made considerable progress. But questions of expediency tended throughout the century to inhibit the development of long-range constructive policies: at first the prior demands of administrative emergency, and in the end, the ever more pressing need for retrenchment of salary expenditures.

1. Classification and Allocation of Responsibility

In some respects, the classification system turned the disrupting effect of expediency to eventual profit. The difficult problem of allocating the civil service personnel suitably in the complicated and changing network of governmental offices was met by the development of a new system of classification far more flexible and varied than the system used by the T'ang. During the first century of the dynasty, the outlines of the system were not clearly cut, as they were to become in the period after 1082. But by the end of this first century the main features of the system had taken form. Formal rank in the service was indicated for the most part by a system of titular but nonfunctional offices. Function was indicated chiefly by the system of commissions. Between these two categories there was a group of assignments which partook of the character of both.

Even though without a definite duty, an official was given a titular office; but it was possible when active for him to bear at the same time titles in each of the above categories. In such a case as we shall see, there was a certain loose coördination in rank between the different kinds of titles. The formal rank of an official as defined by his titular office, and in addition perhaps by his assignment and possibly his honorary office, corresponded to a general range of commissions and charges for which he was considered eligible. His advancement to positions of greater influence entailed a parallel (but not necessarily simultaneous) series of promotions in the functional offices and in formal rank.[1]

The Titular Offices [2]

The titular offices that primarily indicated formal rank in the service were, with very little alteration of detail, the hierarchy of once functional offices whose names had survived from the T'ang, while their functional significance had in most cases been lost. They included such titles as chancellery executives, secretariat executives, executives of the Department of Ministries, ministers, senior lords, directors,[3] and the nominal subordinates of these. Like the T'ang offices from which they were derived, they were grouped in nine grades,[4] each grade in turn being subdivided into two or four subgrades.[5] In the early Sung, however, there is comparatively little reference to the grade of the titular office; each titular office had an exact position in the order of protocol, and this position made it in itself a kind of grade for classifying purposes. The officials also received their basic pay according to their titular office, which for this reason was sometimes referred to as the stipendiary office.[6] (Additional allowances attached to the functional offices a man might hold.)

The titular offices were divided into two major classes: the ad-

---

[1] A failure to make this distinction between the functional and nonfunctional offices has led to some confusion in the description of the governmental organization in WILLIAMSON, II, Chap. VII.

[2] *Kuan* (or *pen-kuan*) 官 (本官).

[3] *Men-hsia shih-lang; Chung-shu shih-lang; Shang-shu tso, yu p'u-yeh; shang-shu; ch'ing; chien.* (For these, cf. Appendix B.)

[4] *P'in* 品.

[5] *Chieh* 階.

[6] *Chi-lu kuan* 寄祿官.

ministrative officials (literally capital and court officials)[7] and the executory officials.[8] A less significant distinction was made within the administrative class between the titular court and the titular capital officials. The titular court officials included all the higher offices, from the chief councilors of state (List: A) down to the five agency chiefs of the Directorate of Astronomical Observation (List: O).[9] Originally a group numbered in the hundreds, it grew rapidly until as early as 1023 it included over a thousand men.[10] Although all court officials attended the greater court convocations, at which the Emperor was present, at fixed intervals, those who were actually present at the regular transaction of court business [11] were much fewer.[12] The titular capital officials included the middle group of offices, from the librarians of the Imperial Library (List: P) down to the chief of the clepsydras in the Directorate of Astronomical Observations (List: Q). The titular executory officials comprised the local administrative staff from the prefectural staff supervisors (List: R) down to the subprefectural registrars and sheriffs and the prefectural inspectors of education and teaching assistants (List: S), the lowest in rank of the civil servants. The two major groups differed in nature as well as in rank; while the officials of the administrative class most often were assigned on commission or otherwise to a function other than that of their titular office, the officials of the executory class more often discharged the functions of their titular post. But it should be noted that in certain cases the holders of administrative-class titular offices also might carry out the functions implied by such office. This was often true, for instance, in the case of censors, and sometimes in that of policy critics or policy monitors. There was also a tendency to preserve some appropriateness in the relationship between a man's titular and functional of-

---

[7] *Ching-ch'ao kuan* 京朝官.

[8] *Hsüan-jen* 選人.

[9] See Early Sung Protocol List, Appendix B.

[10] See Table 3, where data on the numbers of the several classes are found.

[11] The regular sessions or *ch'ang ch'i-chü* 常起居.

[12] See *HCLY*,26,11a. A number of Sung texts agree that the expression "regularly advising official" 常參官 is equivalent to "official elevated to the court" 升朝官, and both terms have been here translated as "court official." There may be some reason, however, to think that the T'ang practice restricting the former expression to the higher ranks of court officials still applied at the beginning of the Sung. Cf. *SS*,158,5b; *SLYYP*,2,3b–4a; Texts 1, 6, 8.

fices. If he served in the Finance Commission, for instance, he might be given a titular office in the Ministry of Finance.

The Commissions [13]

These were the most clearly defined category of early Sung personnel classification. They regularly implied a definite function, and they conferred no formal rank on the holder. Most of the functional offices which we have occasion to consider in this book were commissions. They included such functions as the fiscal intendantship of a circuit, or the administratorship of a prefecture or of a subprefecture. The commissions were equated in rank with the various titular offices, but the titular office might be somewhat lower or somewhat higher than the commission. The rank relationship between commission and titular office was expressed by the form of the commission title, in which the name of the function or unit administered was generally preceded by a term such as "administering," [14] or "supervising," [15] or "provisional," [16] or a combination of these. The exact use of these prefixes varied at different times.

Although certain commissions were normally reserved for men of the administrative class or for men of the executory class, the personnel agencies in charge of the two classes might arrange a temporary transfer of posts from one class to the other if the number of posts assigned to a class was out of balance with the number of officials of that class available.[17]

The Assignments [18]

These were, like the commissions, held in addition to a titular office. They might, and often did, imply a real function. But an official who already had an assignment might also receive a commission. In this case, his function was that of the commission, and the assignment was merely an additional honor. The most conspicuous examples of assignment were the academicians (*hsüeh-shih*) of various kinds and the officials assigned to the three institutes.[19]

---

[13] *Ch'ai-ch'ien* 差遣.

[14] *Chih* 知.

[15] *P'an* 判.

[16] *Ch'üan* 權.

[17] An example of this is found in 1019, when administrative class posts were made available for the executory class (*TK*,38,10a).

[18] *Chih* 職.

Other kinds of title, entirely honorific, will be mentioned below. Confusing as the system seems, it had distinct advantages in meeting emergencies. If an official of high titular rank was no longer wanted in one of the few positions of that rank, or if his services were temporarily needed for an important function of lower rank, he could without demotion be employed in a lower position. Or a lower ranking official could be used temporarily in a higher position without any commitment to give him permanent promotion. Along with this flexibility, it gave the official a degree of assurance that he would not be formally demoted in rank without some serious inadequacy or offense.

Since the governmental structure provided only a relatively small number of posts for technical specialists, chiefly on a very low or a relatively high level, the classification system made no important distinction on technical lines. But efficiency was promoted in another way, by hierarchical specialization of duties, which had made considerable strides. Administrative problems were, in a large proportion of cases, dealt with by orders defining the policy to be followed, leaving the decisions on application to officials on a lower level. Many measures construing the general policy were still published as Imperial proclamations, but these seem often to be merely a formal confirmation of lower level decisions.[20]

2. Recognition and Remuneration

The vital bearing of the official's prestige, financial solvency, and personal contentment on the morale of the service was fully recognized, and in some ways successfully exploited.

The flattery of honorific titles and appellations was invoked with extreme liberality. Dignities, decorations, laudatory epithets, prestige titles, honorary offices, and titles of nobility were generously distributed among both civil and military officials; they might obtain posthumous offices or promotions for their deceased ancestors as well.[21] Such signs of honor, often given automatically, soon lost any

[19] See Chapter III, Note 102 and p. 32.

[20] The development in this respect can be seen when one compares the Imperial proclamations of the Sung with those of the Han. (Cf. DUBS, *History, passim.*) The latter show much greater attention to relatively minor individual cases.

[21] Honorary offices were titular offices granted in name only; such titles were preceded by the words *chien-chiao* 檢校 . Somewhat similar were complimentary probationary titles (*shih chih* 試秩) of capital-official rank, granted to civil aides,

real prestige, and a Sung historian tells us that the only real mark of success to the men of that time was a position in the Censorate, an academic assignment, a post close to the throne, or an important local commission.[22] Such places were for the most part given on the basis of real accomplishment, and represented an honor worth striving for.

Concern for morale was demonstrated by policies such as that allowing an official with elderly parents to transfer to a position near their place of residence.[23]

The practice of granting retirement benefits existed early, and gradually expanded in scope. The motive seems to have been dual: on the one hand to offer the official a prospect of security at the end of his career, and on the other to discourage continuance in office beyond the age of vigor. Retirement at the age of seventy (Chinese style) was both permitted and made increasingly mandatory.[24] (There seem always to have been cases of retirement earlier or later than this, however.) As the system evolved, benefits took several forms. Officials might be granted on retirement a gift of money or silk. Or they might be permitted at that time to nominate a son or grandson for office, and thus ensure their support; this was a form of recruitment through protection. Or they were granted a promotion in titular office and given as a retirement pension half or all the salary

---

and complimentary concurrent offices in the Censorate given under certain circumstances. There were twelve dignities (*hsün* 勳), the highest of which was that of "superior pillar of the state" (*shang chu-kuo* 上柱國). Laudatory epithets (*kung ch'en* 功臣) consisted of a number of conventional expressions, varying according to the office of the official, and added to his title. There were twenty-nine prestige titles (*san-kuan* 散官), and twelve titles of nobility (*chüeh* 爵). (The above are listed or described in *SS*,169,23b–35b.) Posthumously awarded offices (*tseng kuan* 贈官) followed fixed rules, described in *SS*,170,9b–15a. They might apply to three previous generations. By rule, officials were garbed in one of four colors, according to rank. But as early as 977 at least, it became a custom to award an official the privilege of wearing garb of rank higher than his (*SS*,153,1a–b). We are told that by the twelfth century almost everybody among the officials was wearing the red or purple of the two highest ranks (*JCSP*,V,2,1b). In addition, decorations such as the "fish-pouch" (*yü-tai* 魚袋), appended to the belt, were also awarded (*SHY*:YF,6,20a–21b).

[22] *KMPY*,1066/10.

[23] *HCP*,100,13b.

[24] The Chinese system of counting age reckoned one year at birth and added another year for each New Year's Day passed thereafter. The retirement age was, therefore, between sixty-eight and sixty-nine by our reckoning.

for the new office, in money and grain. They might, however, lose all these benefits if their career record was marred by serious offenses such as rapacity, or if they failed to retire at the required time.[25]

It was of course well understood that considerations of morale required the government to ensure a reasonable living standard for its officials. The state provided them, in addition to their money salaries, allowances of clothing and grain, according to a fixed schedule varying by rank and circumstances of employment. During the early years of the dynasty the meager salaries of the lower officials were improved. But with the increasing responsibilities of the state and the growing number of employees, the attempt to maintain the pay schedule at an adequate level became a problem. This was one of the stated motives for attempts to restrict the numbers on the state payroll.

With the passage of years, the problem gradually assumed more serious proportions. As larger numbers gained entrance into the civil service, they came to exceed the available number of posts. When relieved of his position, a man might have to wait some time for another. By the middle of the eleventh century, a minor official might draw his salary only three years out of six or seven. This was felt of course most acutely among the officials in the lower salary brackets. One result of it was the practice, widely condoned even in earlier years, by which officials supplemented their income through engaging in private trade. Such a custom led easily and too frequently to the misappropriation of state property and the abuse of official position through venality and improbity of other kinds. The evil was more readily diagnosed than treated.[26]

To establish a high morale in the service by other means, handicapped by the inadequacy of pay, might seem a disheartening task. But the attempt was made, as we shall see, perhaps encouraged by the dictum of Mencius: "In the absence of a stable livelihood to have a stable heart—only the [Confucian] scholar has the ability."[27] For some, the pride of service and the hope of advancement

[25] Cf. *SHY*:CK,77, esp. 29a; 30a–b; 33a; *YYY*,5,11a–12b; *SLYYP*,5,8a–b.

[26] For the salary scales and periods of unemployment, see *SHY*:CK,57,1a–4b, etc.; *YYY*,2,2b; *LCHSWC*,39,9a; *SHY*:CK,61,1a; *HCP*,11,6b. For clothing, see LPC,2,13a. For commercial activities of officials see CHS:SYSY.

[27] Mencius, I,A,7.

might make a life of strict frugality supportable; for others, private resources filled the gap. In evaluating the success of the civil service administration, nevertheless, we must keep in mind the financial discouragement with which the personnel administrator constantly contended.

3. Appointment and Promotion

The practices by which a civil servant was assigned to his rank and function, and advanced from one step of the structure to another, were necessarily affected by the metamorphosis which the classification system underwent during the first five reigns. Rules of appointment and promotion were subject to constant change, unintegrated, and often seemingly inconsistent. We possess no clear formulation of the system as a whole for any one part of the period. But like the rest of the governmental organization, appointment and promotion gradually acquired an increasing coherence during the first half of the eleventh century.

Even from the beginning of the dynasty, despite the constant change and seeming confusion of practices, the qualifications for the holding of a given office were in considerable degree specified by rules. The existence of these rules gave the official some sense of security in his career. Since all appointments were made centrally, the tenure of his office and his advancement were not subject to the caprice of his immediate superior, although the latter's opinion was not without effect on him. The official normally had no reason to fear demotion or dismissal without formal action and without cause. Beyond affording this sense of security, the rules of appointment were formulated so as to give the official some confidence in his prospect of advancement. At the same time, they sought to stimulate him to greater effort by basing his advancement partly on his achievement. They were planned to ensure that ability might rise rapidly to high position, without disregarding the need for experience.

As these objectives were to some extent conflicting, so were the methods which embodied them. Advancement depended on a number of factors. From the first we find that the more important controlling factors included regular positional sequence, and set terms of office, modified in application by preferential treatment based on the way in which the service had been entered, and by the use of merit ratings, examinations for promotion, and sponsorship. Advancement in titular office seems to have paralleled roughly that in function.

The relative emphasis to be placed on the different factors was the subject of continuous controversy. This reflected a more fundamental difference of opinion: the contest between those who advocated a government of laws, on the one hand, and on the other those who held that good government was to be achieved only through officials of high character, who could not be found by any rule. The latter view, as we have seen, was the more strictly Confucian. The conflict was clearly stated by Su Shih. He says "It will surely be argued that if a distinction is made on the basis of relative ability, without a wholly fixed law, then private likes and dislikes have an opening. I do not consider this to be so. The thing with law is to preserve its basic principles; its additions, subtractions, and evolution will certainly be entrusted to men. . . . If someone insists that one must trust laws, not men; that one certainly cannot place confidence in the men of the world, and needs a fixed rule; I still am not convinced that such a course cannot result in depravity." He holds that the governmental evils of his time stem directly from excessive reliance on paper work.[28] Even WANG An-shih, whose own policies extended considerably the scope of regulative legislation, decried in theory the reliance on rules in personnel matters.[29] Few eminent men seem to have raised their voices to support the opposite theory; yet in practice the proponents of objective rules seem to have carried the day rather more often than the advocates of character as the prime criterion.

This controversy resulted in a certain pendulum swing in the emphasis given the several factors. In the beginning, the exact interrelationship between the different factors is rather unclear, and the use of sponsorship to obtain specially qualified men, for example, seems merely to override the normal requirements set for sequence and duration of office. As time passes, however, there appears a closer integration of the various factors into a single complex but less variable pattern. Rapidity of advancement comes to depend not on any single factor, but on a combination of all the factors. As the rules become better adapted to the requirements and purposes of

[28] *STPCC*, Ying-chao, 2,4b–5b.

[29] *LCHSWC*,69,6a (transl. in WILLIAMSON, II, 370).

government, there is less need to modify them constantly or to make exceptions of special cases.

With the tendency toward systematization, the official of average abilities seems to have acquired a better chance of advancement, while the chances of rapid rise through good fortune or superior ability seem to have diminished correspondingly. Sponsorship, important from the beginning, played a role of ever growing importance as a normal method of promotion.

The Procedure of Appointment

The several offices at the capital which, as we have seen, divided the jurisdiction over appointment and promotion of officials, maintained registers containing relevant information on all civil servants. These registers contained the information derived from the annual merit ratings, and no doubt information from less formal reports which all officials were urged to make concerning the conduct of officials they observed or of whom they had heard.[30]

The registers were consulted in selecting a man for an important position, or in making promotions. Each promotion was preceded by a careful case review,[31] in which the appropriate bureau considered all information on the candidate's character and performance. If an official believed that he had fulfilled the requirements for promotion, he might request an action on his case.[32] In 964, an elaborate system was established requiring the executory class officials eligible for promotion to attend quarterly assemblages held at the capital. The appointments were all made on these occasions.[33] Beginning in

[30] On the personnel offices and this jurisdiction see above, Chap. III, p. 43. Registers of officials are mentioned at least as early as 974, when the Censorate is directed to keep one. In 985 the official in charge of administrative class officials was directed to compile a complete record of their careers, achievements, and faults. YH,119,30a; 127,11b. For reports, cf. texts 26, 55. Such reports might be submitted confidentially, under seal (text 73).

[31] Mo-k'an 磨勘.

[32] TK,39,43a. It was provided in 1057 that the competent bureau should automatically initiate action on promotions, without request from the official in question.

[33] KMPY,964/1st month; 7th month; YH,117,19a; TK,38,5a; SS,158,3a. This practice was called ssu-shih ts'an-hsüan 四時參選. Candidates were to arrive at the capital before the 15th day of the 1st, 4th, 7th, and 10th months. They were to receive their credentials and release from their previous posts on dates varying according to five distance zones, from 1,000 li to over 5,000. The several local governmental units

972, however, the shortage of officials caused by the rapid accession of new territories led the government to waive the quarterly assemblages and make appointments whenever the officials became available. Although the law of quarterly assemblages remained on the books, it became a dead letter.[34]

The Factor of Sequence and Tenure of Offices

At the beginning of the Sung, as we have seen, the lower posts in the local administration were held by men irregularly recruited, held in low regard, and with little prospect of advancement to more important positions. The higher local offices were filled by men from the central administration. But this situation began to change almost immediately. As early as 964 it was provided that even those who won higher grades in the decree examinations or in the doctoral examination in letters should begin their governmental careers in one of the lower civil aide positions in a prefecture.[35] By 993, it was ruled that no official could serve as administrator or vice-administrator of a prefecture who had not first gained experience in the lower ranks of local government. Since prefectural administration was the common gateway to higher office, this requirement applied to practically all important governmental posts, and in the course of time high officials who had not begun in the lower local offices became increasingly exceptional.[36] In this way it was insured that a majority of the officials throughout the government would have at least some direct experience in administration at a level where it touched the people directly.

From very early in the dynasty, the Sung government established a sequence of the offices that the civil servant would hold in the course of his successive promotions. This applied particularly to his promotion through the ranks of the executory class and into the administrative class, for which detailed rules are found at least as early

---

also submitted quarterly lists of their vacancies to the personnel agencies at the capital. Titular capital officials of the seventh grade or lower, at first subject to the same procedure, were soon exempted and placed on the same basis as the rest of the administrative class. The men of the clerical class followed a procedure similar to that of the executory class.

[34] *TK*,38,5b. This waiver was called *fang-hsüan* 放選.

[35] *HCP*,5,10b; *SS*,158,4a.

[36] *KMPY*,993/10; *YYY*,5,13a. It should be noted, however, that exceptions to this rule were possible through special Imperial action.

as 962.[37] Admission into the administrative class was considered the most important step in the ladder of promotion.[38] From the very beginning, there was nothing that can be called the "normal" sequence of offices; instead, the steps of promotion were already differentiated to take into account the factors of merit rating and entrance method.[39]

By the early eleventh century, a similar sequence appears in the promotions of commission given within the administrative class, and we find that an official regularly (apart from special exceptions) held successively the posts of service agent, subprefectural administrator, prefectural vice-administrator, and prefectural administrator.[40] Beyond the last office, already high, it was obviously impractical to determine a uniform career of promotions. Sequence of office in these administrative class posts also was affected by various factors. It is noteworthy that among the factors affecting sequence of office, that of specialization was generally absent. There is only rare evidence of any alteration in the sequence to give a man a post in a field for which he was specially fitted or prepared. This no doubt reflected the generally restricted place given to functional specialization in the governmental structure as a whole, and the emphasis in the Confucian political philosophy on broad outlook and moral worth rather than technical training.

The length of time each post should be held was also subject to increasingly fixed definition. Tenure might be measured in years or "annual merit ratings," [41] or it might be measured by a number of "terms," [42] commonly three years, or by a combination of the two. According to the system as it existed at the opening of the Sung, a certain tenure period was established for each post, theoretically based on the work burden in each case. In 961, however, it was felt that this delayed unduly the advancement of more able men, and in an extreme reaction all rules of seniority were abolished in favor of advancement solely according to merit.[43] Without evidence of special

---

[37] A rule of seniority (*hsün-tzu ko* 循資格) was established in 962 (*HCP*,3,11a; *TK*,39,36b; *KMPY*,962/10).

[38] *TK*,38,12b.

[39] *SS*,158,4a; *HCP*,5,10b; *TK*,39,37a.

[40] *SS*,160,22b; *TK*,39,40b.

[41] *K'ao* 考.

[42] *Jen* 任.

[43] *SHY:CK*,59,1a; 11,6a; *HCP*,2,7b; *KMPY*,961/4; *TK*,39,35a–b.

merit, we are told, a man might remain at the same post for ten years or more.[44] Thereafter, a policy of more equitable promotion was gradually introduced. The expressed motive was pity for those long without prospect of advancement; the morale in the lower ranks of the service may well have deteriorated. The new policy operated partly through the imposition of minimum periods of tenure, which, by restraining in some degree the operation of personal favor and chance, improved the prospect of the average man. It also, of course, inhibited the rise of the more able, except in so far as special provision was made for these.

The exact minimum time requirement for promotion differed from office to office and from period to period. Like the sequence of posts, it varied also through consideration of merit ratings and other factors. A promotion might come after as little as three years, or might take considerably longer.

The rise to administrative class status from the first entrance into the civil service might require as little as six to ten years. In the early eleventh century, the overgenerous practice of general promotions at the time of the suburban sacrifices was abolished, but in other respects a liberal promotion policy seems to have continued.[45] As a result of this, we find by the middle of the eleventh century complaints that the upper ranks of the service were becoming overloaded with men of mediocre abilities and were expanded numerically beyond the needs of the government. At the same time, the rise of specially able men was again retarded. As methods originally reserved for the exceptionally talented were opened to larger numbers, the able were lost in the throng. Around 1050 there was already a list of former executory class men who had qualified for the administrative class but for whom there would be no positions available for two years, and this list continued to expand, creating at the same time a shortage among the civil aides, from whom they had been promoted.[46] An apparent attempt during Jen-tsung's reign to limit annual promotions to the administrative classes to one hundred seems to have proven inadequate.[47] It was complained, moreover, that the short tenure of a given post prevented the official from becoming familiar with its special problems, from securing the coöperation of his staff, and ultimately from carrying through any effective policies and

[44] *TK*,39,40b.
[45] *TK*,39,39b; *YYY*,2,1a.
[46] See Chap. X, p. 164.
[47] *TK*,39,37b.

demonstrating his capacities, whether good or bad. As a result, there was continuing agitation to increase the restrictions on promotion and on the operation of the several methods of advancement.[48] The roster of officials in certain categories of the administrative class was fixed at a definite number.[49] Promotion in local commissions was subjected to minimum time requirements as early as the reign of Chen-tsung, when two terms of service were stipulated for each of the successive commissions: service agent, subprefectural administrator, prefectural vice-administrator, and administrator.[50] By 1028, this requirement had risen to three terms of each. It was, however, quickly modified to allow the counting of terms falling short of the nominal three years, and under certain circumstances one term of the three might be waived.[51] The promotion in titular office, while it followed a pattern parallel with that in commission, was nevertheless not exactly simultaneous, and indeed, rather had its own rules of seniority.[52]

[48] SUNG Ch'i thus complained in about 1041–1048 (*SCWC*,28,9b), and WANG An-shih a decade or so later (*LCHSWC*,39,13b–14a).

[49] Under Ying-tsung the number at the rank of junior lord of the nine courts or vice-director of the directorates was limited to seventy. Cf. *LPC*,2,11b; *TK*,34,29b.

[50] *TK*,39,40b. Quoting a statement of CHANG Fang-p'ing in 1048, the innovation is ascribed to the period 1008–1016. According to a ruling of 1015, the time was modified for circuit intendants according to distance of their posts from the capital, two and a half years in nearer areas and two in more distant.

[51] The proclamation of 1028/1 itself provided vaguely for exceptions on ground of merit or numerous sponsors (*SHY:CK*,11,2b; *HCP*,106,2a–b). In the ninth month it was amended to reduce the required terms by one if there were five sponsors (*HCP*, 106,18a; *YYY*,3,7a. The latter source dates it the same cyclical day of the seventh month). This in turn raised objections because it made no provision for the man of proven worth with no sponsors, and in 1030/8 candidates for promotion were re-divided into three categories: (a) men with no record of private offense, and no more than minor administrative delinquency, who would serve at least two terms before promotion; (b) men with a private offense (not rapacity) or a more serious administrative delinquency, who would serve the normal three terms; and (c) men with record of grave offense, whose cases should be considered individually. Those guilty of rapacity were not under any circumstances to be promoted at all. This scheme seems to have allowed no latitude at all on the ground of sponsorship (*HCP*,109,9a; *SHY:CK*,11,3a). For the above legal terminology, see below, p. 171. In the meanwhile, provisions for short terms also appeared. In 1029/8 it was permitted that men transferred in good standing before the expiration of their term might count two years as a term. Three months later, they were permitted to count two terms aggregating three and a half years (*SHY:CK*,11,3a).

[52] Cf. *HCP*,109,9a; 14a; text 66.

The Factor of Entrance Method

From the very beginning of the dynasty, the way in which an official had entered the service played an extremely significant rule in determining the speed of his rise. He received preference generally proportionate to the difficulty of the process through which he had passed, the intensity of the competition he had met, and the standing he had won in comparison with his competitors. The result favored greatly those who had qualified through examinations.

The factor of entrance method affected future careers in at least four respects: the appointment first given, the extent of promotions given on subsequent occasions, the length of tenure required before promotion, and eligibility for certain special posts.

Except for the opening years of the dynasty, when rather extraordinary appointments might be given to new examination graduates, the difference in initial appointment was not great. New men in general received posts of the lowest civil service grade: prefectural inspector, or subprefectural registrar or sheriff. Such difference as there was lay in the importance of the place where they would be stationed, which ranged from the largest to the smallest prefectures or subprefectures. For the determination of appointments and promotions, candidates were divided into three general groups: those formally qualified, those lacking formal qualification, and men of the three least favored categories.

The term "formally qualified" [53] in this context applied to those who had passed doctoral examinations, including (later in the period) those who, having passed the military doctorate,[54] had transferred to the civil service.[55] Among the doctoral graduates, further distinctions were drawn. The best posts went to the doctors in letters, the next to those in the nine classics, the third best to a category including all the other doctoral fields except the concentrated classical study and military doctorate, and the last two named fields comprised a fourth category.

The group "lacking formal qualifications," [56] including a number

---

[53] *Yu ch'u-shen* 有出身.　　　　[54] *Wu-chü* 武舉.

[55] Those who had transferred from the clerical service were called "formally qualified clerical service men" (*liu-wai ch'u-shen* 流外出身), and the term "formally qualified" was applied to certain other groups also. But it is clear that for purposes of promotion, the term has a more limited sense. See, for example, *SS*,169,14b–15a.

[56] *Wu ch'u-shen.*

admitted through transfer from the military and in a variety of other
ways without examination, came next. Finally, the three least favored
categories [57] included those recruited from irregular status, those recruited from the clerical service, and those who had received "qualification through contribution." [58]

After their initial appointment within the service, the men who
had entered through doctoral examination enjoyed a still greater advantage. Each time they were promoted, they might advance much
more than a man without the doctoral degree, and thus rise from the
ranks of the executory officials to the administrative more rapidly. [59]
Once in the administrative class, they continued to enjoy this advantage. Here, in the reign of T'ai-tsung, only the graduates of the
decree examinations and the doctors in letters and the nine classics
were favored, but they might jump in three promotions to a position
which would require six for others. [60] Eventually the favor was extended to all holders of doctoral degrees within this class also, while
those who had won the place of first palace graduate were permitted
on occasion to make still greater jumps in rank. [61]

The factor of entrance method also on occasion made a man eligible for promotion after less than the period of service normally
required. The differentiation of groups receiving this advantage resembled that connected with initial appointments. [62] Finally, a favor
accorded to a more limited number was that of early eligibility for
an assignment in one of the three institutes. In the earlier years of
the dynasty, it appears that men who had passed the decree examinations and the five highest recipients of the doctorate in letters

[57] *San-se-jen* 三色人.

[58] *SS, loc. cit.; SS*,158,10a–11b. These passages do not make any distinct provision
for the men recruited through decree examinations, through facilitated examinations,
or through protection. That the last named were treated as a less favored group
appears from evidence elsewhere. See above Chap. IV, Note 81. The military doctorate
was first established early in the reign of Jen-tsung, abolished for a while in the
middle of the century, but revived in 1064. *LPC*,2,5a.

[59] *SS*,158,2a; *SS*,169,13b–14a.

[60] *SS*,158,7a–b.

[61] *SS*,169,1a; *JCSP*,I,6,2a. As an exception to the tendency to grant preference only
on grounds of proven ability, it appears that relatives of empresses or of certain of
the highest officials received a certain advantage over the ordinary nondoctoral candidates, though less than that accorded holders of doctoral degrees.

[62] *SS*,169,15a–b. Illustrations of the practical advantage of a doctoral degree are
given in Chap. IV, p. 60.

were allowed to take an examination which would qualify them for service in the Institute of History, the Chao-wen Institute, or the Chi-hsien Library. Later, this privilege was extended only to the decree examination graduates and the first palace graduate, after one or two terms in another office.[63] Service in the institutes, as we shall see below, opened the way for a rapid ascent to the highest positions.

The Factor of Merit Ratings

The use of merit ratings as a factor in promotion is found throughout the first century of the Sung, under rules that varied greatly in detail. They applied to officials of all kinds, but the greatest stress was on those employed in local government, whose character and efficiency were naturally less easily ascertainable by the central authorities than were those of men stationed at the capital. Rules for rating of prefects and subprefects were formulated as early as 962, while similar rules for officials at the capital took form under T'ai-tsung's reign.[64] At least as early as 964 it was stipulated that the ratings should take place annually (for executory class men), and this remained the rule thereafter.[65]

The rating appears most usually to have been done by regular administrative superiors. We have early mention of the marking of both subprefectural and prefectural officials by the prefectural administrator.[66] The fiscal intendant and his assistant, however, had special responsibility for the merit ratings in his circuit, including apparently those of the lower officials. The judicial intendant also shared this responsibility, in a lesser degree.[67] Special bureaus at the capital were in turn responsible for the rating of the circuit intendants and the officials of the central government.[68]

[63] *TK*,38,17b,18a. Examinations for admission to institute assignment were also permitted to men sponsored for the purpose, and others were appointed by the regular commissioning process. See below, p. 98.

[64] *TK*,39,37b; TTS:KHCT,34.

[65] *HCP*,5,11a; *SS*,158,4b.

[66] Cf. *SS*,158,3a; *HCP*,5,4a.

[67] In 1043, Ou-yang Hsiu pointed out that this duty could not be adequately discharged by the already overburdened fiscal intendant, and advocated that a new official be specially created for the task. It is not clear that such action was actually taken (*HCP*,141,3b–4a; *KMPY*,1043/5).

[68] See above Chap. III, p. 43.

The matters on which an official was to be rated varied greatly. Many of them, however, have one interesting thing in common: they were verifiable facts, and did not call for subjective appraisal by the rating official. In 962, for instance, prefects and subprefects received credit if their concern for popular welfare was evidenced by a population increase of as much as 10 per cent. They were similarly to be penalized in rating if their neglect of public welfare resulted in a 10 per cent population decrease, or if their inefficiency resulted in a 10 per cent decrease in revenues or in a fine.[69] The same year recognition was proposed for sheriffs and subprefects who succeeded in apprehending brigands within a stipulated sixty-day period, greater if the arrest required a fight. For failure to apprehend the culprits, the officials were to be penalized.[70] Or again, local officials were to be credited if the various public properties in their charge were kept in good condition without overburdening the people of the district, and demerited if the properties deteriorated.[71] An important criterion in rating was freedom from corruption or private offense. Here we have once more a verifiable fact.[72] It is clear that this emphasis on objectivity was not accidental, but the result of a conscious fear of partiality in merit ratings, voiced in the slogan "trust laws, not men." There were, it is true, strict admonitions against personal favor, and punishments for any demonstrated injustice in ratings, or even for incompleteness.[73] But such laws were difficult to apply.

Nevertheless, Confucian opinion obliged the government to attempt at the same time some rating on the basis of more fundamental if less easily ascertainable facts. According to a rule of 1004, for instance, the local officials were to be ranked by the fiscal intendants in three categories. The highest included those who were just, diligent, incorrupt, efficient, and kind to the people. Next came those who were efficient but without a particular reputation for incorruption; or spotless in character but without their administrative competence being noised about. Lowest were the timorous, weak, covetous, and coarse.[74]

---

[69] *TK*,39,37b.

[70] *Ibid*.

[71] TK,39,38a.

[72] Cf. *HCP*,24,5b; 34,3b; 102,2b.

[73] *TK*,39,38b; *Hsing-t'ung*, 9,2b.

[74] *TK*,39,40a. For other similar rules see *KMPY*,976/11; *HCP*,17,20b.

The grades achieved in the merit ratings seem usually to have affected the speed of promotion rather than the sequence of posts. A good rating would reduce the tenure of a post normally required before promotion, a poor one would increase it.[75] Sometimes fines of as much as a month's salary, or even more, were imposed.[76] A succession of poor ratings might lead to demotion or dismissal.[77] When a man's record bore evidence of a serious offense of any kind, his advancement might be severely checked.[78] For discovering the existence of faults for which prosecution was in order, the intendants were strictly accountable.[79]

When an official's shortcomings were not so tangible in character, however, his superiors no doubt tended to overlook them when making a rating, and critics of the mid-eleventh century complain that the personnel offices tended to disregard the merit factor except in flagrant cases, basing their decisions instead largely on seniority and other factors more routine in application.[80]

The Factor of Examinations for Promotion

While merit ratings, as we have seen, applied to all officials, the examinations for promotion affected primarily the exceptional men. In general these examinations seem not to have constituted a regular step in the promotion procedure, but might be taken to demonstrate special proficiency. Some were rather general in character, while some were designed to find men for positions requiring certain special aptitudes. They differed in difficulty and in the extent of the promotion which might result.

The most difficult and rewarding were the decree examinations.[81]

[75] Cf. *TK*,39,38b; *SCKY*,5,7a. By a rule of 1061, men were specially reported after receiving an excellent or a poor rating for two successive years (*HCP*,195,3a).

[76] E.g., in 962, for failure to apprehend brigands (*TK*,39,37b); or proposal of SUNG Ch'i (*SCWC*,28,10a).

[77] *Ibid.; TK,* 39,44a.

[78] Cf. *TK*,39,40a.

[79] The rule governing intendants' responsibility in this was made more strict in 1009 (*HCP*,72,18a; *SHY:CK*,42,58a; *KMPY*,1009/11).

[80] *PHSKTY*,3,47a; *HCP*,208,10b–11a. We are told that a case of 1066 was the first demotion for poor ratings, under a law of 1061 (*TK*,39,44a; *HCP*,208,6a–b; *SHY:*Ck, 59,8b). But officials as high as circuit intendants could on occasion be treated severely on the basis of merit ratings, as demonstrated by a case of 1011 (*CKFC*,47,12a).

[81] *Chih-chü* 制舉.
This outline of the decree examinations is based on NCC:STCC.

These were intended to find men qualified for specially difficult work and afford them a means of rising rapidly to a place of responsibility. Since the purpose was to discover new talent, higher officials were not permitted to take them.[82] They were open not only to men in the civil service, but also to those who had not yet qualified for entrance. Thus, in a very restricted degree, it became a method of recruitment to the service as well as of promotion. Moral character as well as scholarship were considered in selecting the candidates, who applied for the test on their own initiative or were recommended by the local authorities.[83]

The examination consisted of two parts. The initial examination, held after 1029 in the Imperial Archives building, came to be known as the "examination at the Archives." [84] For those who survived the first test, a second part, the "Imperial examination," [85] was conducted by the Emperor personally. The subject matter of the two parts was similar. One day was allowed for each. According to the rules formulated for the Archives examination soon after 1004, it included six discussion questions, each of which called for the explanation of a given quotation. From early in the reign of Jen-tsung, each answer was to be over five hundred words in length. In order to identify the quotation and understand its implications and the controversial points it might contain, the candidate needed a familiarity with not only the nine classics, but also with the dynastic histories, the historical work called the *Discourses of the States*,[86] and the philosophical works attributed to Mencius, HSÜN K'uang, YANG Hsiung, KUAN Chung, and WANG T'ung. It was also necessary to know well the commentaries on all of these.

[82] The rules became gradually more severe, eliminating as candidates all circuit intendants, and men employed in the three institutes, Censorate, Secretariat-Chancellery or Department of Ministries, or else those ranking higher than professor of Imperial Sacrifices (List: M).

[83] From early in the eleventh century, they were to be approved by the Secretariat-Chancellery before admission to examination. From 1046, recommendation became mandatory. Like recommendation as a method of recruitment, the decree examinations were in fact an outgrowth of the Han recommendation system.

[84] *Ko-shih* 閣試.
Earlier, it was held in the Bureau of Academicians, and then in the Secretariat-Chancellery.

[85] *Yü-shih* 御試.

[86] *Kuo Yü.*

For the Imperial examination, according to the rules followed from 964 on, one question only was set. The required length of the answer (sometimes waived) was over three thousand words. The question was usually devised by the Emperor with the assistance of the chief councilors of state, and posed a complicated problem calling for subtle reasoning and argument. It might, for instance, concern the right or wrong of some political action of the past.[87]

Because of its difficulty, the examination was given rather rarely. From the founding of the Sung until 1067, candidates succeeded in qualifying for the Imperial examination in only seventeen years, and during this time only thirty men passed! Of these, three were from outside the civil service.[88]

Equal in importance with the decree examinations, and more often employed, were the examinations leading to an assignment in the three institutes. Such assignment was eagerly sought, having a prestige entirely disproportionate to the relatively low rank it bestowed. It was a short cut to the highest positions in the government. During the early Sung, it became customary to recruit from the institute officials men to be Han-lin academicians and drafting officials in the Secretariat. From the latter two groups, in turn, the councilors of state were frequently chosen.[89] During the mid-eleventh century, the gradual reduction in the numbers admitted to the institute examinations reduced the effectiveness of the practice, but the institutes continued to serve as a reservoir of talent for more important offices

[87] Although the examinations seem to have been rather similar, the degrees awarded carried different names. Most often it was called *hsien-liang-fang-cheng* 賢 良 方 正 ; in 1030 and 1034 the degree of *mao-ts'ai-yi-teng* 茂 材 異 等 was given; in 1034, 1042, 1057, and 1061 there was given the *ts'ai-chih-chien-mao* 才 識 兼 茂. Two or even three kinds of degree might be given the same year. The texts mentioned are known to have been used in the examinations toward the end of the eleventh century.

[88] One man—CHANG Fang-p'ing—passed it twice. On the first occasion he was promoted from outside the service to the position of subprefectural administrator (in the administrative class). On the second occasion, he was promoted to prefectural vice-administrator. In 1007, the decree examination graduate HSIA Sung was promoted from recorder of a subprefecture to titular executive assistant of the Court of Imperial Banquets (administrative class) and subprefectural administrator. The exact degree of promotion was not uniform. After 1067, the decree examinations were still more restricted in scope. During the following two centuries, the Imperial examination was held five times, and passed by eleven.

[89] Cf. *HCP*,208,15b–17a; *TK*,54,30a–b.

until the custom received the coup de grâce in the reorganization under Shen-tsung.[90]

We have seen that the privilege of taking the institute examinations was one of the advantages that rewarded high standing doctoral graduates. This privilege extended also to all graduates of the decree examinations. Others might gain it through the recommendation of officials of the Secretariat or Bureau of Military Affairs at the time of their first appointment to those organs. Finally, officials might be appointed, apparently without examination, as a reward for long and meritorious government service. Increasingly severe regulations sought to protect the institutes from favoritism by excluding as candidates the relatives of high officials.[91] But as the numbers permitted to take the examinations decreased, the personnel included an increasing proportion of veteran officials, and the attempt at the end of Ying-tsung's reign to revive the older practice was thwarted by the change in leadership at the death of that sovereign.

In addition to these examinations of special importance, there were a number of others on different levels of importance and for various special purposes. Appointment as a special drafting official of the Secretariat was normally preceded by an examination.[92] We find references also to examinations given to test potential legal officials in their knowledge of law and in their skill in its application.[93] The old person-speech-writing-decision test [94] appears in the Sung to have lost the important role it had held in the T'ang as a method of appointing lower officials. Although references to it at the very

[90] HCP, loc. cit.; SCSS,9,148; TK,38,17b–18a; OYWC,101,9b–11a; 119,2b–4a; TK,56,27b; SS,169,1a; JCSP,I,6,2a; text 141. Even in the reign of Ying-tsung, we are told, eight out of thirteen leading officials rose from the institutes. Cf. OYWC,114, 8b–11a.

[91] LTKS, 1, passim; LPC,2,10a; KMPY,1043/10; SHY:HC,33,1a. The examinations required the composition of one poem and one poetic description (TK,38,18a).

[92] KMPY,997/4. The examination consisted in composing three items each of edicts (chih 制) and announcements (kao 誥), of 200 words, and one each of 100 words.

[93] For example, in 962 it was permitted that legal officials (and civil aides?) be tested in law instead of in a writing-decision test (HCP,3,9b). A similar legal test was required in a proclamation of 986, apparently for local officials of all ranks (YYY, 3,5b). In 1028 officials were permitted to request an examination in law, presumably to qualify for positions in the Ministry of Justice and the High Court of Justice. They were required to have sponsors, and were tested on the basic laws, the commentaries on them, and on their ability in rendering decisions (TK,38,10a).

[94] Shen-yen-shu-p'an 身言書判.

beginning of the Sung seem to imply that it was required for all officials of the executory class, later references appear to give it a much more restricted role, as an examination through which executory class officials might gain a somewhat accelerated promotion.[95] The subject matter seems very similar to that of the preëminence examination,[96] with which it was closely associated, if not actually merged. Both examinations were abolished in 1034.

The Factor of Public Opinion

Public opinion played a certain role in connection with promotions and assignments to specific local posts. As we have seen, Confucian thought attributed theoretical importance to the voice of the people as a guide to the sovereign, and practical considerations added their persuasions to make the government rather sensitive to the reactions of the local community.[97] It is evident that at least on occasion during the first two reigns, local residents and functionaries could and did petition the government in the hope of retaining good officials.[98] But China had not formulated any systematic method (such as majority vote) for expressing the cumulative popular will. Both the centralized conception of the Sung civil service, and the merit principle which theoretically determined promotion and the distribution of duties, moreover, were in natural conflict with the principle of selection on the basis of popular partiality alone. Such partiality might help to demonstrate an official's merit, but was only one of several necessary criteria.

[95] *YH*,116,1a–2a; *HCP*,110,2a–b; *YYY*,1,2a–b; *TK*,38,6a; *KMPY*,1034/2.

[96] *Pa-ts'ui* 拔萃.

[97] Cf. below, pp. 116–117.

[98] These petitions, it seems, were sometimes taken to the capital by local deputations. In 963 such deputations were forbidden, but the local people were permitted to submit petitions through the regular channels if they wished to retain an official of exceptional accomplishment (or erect a memorial in his honor!). Such petitions were forbidden altogether at the beginning of Chen-tsung's reign (Text 4), but the practice seems to have continued, as evidenced by a reference of 1043 (*OYWC*,103,4a). In the last-cited case, an official's popularity in his former post is adduced as a reason for his reappointment there and as a demonstration of his worth. Historians quote evidence of popular approbation and affection as a mark of a good official. Cf. biographies of Chou Tun-yi and Ch'eng Hao (*SS*,437,2b–3a; 6b).

The Factor of Avoidance [99]

This was a more important part of the system, and filled a vital place in protecting official probity. It provided that officials related by blood or marriage should not have close contact in their official work. In this way it was hoped to prevent family ties from making it difficult for a man to carry out his duties impartially.

Such a principle, useful in any government, was particularly important in China, where the strong ethical emphasis on family responsibilities might easily have priority over administrative responsibility to the state. For the most part this principle would not hinder promotion, but merely bar activity in certain geographic areas or branches of the central government. If, however, a man had a relative serving in a high post, such as chief councilor of state, avoidance might keep him from attaining very high posts so long as the relative continued in such office. In general, avoidance prevented relatives not only from working in the same office, but from holding positions which, even though in different offices, involved a close working relationship.[100]

Although the practice of avoidance is found relatively early in the dynasty, we do not have evidence that the rules were clearly formulated until somewhat later. In 1041, a rule was adopted defining the exact degrees of relationship affected. They extended even to third cousins and to nonsib relatives beyond the mourning degrees.[101] A proclamation of 1063 regularized the application of avoidance in local government.[102]

[99] *Pi ch'in hsien* 避親嫌.

[100] For example, in 1018 Lü Yi-chien was obliged to resign the post of censor of miscellaneous affairs because a relative was executive censor (*SHY:*CK,63,1a). In 993, WANG Tan resigned as special drafting official of the Secretariat because a relative was assisting civil councilor of state (*ibid*). In 1038, because his father was serving in the latter office, a Han-lin academician resigned his post (*SHY:*CK,63,1b).

[101] *SHY:*CK,63,2a. The avoided relationships were defined as: 本族總麻以上 親 及 有 服 外 親 無 服 外 親. A ruling of 1058 excepted relationships through a deceased wife (*loc. cit.*, 3a).

[102] Subprefectural officials might not work in the same subprefecture with relatives; prefectural and circuit officials were similarly restricted. In each case, they were to be transferred to a neighboring unit of similar rank (*ibid.*, 3b). There is evidence also of an official avoiding his native place (*SHY:*CK,61,38a ff). Exchanges of posts were sometimes made for other reasons: lack of special qualifications (as experience on the border), personal incompatibility with the local inhabitants, or personal convenience,

A special case was presented by the relatives of Empresses and Imperial concubines, who by a rule of 1050 were prevented from holding posts in the Secretariat or Bureau of Military Affairs, and thus were barred from the Council of State.[103]

The principle also found an important use in safeguarding the objectivity of personnel administration. Officials of the Bureau of Administrative Personnel were in 1033 forbidden to act on the case of a relative. Should such a case fall to them, they were required to turn it over to a colleague in the bureau.[104] By a similar rule, examination candidates related to examiners were specially examined by another official designated for the purpose.[105]

These were the main factors other than sponsorship that in varying combinations determined the rapidity of a man's advancement in the civil service. It remains to examine the operation of sponsorship and its relation to the other factors of the promotion process. In doing so, we shall see in closer perspective the motives and conditions that affected the operation of the factors we have already considered.

---

as proximity to aged parents (*ibid.*). Exchange between fiscal intendants is found in 1045 (*op. cit.*, 63,2b).

[103] *LPC*,2,11a; *KMPY*,1050/int.11.

[104] *SHY*:CK,63,1b.

[105] Such avoidance is found in 962. The special examination in such cases was known as the *pieh-t'ou* 別頭 examination. *SHY*:HC,3,1b–2a; *YYY*,5,1a–b.

VI

THE OBJECTIVES OF SPONSORSHIP: USES
AND SCOPE

As we noted in the preceding chapter, sponsorship was one of the several factors which together affected the rapidity and the extent of an official's rise in the civil service. Its place was in some ways intermediate; it was less selective and affected larger numbers than did the decree or institute examinations, but it was more selective than promotion through sequence and tenure, merit rating, or entrance method.

Its objectives are presented with considerable clarity in the memorials and proclamations that are left to us. They tell us of the widely varied offices that sponsorship was designed to fill. They describe the role it was intended to play in discovering men of superior character and outstanding talents. They make clear also the role it ought to play in broadening the opportunity for advancement and raising the morale of the civil service.

1. The Molders of Policy

When we consider the objectives that shaped the early Sung institution of sponsorship, we immediately ask "Whose objectives?" We are not here concerned with all the individuals who acted as sponsors, but with those who in one way or another conceived and directed the acts through which the institution was brought about. Who were these initiators? The answers available are not entirely satisfactory. Of some hundred and fifty measures of various kinds on the subject recorded in the *Sung hui-yao*, I have been able to trace there or elsewhere the authorship of barely a quarter. This is too limited a ground for generalization and permits us only to note certain apparent trends.

In the cases covered by our data, the initiative for action comes from three general groups in approximately equal degree: (a) agencies directly responsible for personnel administration, (b) agencies of general jurisdiction, and (c) agencies whose duties lay specifically in other fields.[1] The personnel administration agencies here active are the Secretariat-Chancellery (acting both as a supervisory organ, and, in the case of higher officials, as a personnel agency) and the Bureau of Executory Personnel.[2] The suggestions from these agencies range from the proposal of general rules and regulations to requests for the use of sponsorship to meet the need of particular situations.

The agencies of general jurisdiction found active in this field are the members of the Council of State, the censors, and the policy-criticism officials.[3] The proposals of this group, as we might expect, concern chiefly the improvement of general procedures of sponsorship rather than its use on specific occasions.

The third group includes agencies and individual officials of all kinds and all ranks. Their concern seems most often with the application of sponsorship to their special fields of activity, but they too propose measures of a more general character.[4] On the whole, it

[1] In the category of measures or initiated actions I include all proposals for new rules on sponsorship, or for the use of sponsorship, or for its manner of use on a particular occasion, so far as the initiative was taken by the proposer. I do not count here cases in which the official or agency proposing an action seems merely to be acting in response to previous legislation or directive and offering no modification of the predetermined policy.

[2] In the case of the Secretariat-Chancellery merely the agency is indicated as author, while in the case of the Bureau the spokesman is sometimes one of the associate supervisors. It is surprising that the Bureau of Administrative Personnel does not figure here. It may be that the latter bureau, directly subordinate to the Secretariat-Chancellery, reported through it, while the Bureau of Executory Personnel, nominally a part of the Ministry of Personnel in the Department of Ministries, reported independently.

[3] Proposals come from censors of various ranks: executive censor, censor of miscellaneous affairs, and investigating censor. In addition, proposals also come from censors who are serving as supervisor or associate supervisor of the Bureau of Executory Personnel.

[4] The High Court of Justice proposed a new rule on the application of guaranty in 1011, and in 1018 a supervisory judge of the court requested a modification of it. In 1024 the Bureau of Judicial Investigation, the Ministry of Justice, and the High Court of Justice were instructed to restudy the subject together. In 962 a rule on legal enforcement of sponsorship rules was proposed by a special drafting official of the Secretariat. In 994 the Institute of History, by request, studied the historical precedents for recommendation by high officials. The Finance Commission in 996 requested recommendation of local service agents, and in 1040 in time of military emergency a supervisory official of the Commission requested that fiscal and judicial intendants

seems from this limited evidence that the system of sponsorship
grew from the aggregate interests, needs, and views of officials in all
parts of the government. The system at each step of its growth of
course required the sanction of the chief policy-forming bodies. But
the coöperative and representative way in which it grew no doubt
helped to make it workable, and also no doubt helped to account
for the seeming inconsistencies and conflicts of purpose which appear during the course of its development.

2. The Scope of Uses for Sponsorship

The most obvious objective of those who promoted sponsorship,
and one which stands out most clearly in the early proclamations,
was simply to find the man best qualified for a post or rank which,
whether high or low, was critically important, and to speed the rise
of the able man to the place where he was most needed. Sponsorship
provided a simple, rapid, and effective method of selection.

The measures enabling sponsorship usually indicated specifically
the use to be made of it: selection for a class of the service or for
specific titular offices or posts. The posts and ranks which were filled
through sponsorship during the first five reigns of the Sung included
very nearly the whole possible range in relative height and in kind.
They included titular offices, commissions, and assignments. Practically nothing was excluded, in fact, but the highest posts and ranks
of the central government at the one extreme, and the lowest local
posts at the other.[5] The rapidity with which sponsorship was applied
to all these purposes is surprising. Although the northern states of
the Five Dynasties appear to have limited the practice merely to
the selection of executory officials, we find within the first decade
of the Sung instances which either exemplify or foreshadow all the

---

recommend men skilled in border matters. In 1005, a fiscal intendant requested the
curtailment of sponsorship by administrators of border prefectures. In 1018 an auxiliary
academician of the Bureau of Military Affairs proposed a rule to help curb the use of
influence in making recommendations. In 1027 a registrar of Hsiang-fu subprefecture
in K'ai-feng requested that a previous action be extended to apply to K'ai-feng. Two
proposals were anonymous sealed memorials, one (1015) calling attention to a local
need for sponsorship, and one (1016) proposing more severe qualifications for
sponsors.

[5] As noted in Chapter IV and below, through the limited use of sponsorship for
recruitment of the service, it occasionally filled even the lowest posts, but this was of
minor importance.

major future uses. Sponsorship was used for appointment in both the executory and administrative classes, and within these classes both for titular rank and for function. For later periods it remained only to make further use of the method so rapidly devised for the needs of the dynasty's founders, and to modify its emphasis to meet altered conditions.

The Filling of Functional Offices

In the great majority of cases, the documents on sponsorship concern themselves with finding men for specific functions rather than with singling men out for promotion in rank. In some cases, however, as we have seen, the titular office was also functional, and sponsorship then operated for both purposes simultaneously.

In the executory class. This was particularly true of the executory class, where title and function usually corresponded. The sponsorship of officials for posts of the executory class, inherited from the Five Dynasties, remained important during the early Sung. The texts preserved, however, refer only rather sporadically to its use for any single office. It is hard to say whether this reflects merely the accident of textual transmission, or an actual variation of emphasis in the practice. There is some evidence to support the latter interpretation.

The critical need for reliable local officials during the opening Sung years was not quickly alleviated.[6] The struggle to secure control of the local units continued through most of the reign of T'ai-tsung.[7] This period shows the most frequent references to the sponsorship of executory officials.

Of sponsorship for the lowest rank, that of prefectural inspectors and subprefectural registrars and sheriffs, the first five Sung reigns show no evidence.[8]

The greatest concern seems to have centered on the office of subprefect, so vital in linking the people and government. Repeated proclamations of the Five Dynasties and the first on sponsorship in

[6] See above, p. 27.

[7] In 987 and 989, for instance, it was still found necessary to order the local administrators not to appoint subordinates summarily, without reference to K'ai-feng (texts 15, 16).

[8] The latest instance of which I have evidence is that of 927 in the Latter T'ang (*WTHY*,4,12a).

the Sung seek men for this office.[9] These proclamations are followed by a gap of nearly twenty years. This gap begins just at the time when T'ai-tsu resorted to the radical step of commissioning court officials to administer subprefectures, in the hope of improving their very low efficiency.[10] Such a measure could be applied to only a few of the most important units, however, and the problem of the many others remained. We read in a proclamation of 981:

"At present . . . our territories are expanding and developing; the subprefectures are many and difficult to administer so that all are in need of officials. Some places have not been filled for years. In weighing the decision of appointments, there is adherence to seniority without discrimination. The prefectures are corrupted by their lower officials." [11] During the following years, therefore, the post receives continuing stress in sponsorship. On occasion men are sought for a particular region, or a place of special importance.[12] Sponsorship, no doubt assisted by accelerated promotion in other ways, seems to have alleviated the difficulty, and before the end of Chen-tsung's reign there was an overabundance of subprefects.[13] Perhaps for this reason nothing further is heard of their sponsorship until in 1029, when their inferior quality again attracted notice. A complainant remarked that, "if among those presented at court by the Bureau of Executory Personnel there were any old and feeble, they would be made subprefects." [14] In response to this need new conditions were formulated, providing for the subprefects' regular annual recommendation. The new rules seem to have continued in force thereafter, with occasional amendment of detail.[15]

[9] 927,954/5,957,958,962 (text 1). For the proclamations before 960, see Chapter I, Note 18.

[10] HCP,4,13b.

[11] Text 10.

[12] For Ho-pei in 991 (text 18). The reason for the need is not apparent, but its urgency is suggested by the requirement that sponsors who were on commission out of the capital should send their recommendations by post. For subprefectures of five thousand or more households (in the largest size classification) in 993 (text 25).

[13] In 1001 some fifteen subprefects or subprefectural administrators were called for (text 39), while in 1019 subprefects were given places normally reserved for men of the administrative class (TK,38,10a).

[14] The nonextant Cheng-yao of CHANG T'ang-ying, quoted in HCP,108,11b.

[15] Rules of 1029 in text 109. The amendments of 1040 in text 117, and of 1066 in text 152. Subprefects also had a place in the scheme of sponsorship briefly tried in 1043, discussed below.

References to recommendation for other posts of the executory class, those on the prefectural staffs, are much fewer. The reasons for this are not obvious. Perhaps, having less independence and direct contact with the governed than the subprefects, they were considered less vital. The upper prefectural staff positions, being of higher rank, stepping stones to the administrative class, and under the eye of the prefectural administrator, were perhaps more eagerly sought, and perhaps adequately filled without sponsorship.

Some proclamations on recommendation of subprefects couple with them prefectural inspectors, who were of similar rank.[16] Reference to sponsorship of men for the upper prefectural staffs is found (except for instances in the Five Dynasties and the opening years of the Sung) only rather later.[17] In 1004 a critical shortage of men for these positions was noted, particularly in the circuits of Ho-pei and Hsi-ch'uan. Recommendations were called for, first in these areas and later for the Empire as a whole.[18] In 1060, after a long silence, we learn once more that the upper prefectural staffs were short of officials, many places lacking from eight to ten, and recommendation was again specially invoked.[19] These were clearly exceptional cases, calling for special attention. It seems on the whole probable that men were also sponsored for such posts in the normal operation of the system, although I have found no order providing for this. I have in any case no evidence that they were ever specifically excluded from recommendation.

To gauge the importance of sponsorship as a method of filling executory posts, we need to know not only what kind of post was filled, and on what occasions, but how many of the existing vacancies were filled through this method on each occasion. Here our data are very scant and far from precise. A few instances supply

[16] Those of 927,954/5,957,958,962,991. See Note 18, Chapter I, and texts 1, 18.

[17] There were calls for recommendation of staff supervisors in prefectures of different grades in 927 and 957. In 958 and 962, they were for unspecified upper prefectural staff positions (*ibid.*). A regulation of 963 concerns the recommendation of prefectural general secretaries, and implies that men of inadequate qualification for the post were being recommended by the regional commander, although we have no record that such recommendation had been ordered (text 3).

[18] Texts 42, 43. In 1005, men on the border were excluded as candidates for these positions because of the difficulty of checking their records (text 46).

[19] Text 144. In 1066, new regulations on sponsorship cover recommendations for these posts among others (text 152).

evidence that the number of men to be recommended would probably suffice, or more than suffice, to fill the vacancies at hand. In such cases, unless a few other candidates with still better credentials were already at hand, sponsorship very possibly entirely replaced other methods of selection.[20] But these instances were all cases of special need, and they fall within the first half century of the Sung. It is not clear that when recommendation for executory posts became a regular procedure, it filled a major proportion of the vacancies. FAN Chung-yen and HAN Ch'i in 1043 claim, on the contrary, that seniority still played the dominant role.[21]

In the administrative class. The employment of sponsorship for administrative class posts, both local and central, left evidence of much greater governmental interest than its use for those of executory class.

In the administrative class, in contrast with the executory, most functional offices were not titular, and recommendation for functional offices of this class did not necessarily imply a promotion in titular rank. Except for two isolated cases, this phase seems to have developed under T'ai-tsung, beginning about 982. From that time it was used for important posts both in the local units and in the central administration.

At first its use for any particular office seems often sporadic, and connected with some special occasion such as a governmental reorganization involving the establishment of new posts. The creation in 963 of the commission of prefectural vice-administrator, for instance, was followed the next year by a call to sponsor candidates

[20] In 993, when men were to be sponsored for subprefect in places of five thousand or more families, 97 sponsors were named, each to recommend two candidates (text 25). Subprefectures of that size were in the largest of the five population categories (*TK*,63,28a) and would number only a fraction of the some twelve hundred subprefectures in the Empire. Therefore 194 men might easily fill such posts even if a very large proportion of the places in that category were vacant. In 1004, when 78 vacancies were reported among upper prefectural staff officials of two areas, fiscal intendants of all circuits were directed to recommend men for the posts (text 42). There were at this time seventeen circuits, and there was apparently no limit to the number each sponsor might name. Later the same year, all court officials were named to sponsor men for the same office, each two sponsors selecting one candidate (text 43). There were at this time some four hundred court officials and some two hundred and fifty prefectures, each employing from three officials to one or none of the rank to be sponsored.

[21] *HCP*,141,12b–13a.

for it.[22] The gradual reorganization of the finance commission between 983 and 1003 was accompanied by the use of sponsorship for the key position of supervisor and for other duties, on at least five occasions.[23] The expansion of the Censorate at the turn of the century also exemplifies the way in which sponsorship was applied directly to immediate personnel needs.[24] The sponsorship of officials qualified for legal work or academic assignments at this time still further reflects a response to special demands.[25]

For some posts, particularly those both numerous and important, such as those of fiscal intendants of circuits or administrators of prefectures, the continuing need resulted in a more frequent resort to

[22] Text 5. The next instance of sponsorship for this office was 990 (text 17). A proclamation of 1005, curtailing the recommendation of men in border circuits for this post, suggests that it had continued thereafter (text 46).

[23] 982 (text 13), 993 (text 24), 994 (text 28). A special need for local service agents was met through sponsorship in 996 (text 29), and again in 999, when men were needed for unstipulated financial duties (text 36). Recommendation for service agent appears again in 1018 (text 86).

[24] The office of censorate investigator (*t'ui-k'an*) had been established either in 990 (*KMPY*,990/5) or in the period after 998 (*SS*,164,4b), with a complement of ten men (latter source) or twenty (former). Recommendations for these posts were called for in 1001 (text 38) and again in 1002 (text 41). On the latter occasion recommendations were also requested for the older post of investigating auxiliary (*t'ui-chih*). In addition to the above and the heads of the organ, orders of 1012 and 1017 further established a minimum number of six regular censors, to be on duty in the Censorate (*SHY*:CK,5a–b; *HCP*,89,4a–b). In 1019, while Wang Ch'in-jo was Chief Councilor, this rule was reversed, but Wang was dismissed soon afterward (*KMPY*,1019/4–1019/5). Thus we find that in 1020 there was a call for recommendation of men to be censors (text 90), and in 1023 for censors and critic officials (*KMPY*,1023/4).

[25] The number of law clerks in the High Court of Justice had been increased in 997, and in 999 the number of reviewing officials (*hsiang-tuan*) was fixed at eight (*SHY*:CK,24,3a). These officials substituted for the assistant justice or revisory judges, and were exceeded in authority only by the supervisory judge and his assistant (*SHY*:CK,24,1a; *SS*,165,1a). In 1002 their sponsorship was directed (text 41). Recommendation of men for undesignated but seemingly important legal work was again directed in 1014 and in 1020 (texts 65, 90). In 1005, at a time when the expansion of public education was receiving attention, the recommendation of ten men to be auxiliary lecturers of the Directorate of Education was ordered (texts 47, 48). This post, established in 994, was equivalent to that of professor, which was not then in use (*TK*,57,15a; 19a; *SS*,165,12a). Earlier in the same year, the Emperor had paid a personal visit to the Directorate (*KMPY*,1005/5). In 1007, another school of the Directorate was founded in Ho-nan-fu, the western capital, calling for a further staff expansion (*SHY*:CK,28,2a).

sponsorship, even under T'ai-tsung and the earlier reign of Chen-tsung.[26]

The question once more rises, as it did in connection with sponsorship for executory class positions: did sponsorship during the first half century play an exclusive role in finding men for the needs we have just noted? In cases when only one or two places were in question, it seems probable that when recommendations were ordered, the men recommended would receive the positions unless they were for some reason unsuitable. Of cases where a larger number of posts is in question, we find, as with executory positions, only a few pertinent examples. Here, too, in such cases as we have, it seems that there were an ample number of men sponsored to fill the available positions.[27]

From the middle of the reign of Chen-tsung at least, while the application to special situations continues, the tendency toward a more common use of sponsorship becomes apparent.[28] The norma-

[26] Calls for recommendation of fiscal intendants are found in 982, 990, 992, 994, and 998 (texts 13, 17, 20, 28, 30). Those of 990 and 998 include also assistant intendants. The other circuit intendants existed only rather irregularly during the earlier period. Calls for prefectural administrators appear in 990, 998, 999 (twice), 1004, and 1007 (texts 17, 32, 34, 35, 44, 51). That of 1004 mentions specifically large prefectures with regional command or border prefectures. Calls for administrative class administrator of subprefecture are understandably fewer, since this unit was more often under a subprefect of the executory class. There are, however, two instances, 999 and 1001 (texts 35, 39).

[27] In 964, when there were only some 129 prefectures of all kinds (SS,85,1a–2a; NCC:TLCKY,I,6,8–9), forty-five sponsors were to recommend one man each to be vice-administrators of those with regional command, one of the more important categories (text 5). In 982, eleven sponsors were to select one man each to be a fiscal intendant (text 13). I am not sure how many of these were to be appointed, but in 993 there were ten fiscal intendant circuits (NCC, loc. cit.). In 996, when "over fifty" service agents were needed, eighty-four sponsors were to name one man each (text 29). In 1004, seventy-two sponsors were to name one man each for prefectural administrator, in a border prefecture or a large one with regional command, and in 1007 fifty sponsors were to name two each, to administer a prefecture of the latter category (texts 44, 51). At this time it appears that there were some two hundred and fifty prefectures of all kinds, so that the vacancies in both instances would hardly equal the number of recommendations.

[28] In addition to later examples of special use for central posts already indicated, other instances of special later uses may be noted. In 1014 men were called for with broad knowledge of civil government, or ability to handle difficult and troublesome offices, or reliability suitable for border defense positions (text 65). In 1018, men to be service agents, of titular capital rank, were required (text 86). In 1029, men were

tive proclamation of 1010 foreshadows this tendency in its listing of specific commissions to be given through sponsorship:

(a) Special duties at Court.

(b) The administration of prefectures and subprefectures whose affairs have fallen into disorder.

(c) The undertaking of special commissions for the Finance Commission, the Bureau of Judicial Investigation, or other central government organs. These might be matters normally within the jurisdiction of the circuit or prefectural authorities, but beyond their competence because of special difficulty or unusual nature. Among the cases specifically indicated were those where unfinished business called for reinvestigation and possibly the reversal of decisions.

It is readily seen that the positions to be given, according to this list, are all commissions of an unusual nature. There is no mention of promotion in titular office, or even nomination for the more usual functional offices. But whether or not it was intended at this time, the new form of recommendation soon received far broader use than that here implied. In 1015 we see already the beginnings of a regular routine for promotion in local commissions through sponsorship, affecting the offices of judicial intendant, prefectural administrator, and vice-administrator, the latter two offices differentiated according to importance of place.[29] By 1018, a formula appears defining the sequence of promotions through sponsorship from the post of subprefectural administrator through prefectural vice-administrator and administrator; it is refined to allow for differences of seniority as well as for importance of the places assigned.[30] At the same time and continuing through the reigns of

---

sought for undesignated difficult commissions (text 108). Or in 1051, men were sought suitable to administer five designated prefectures or to be vice-administrators of two others, all in the Ssu-ch'uan area (text 129), and in the following year for employment in important border affairs (text 132).

[29] The controlling factors in this formula were length of service and number of sponsors. The posts given the preferred category were judicial intendant or administrator of large prefecture with regional command. The second category received posts of vice-administrator of a large prefecture with regional command, or administrator of a smaller prefecture (text 67).

[30] The sequence was from subprefectural administrator to prefectural vice-administrator to administrator. If a candidate had already attained the status of expectant (ho-ju 合入) vice-administrator or vice-administrator, he would be stationed in a more important prefecture, one with regional command (text 83).

Jen-tsung and Ying-tsung, we find increasingly elaborate rules determining the methods by which men were to be recommended for such administrative class functions. These regulations (which will be discussed later) make it abundantly clear that sponsorship had become a normal method of selection for functional office.

As it became a normal method of selection for function, the application of sponsorship was modified increasingly to take into account the other normal factors in promotion. Thus it affected the advancement of a greater number of officials, but played at the same time a less exclusive role in any single case. And there is evidence, even late in the reign of Jen-tsung, that simple seniority remained a controlling factor in the placement of many, perhaps most, local officials.[31]

Promotion in Titular Rank

Sponsorship for titular rank, as already noted, receives less attention in the documents than that for specific duties. It was concerned primarily not with selecting men for promotion to a particular titular office, but with promotion to the administrative class as a whole. Here it performed an important function.

During the last three of the reigns we are considering, men entering the administrative class through sponsorship were given a titular office in the group of capital officials. During the reign of T'ai-tsu and the earlier part of that of T'ai-tsung, however, this does not appear to be so. In three or four cases at least men of the executory class were to be sponsored directly for court rank.[32] Peculiar to this same period was the recommendation of men to be promoted from titular capital rank to titular court rank.[33] In 993,

[31] See the memorial of Fan Chung-yen and Han Ch'i in 1043 (*HCP*,141,12b–13a) and that of Pao Ch'eng, written probably not long before 1062. (*PHSKTY*,3,47a). Both complain that the Bureau of Administrative Personnel in selecting prefectural administrators and vice-administrators, and subprefectural administrators, regularly adheres to seniority and ignores merit, and they advocate a greater stress on sponsorship.

[32] The first instance, in 964 (text 5), was remarkable in providing that executory class officials might be recommended for the administrative class commission of vice-administrator of a prefecture with regional command. Although this post was later filled by capital officials, its first holder was a court official (*TK*,63,15a), and it seems probable that in this case a simultaneous promotion to that rank would be implied. This was followed by proclamations of 967, 970, and 985 calling for recommendation for court titular rank, with no specified commission (texts 6, 8, 14).

[33] 967, 970, 985, 992 (texts 6, 8, 14, 19).

we find the first instance of recommendation for capital rank. It is followed by others, and simultaneously the references to recommendation for court rank disappear.[34] While the normative proclamation of 1010 made no direct reference to annual sponsorship for promotion to the administrative class, we find from about that time the formulation of rules which seem to presuppose such a practice.[35] In any case, proclamations of 1012 and later explicitly apply to it.[36] At the same time, the regular use of sponsorship for the recruitment of the administrative class did not exclude the special recommendation of executory class men for the administrative class to meet some particular need, as later proclamations show.[37]

The attributes demanded in candidates for sponsorship, and the rapidity of their promotion, which we shall examine later, will suggest the importance of the system for promotion of the specially qualified to the administrative class. It is harder to judge the place that sponsored men occupied quantitatively among administrative class recruits. Two kinds of evidence suggest that it was considerable. One is the apparent difficulty, during Jen-tsung's reign, of obtaining promotion to the administrative class without sponsorship, and the resulting eagerness for recommendations.[38] The other is the fact that tightening of sponsorship requirements was repeatedly resorted to in the hope of curtailing the too rapid expansion of the

[34] 993, 996, 1005 (texts 25, 29, 47, 48). The last two are again examples of recommendation of executory class men directly for administrative class commission.

[35] An earlier proclamation of 1010 establishes requirements of service in previous position before sponsorship, and applies them to candidates from the upper prefectural staff among others. They would presumably be sponsored for titular capital rank (text 54). The same is true of the normative proclamation (text 55). An anonymous memorial of 1015 remarked that executory class officials with many recommendations generally receive titular capital offices (text 69).

[36] Text 59. Subsequent regulating proclamations will be discussed below.

[37] E.g., 1018, when a selected group of censors were to sponsor men to be service agents (text 86), or 1020, when men were similarly to be recommended for prefectural administrator of titular capital rank (text 90).

[38] In 1024 the censor Li Hung notes that the requirement of five sponsors for promotion from the executory class results in a begging for recommendations by those who have only one or two. This resulted in a reduction in the required number of sponsors (text 97). The situation is illustrated also by two cases of that year in which the lack of sponsors is said to have effectively prevented the rise of executory officials, otherwise deserving, for many years. One of them had no fault in his record, and had served for fourteen years. The Emperor by special action made them titular capital officials (*TK*,39,40a; *HCP*,102,1b).

administrative class.[39] This effort continued until the end of the period we are considering. Aside from its part in the recruitment of the administrative class, sponsorship played a less conspicuous role in titular rank promotion within that class.

As we noted earlier, sponsorship for titular office obviously accompanied that for function in cases where titular and functional office coincided. Apart from the executory class, the most conspicuous examples of this were in the Censorate. Promotion in titular office also might be incidental to a promotion in function, achieved through sponsorship.[40] For a brief period the practice assumed a larger role and became not only a regular but a principal, if not mandatory method of titular promotion. Under a scheme proposed by FAN Chung-yen in 1043 to prevent the automatic rise of mediocre men to higher positions, recommendation by five sponsors was required at each of three key points on the ladder of titular office promotion.[41] The new extension of sponsorship soon came under attack because of its encouragement of sycophancy (as we shall see later) and was repealed in less than two years.[42] Such an attractive panacea was not easily forgotten, however, and we find it advocated again in the following reign.[43]

[39] CH'EN Fu-liang so construes measures of Jen-tsung's reign (TK,39,37b), as does CHIA Yen (SHY:HC,28,2b; TK,38,16a). As the latter points out, the continuing recommendations thwarted the effort, and in 1065 he secures a proclamation urging sponsors not to fill their quotas unless they have men of special merit (texts 150, 151).

[40] An interesting example occurred in 1015. A man was at first given a promotion involving change both of commission and of titular office, but because his previous promotion was too recent, a simple change in commission was substituted (text 66). A rule of 1007 seems to imply that a recommendation might be specifically for commission only, or for titular office as well (text 50).

[41] Unfortunately, SHY lacks a detailed text of this extremely interesting scheme. Abbreviated versions are to be found appended to SHY (text 123), and in KMPY 1043/10 and HCP,144,8b. The three key offices for which sponsors were required were (1) those of assistant office or division chief in the Department of Ministries (L), (2) office or division chief in the same (L), and (3) junior lord of one of the nine courts or vice-director of a directorate (J). SHY does not indicate any way of circumventing the requirement, but KMPY says that, lacking sufficient sponsors, the candidate must wait two years more. KMPY seems to say (the interpretation is not certain) that sponsors are also required for promotion of titular capital officials. Also, according to KMPY, promotion to the titular ranks of senior lord of a court or director of a directorate, or policy critic-adviser was to be made only by special directive. The same was to be true of titular positions in the Secretariat-Chancellery.

[42] Text 123.   [43] Cf. HCP,208,11a (1066).

VII

THE OBJECTIVES OF SPONSORSHIP: PERSONAL QUALITIES AND GROUP MORALE

The documents which embody early Sung policy on sponsorship describe with great care the qualities which a candidate should have. The desirable traits of character are repeatedly stipulated, and the requisite skills, abilities, and experience are set forth still more regularly and carefully. Qualifications of other kinds receive attention with varying frequency.

We shall see that in the earlier period there was a general tendency to stress qualities which were in practice difficult to assure through other methods of advancement. These qualities remained important in later years also, but were joined with new considerations which accompanied the integration of sponsorship with the more normal methods.

The qualities required for different ranks and functions did not differ greatly, though we shall note certain qualities which were more often considered for special positions.

1. Personal Character

It is not surprising that personal character, which occupied such an important place in Confucian political theory, received stress in sponsorship. This seemed, of all Sung promotion methods, the best adapted to favor the man of worth, the *hsien-jen*. Those who complained of the character of officials in their day often turned to sponsorship as the most promising tool of reform.[1] Though they often perceived its shortcomings in practice, they looked for remedies through its improvement rather than the substitution of other methods.[2]

[1] See, for instance, the address of FAN Chung-yen in 1043 (*KMPY*,1043/10), or that of CHANG Fang-p'ing in 1048 (*TK*,39,40b), or one of PAO Ch'eng (*PHSKTY*,3, 47a). *Hsien-jen* 賢人.

[2] Cf. the address of CHIA Yen in 1065 (*SHY*:HC,28,2b).

When they translated the general stress on worth into more specific terms, the traits most often called for were rather more concrete and practical than we might have expected after reading the eulogies on the worthies of old with which measures were often prefaced. Vigor, for instance, stood near the top of the list. Most often it was sought in the forms of effort, achievement, and industry.[3] Somewhat less often—and especially for more important positions—there was emphasis on firmness and freedom from timidity.[4]

Discipline was mentioned even more often than vigor. Most often it appeared as freedom from the misuse of authority, presumption, or impropriety.[5] It also took the positive form of reliability, or understanding of the proper code of a public servant.[6]

Caution is among traits sought for more important posts.[7] We find mentioned also such traits as filial piety, staunchness in friendship, and conduct dictated by conviction, not shifting to suit the exigencies of ambition.[8] It is interesting to note the regularity with which proper conduct was stipulated in candidates for academic positions.[9] The candidates' concern for the popular welfare, and considerate administrative methods, were stressed now and again.[10] The encouragement of this concern was prompted not only by Confucian principle, but by vivid memories of the dangerous uprisings that had crippled the T'ang government. This motive shows occasionally in the more specific requirement that the candidate shall not have given rise to disturbances through his harshness! [11]

[3] For instance 962 (text 1), 1007 (text 50), 1029 (text 109), 1044 (text 122). In 993, the aged and decrepit are among those excluded (text 24), and again in 1050, when an age limit of sixty was set (SHY:CK,48,2a).

[4] For instance in 985 (text 14), 992 (text 20).

[5] For instance 1024 (text 97). Most references to this are under Chen-tsung or early in Jen-tsung.

[6] For instance 993 (text 23), 996 (text 29).

[7] For instance 998 (text 30).

[8] As in 1059 (text 143).

[9] For example, in 1005 in candidates for lecturer in the Directorate of Education (text 47), or in 1057 in those for institute assignment (text 141).

[10] In 1044 a proclamation requires men who have practiced "government through love of the people, not emphasizing resort to punishment, but gaining voluntary obedience" (text 122), while in 1061 another stresses "genuine kindness to the people" (text 145).

[11] As in 1015, where candidates are admonished not to "pervert the law with cruel punishments, leading to the rise of trouble" (text 69). Or 1029, where the candidate in collecting taxes "shall not go to the extent of pressing and annoying" (text 109).

But far greater than the concern with all these traits was that shown by the innumerable stipulations that the candidate show a record free from corruption and penal offense. These last considerations were of course vital to the functioning of government. They were in addition criteria which could be applied far more objectively than some of the others mentioned.

The governmental concern with past record was manifested not only in frequent repetition, but in the distinction of past trespasses by degree and kind. Corruption was clearly held to be the most serious kind of offense, and the man who profited directly therein the worst offender. Among those who had offended in ways other than corruption, a distinction was drawn between men guilty of "private offenses" (those committed with a presumed intent to further private interest), and those guilty of administrative delinquencies (those committed without such motive).[12] Administrative delinquencies were considered less serious. While both public and private offenses would count against a candidate, only corruption would usually bar him irrevocably from recommendation.[13]

The mere enumeration of desirable traits, such as we find in proclamations, of course, leaves some room for interpretation. Is it perhaps a simple gesture of compliance with conventional principles? Or does it show a genuine intent to encourage certain kinds of men? If the latter, is it only a reminder of the importance of character, or an effort to remedy a serious existing deficiency in the service?

The proclamations themselves answer our questions in part. With respect to certain traits they go beyond exhortation and lay down courses of action which suggest that the governmental concern was serious, and the encouragement of the trait (or discouragement of

[12] Corruption (rapacity) was one form of private offense. For further discussion of these types of offense see Chapter X, p. 172.

[13] The exact details of this varied from time to time. See, for instance, the rule of 1024, which barred those guilty of corruption, self-interest, excesses, presumption, and stubborn evasion, or of an offense liable to a sentence more severe than forced labor. But the text seems to imply that candidates were admissible if guilty of an offense technically "private" but not actually committed with private intent (text 97). Other modifications may be seen in texts 109 (1029) and 144 (1060) and other texts discussed later in connection with guaranty. The requirements were somewhat stricter in the case of candidates recommended to administer border prefectures, where supervision was more difficult. A measure of 1023 (*HCP*,101,3b) required such men to be specially investigated. Any whose record showed conviction for a private offense of any kind or demotion in commission were to be excluded.

its opposite) a real problem. These actions will be discussed in the following chapter, but we may note here that they included the authorization of supplementary reports on officials' conduct, the checking of records by the personnel bureaus, and if the demonstrated qualities were unsatisfactory, the delay of action pending special instructions. They included also rewards and penalties both for the sponsor and the man recommended; the candidate's lack of the required qualities might cause prosecution of the sponsor under the laws of guaranty.

The aspects of character that these disciplinary measures are designed to promote are on the whole those most often mentioned in the calls for sponsorship: vigor, discipline, and incorruption. These qualities were clearly both vital to the functioning of an organization, and susceptible to fairly objective appraisal. The interest in them, we may safely conclude, was no matter of formalism. We need not judge that the interest in other qualities was less sincere; but it was presumably less urgent.

2. Skills, Abilities, and Experience

In describing the kind of man eligible for recommendation, the proclamations showed the concern of their authors with administrative ability, training acquired through study or practice, and experience as indicated by positions previously held and length of service.

Ability might be referred to in general terms, but more often specifically in application to administrative problems. Occasionally it might be of a kind qualifying an official to cope with important positions and problems of special difficulty.[14]

The training specified was most often general, with the customary emphasis on classics, literature, and history. While the educational requirement was particularly stressed in candidates for academic positions, it was not at all confined to that sphere.[15] In 1022, in fact, it became a rule that all candidates for promotion

---

[14] For example, see references to general ability and intelligence in 992 (text 20). Or, in 981 and 1061, extraordinary methods of administration (texts 11, 145). Or, in 996, having administrative efficiency and ability to bear responsibility (text 29). Or, in 1014, extensive knowledge of civil administration and ability to take charge of complex and difficult departments (text 65). Or, in 1029, suitable for difficult commissions (text 108).

[15] E.g., 981 (text 11), 993 (text 23), 1005 (text 47), 1057 (text 141).

through sponsorship to the administrative class must have doctoral degrees.[16] I have found no evidence that this requirement was ever abrogated during the period under consideration. For lower positions, a doctoral degree also secured preferential treatment in some cases, though it does not seem to have become mandatory.[17] Reference to training of a more specialized kind, qualifying the candidate for such fields as law, finance, or teaching, also appeared occasionally.[18] The paucity of these references, however, throws into greater relief the general tendency to favor a humanistic rather than a technical training, and the related administrative policy of transferring officials freely from one administrative field to another so that they would acquire a rounded view of governmental problems.

It was understood that a part of the civil servant's training could be acquired only through actual experience with administrative problems. It was not desirable to recommend a man who had but recently entered the service because he "might not yet be versed in the requirements of an official position." [19] The requirements of experience were gradually formulated to meet the demands of each position for which a man might be sponsored. Because of the varying needs, and perhaps for the sake of emphasis, some statement of the requisite experience appeared in almost every order empowering sponsorship. According to the post to which promotion was contemplated, the proclamation usually defined rather precisely the class of the service or the functional post from which a potential candidate should come, often the length of his service there, and

[16] Literally, formal qualification (ch'u-shen). For the interpretation of this phrase, see above, Chapter V, Note 55. Text 92.

[17] E.g., in 1029, when the requirement of previous service for candidates for sub-prefect was reduced from four years to three in the case of those with a doctorate (text 109). In 1060 such a degree won a reduction of previous service requirement from five years to four, for candidates for civil aide (text 144). In 1066, such a degree won a reduction from four years service to three for such candidates (text 152).

[18] E.g., in 1014, men trained in penal statutes (text 65), or in 1027 men suited to difficult commissions of a fiscal or penal kind (text 104), or in 1026 men with a deep understanding of the meaning of the Classics and who excelled in lecturing (text 101). In 1066, OU-YANG Hsiu said that officials recently selected for high office were largely men "strong and efficient in finance and law," to the unfortunate neglect of the kind of scholar recruited through the institutes. This, however, was because sponsorship for the latter positions had been neglected (HCP,208,16a; SCSS,9,148; TK,38,17b).

[19] Text 52.

sometimes the posts he should have held in his earlier career.

In practice, the consideration of experience was but one of the reasons for stipulating that an official advance through a regular sequence of posts, and that he hold each post for at least a certain minimum period and not more than a certain maximum. Regularity of promotion was important also as a means of encouraging morale on the one hand, and, on the other, of regulating the number of officials in the higher brackets of the civil service. It is often difficult to say which of these motives was the primary consideration in a given piece of legislation.

Like formal requirements of other kinds in connection with sponsorship—and, as we have seen, in connection with other methods—the experience standards tended to become more rigid with the passage of years. Although sponsorship was employed as a way of expediting the advancement of abler men, the experience requirements seem for the most part only a shade less severe than those set, at a given time, for promotion by less selective methods. This shade of difference was nevertheless a very real one, and as we shall see in another chapter, it combined with other advantages to make recommendations eagerly sought.

The promotion permitted on a single occasion seems from the beginning to have followed a rather consistent policy. Subprefects were generally recommended from among the prefectural inspectors and subprefectural registrars and sheriffs.[20] Candidates for civil aide positions were recommended from this group and from that of the subprefects and executive inspectors.[21] Candidates to be raised through sponsorship to the administrative class rank seem to have come not only from the civil aides, but from lower executory officials as well. (This was true not only of sponsorship for titular capital office, but also for titular court office in the early period when that

[20] E.g., 991, 1001, 1029 (texts 18, 39, 109). The last seems to have established the practice as a rule. A proposal of FAN Chung-yen in 1043 provided in addition for recommendation from men recruited—newly, it seems—from the clerical class. But it is not clear that this proposal was adopted (text 120). In some cases, the eligible group was not defined.

[21] Two instances of 1004 (texts 42, 43) say merely from prefectural and subprefectural officials, without specifying the groups. Two of 1060 and 1066 (texts 144, 152), specify both groups. The former group was qualified for sponsorship for civil-aide subprefectural administrators in FAN's proposal of 1043 (HCP,141,12b–13a) and perhaps in 981 (text 10). The latter in 1029 (text 109), and perhaps in 1001 (text 39).

rank was conferred directly on executory class men.)[22] In many
cases such recommendations are called for without indicating what,
if any, commission within the administrative class would be given.
In such cases, it is not clear whether the promotion in rank would
be accompanied by an immediate change in function or not. But
sponsorship directions often indicated a definite change to be made
in the candidates class and function simultaneously. In such cases,
men were sponsored for lower commissions of administrative class
rank, such as service agent or subprefectural administrator. At the
same time, administrative class men were also sponsored for these
lower positions in the class.[23] In general, it does not appear that the
lowest executory group—the sheriffs, recorders, and inspectors—
could be sponsored for so great a promotion.[24] For all local commissions above these, except for the early years of the dynasty it
seems that only administrative class officials might be recommended.
Usually the candidates already held the commission next lower in
rank.[25] Considering these promotions as a whole, the smaller of

[22] Candidates for court office might be from the capital official class, the civil
aides, or undesignated lower executory officials (texts 6, 8, 14). In 992 they were from
capital officials only (text 19). For capital office, they might be from the civil aides
or from lower executory officials in 993, 996, 1012, 1020, and the FAN proposal of
1043 (texts 25, 29, 59, 90, 120). The functioning of the rule is exemplified by a case of
1006, in which a judge (apparently in an encampment prefecture) was promoted
through sponsorship to titular executive assistant in the Court of Imperial Banquets
(upper capital class) and given the post of auxiliary lecturer of the Directorate of
Education (text 48). In 1018, the groups of civil aides and of subprefects and executive inspectors were specified, and the latter again by FAN in 1043 (text 86; *HCP*,141,
12b–13a). But we have no specific evidence of their recommendation from any still
lower group. (See, however, unclear cases in Note 24.)

[23] The evidence at hand is rather slender for generalization. Service agents were to
be sponsored from civil aides and lower executory officials in 996 and 1018 (texts 29,
86). The latter restricts the lower executory officials to subprefects and executive inspectors. Subprefectural administrators were to be sponsored from court rank (999),
and capital rank (1001), the latter including (1043) those commissioned as service
agents (texts 35, 39; *KMPY*,1043, tenth month). They might on occasion also be
from civil aides and unspecified lower executory officials (1020, text 90); possibly
this was intended also in 993 (text 25). The FAN proposal of 1043 included as candidates the civil aides and also subprefects and executive inspectors (*HCP*,141,12b–13a).

[24] A vaguely worded text of 981 may indicate an exception to this practice (text
10), and less probably the similarly vague text of 1001.

[25] In 964, for the important post of vice-administrator in a regional command prefecture, not only titular capital officials, but civil aides and unspecified lower execu-

them did not exceed those possible by more routine methods, and it appears that even the greater did not exceed radically the rises possible by other means.[26]

tory officials might be recommended (text 5). Thereafter, we have evidence only that administrative class officials were eligible, even in ordinary prefectures (990, 1015 twice, 1051: texts 17, 66, 69, 129). Among these, those holding the lowest local commissions, the service agents, were seemingly not eligible. Rather, men were sponsored from among the subprefectural administrators (1018, 1051, 1043/5, 1043/10/28: texts 83, 129; *HCP*,141,12b–13a; *KMPY*,1043/10). The texts of 1018 and 1043 indicate that this was an established rule. For the commission of prefectural administrator, men were to be sponsored either from the administrative classes in general (990, 1004, 1015, 1051: texts 17, 44, 69, 129) or specifically from the court officials (998, 999 twice, 1007, 1020: texts 32, 34, 35, 51, 98). A rule of 1018 (text 83) provided that they previously hold the commission of prefectural vice-administrator, and instances of 1028 (*HCP*,106,5b) and 1051 (text 129) in which they were recommended from among subprefectural administrators were clearly emergency measures for a border area. Even then, it was provided in the latter instance that they would carry out the duties of the post, but not receive the official status at once. Orders on the sponsorship of fiscal intendants and their assistants called for court officials. An exception, in 992 (text 20), allowed capital officials in words which indicated a concession for cases of special merit.

[26] For the routine sequence of offices, see above, p. 87. We are told that under T'ai-tsung administrative class officials having in addition an assignment might be made prefectural administrator (*HCP*,102,7b), while in 990, through sponsorship, a mere capital official might receive the same commission (text 17). About 1004, a man with assignment might be made only vice-administrator of a small prefecture (*HCP, loc. cit.*) while by sponsorship a capital official might receive the same post in a regional command prefecture, or that of full administrator in a border prefecture (text 44). By 1015, such men might be recommended only for vice-administrator of a border prefecture (text 69) while as late as 1024 the rule for assignment men remained as before (*HCP, loc. cit.*), thus equalizing the opportunity afforded by the two methods. When we compare our information on promotions through sponsorship with that available on promotion through decree examinations, there appears again to be a general resemblance, as one can see by comparing our evidence with the instances of decree examination tabulated by Professor NIEH (NCC:STCC,27–29). The rank of civil aide was given through the examinations to men of the subprefectural recorder or sheriff class, as through sponsorship. Men of the same low rank might achieve titular capital office through the examinations, though it is not clear that so great a promotion was given through sponsorship. On the other hand, men were promoted through the examination to titular court office from capital rank, and at least once from the civil aides, while by sponsorship they appear to have come from lower executory ranks as well. Except for the promotion of a subprefectural recorder to prefectural vice-administrator in 1007, the men given this post through the examinations come from the administrative classes, as usually also through sponsorship. Information on promotion to other commissions through the examinations is too

To the stipulations concerning the previous office and rank of the candidate for sponsorship, which as we have seen were found from the beginning, others were added before long setting a minimum term of previous service. When the seniority principle was applied to sponsorship, the latter of course lost some of its value as a way of expediting the rise of the more able. But when the widespread and sometimes undiscriminating use of the recommending privilege, which we shall note later, brought an unmanageable number of recommendations, the service requirement presented a welcome and convenient method of simplifying the administrative task. Concern with the candidate's experience evidently played a part in setting up the service requirement, but it was not the sole guiding motive.[27]

Once introduced, the seniority requirements gradually acquired greater emphasis and strictness. Evidence of such requirements appears earliest in reference to executory class officials. Their length of experience came under reconsideration several times in Chentsung's reign, and in 1029 a rule was established which seems to have solved the problem temporarily. It required some nine or ten years service before promotion to the administrative class: Three (or four for men without degree) in the rank of prefectural inspector, subprefectural recorder or sheriff; one three-year term each as subprefect and as titular civil aide administering a subprefecture. An additional year of service was exacted of any who had committed a private offense. Later in Jen-tsung's reign and under Yingtsung, the requirements were again relaxed somewhat.[28]

---

scattered for any generalization. The instances of promotion through decree examination are too few to indicate clearly the underlying policies, but in general the practice of the first five reigns betrays little long-term change, though many variations in individual cases.

[27] For concern with the factor of experience see, for instance, text 75 (1016) where, although the candidates in question hold military title, they are to be qualified for civilian administration also. Excluded as candidates are those who are "young and inexperienced in affairs." For the motive of restricting numbers, see *TK*,39,37b.

[28] A move toward the regulation of service in connection with sponsorship was evident as early as 981, when men of the inspector-recorder-sheriff class appointed through sponsorship to administer subprefectures (whether as executory or capital class men is not clear) were to serve three years in their *new* position before being considered for further special promotion (text 10). In 1009 it was established as a rule that civil aides, prefectural, and subprefectural officials should have served over one term before their recommendation (text 52). The following year this

In the case of recommendations for administrative class commissions, length of service also clearly played an important part in determining the treatment of individual cases, but we lack evidence that the service requirements were so clearly and rigidly stated. A case of 1015 indicates that three years service in a titular office was adequate, if the number of sponsors was sufficient, before a change in such office through sponsorship, while a lesser period might not be. A man with shorter service might, however, be eligible for promotion in commission.[29] A policy was adopted the same year differentiating sponsored candidates for commission, according to length of service as well as number of sponsors, and giving higher commissions to those making a better showing in those respects. We lack, however, data on the exact interpretation of these criteria.[30] A policy followed in 1018 relates the sponsorship practice more closely with the ordinary rules of seniority, allowing the sponsored candidate a slight advantage either in time or degree of advance-

---

qualification was made more specific, requiring for recommendation three terms of service, reaching a total of six years, since the last previous promotion. A case of 1014 seems to refer to this rule (texts 54, 65). For a while, beginning in 1017 and still effective at least in 1024, the requirement was relaxed to four years (texts 80, 97). The rule of 1029 is described in text 109. A scheme of 1043, which may not have been fully implemented, continued the 1029 requirement of three or four years as inspector-recorder-sheriff but allowed recommendation on the basis of this service directly for civil-aide subprefectural administrator. In this rank [? *chih-kuan chung ling-lu* 職官中令錄], they required only five years of service before recommendation for capital-official subprefectural administrator (*HCP*,141,12b–13a). The shortage of expectant civil aides in 1060 produced a formula again somewhat less strict than 1029, under which men both of subprefect-executive-inspector and of inspector-recorder-sheriff rank might after four years of service (five for men without degree) be recommended for civil-aide posts (text 144). In 1066 this requirement was further reduced to three years (four without degree), and to be recommended for subprefect, no more than one year in the inspector-recorder-sheriff group was needed (text 152).

[29] Text 66. A prefectural administrator with three years service in titular rank was recommended for change in titular office and promotion to commission of fiscal intendant or assistant intendant, and a man recently promoted to capital class and acting as Lo-yang police supervisor 軍巡判官 for change in titular office and the commission of prefectural vice-administrator. Both were given promotion in commission, but the second was denied change of titular office, partly on grounds of seniority.

[30] Text 67. Those with more sponsors and service were to be made administrators of large regional-command prefectures or judicial intendants; the others, vice-administrators of such prefectures or administrators of small ones.

ment.[31] For a short time after 1028 the seniority relationship with other methods was formulated precisely, allowing a man with sufficient sponsors a reduction of one term in the recently set three-term service requirements. After two years, the rule was amended to allow the same reduction for all candidates with good records, whether sponsored or unsponsored, and thereafter no clear concession in seniority rules seems to have been allowed sponsored candidates, although in special cases they seem to have enjoyed some latitude.[32]

The equalizing of minimum seniority requirements for sponsored promotions with those for promotions through other methods did not, however, mean that the rapidity of promotion had been equalized. Whether through an oversupply of officials in certain ranks or from other causes, the period of waiting for promotion might in the normal course be considerably longer than the prescribed minimum. The preference which might be gained through sponsorship or another favored promotion routine therefore invested these methods with an attractiveness apart from and above any reductions in minimum waiting periods.[33]

[31] Text 83. Recommended men were to move from subprefectural administrator to prefectural vice-administrator, or from there to administrator, the text implies, before the time normally required by seniority rule. If already qualified by seniority, they would receive a somewhat greater promotion to the same post in a regional-command prefecture.

[32] See above, Chapter V, Note 35. In a case of 1029/9 it was permitted to recommend for difficult commissions prefectural vice-administrators who had served only one term, still less than the time permitted under the recently amended rules (text 108). A proclamation of 1043 specifically states that sponsored candidates for prefectural administrator and for vice-administrator should have the proper seniority in the immediately lower post (HCP,141,12b–13a). An emergency measure of 1051 still observes the form of seniority: to supply needed administrators and vice-administrators in certain Szechwan prefectures, it was permitted to recommend capital-official administrators of subprefectures who had served one full term plus one year of the next, or one term of at least a year plus two years of the next. After three years of service in the new post, the man would receive merely the official status of a new prefectural vice-administrator (text 129).

[33] The scheme briefly tried in 1043, making sponsorship practically mandatory for promotion, will be discussed below. According to two sources, it again favored the sponsored candidates in the matter of time requirements, in this case for promotion in titular court office. At three rungs of the promotion ladder it required three years' service of a candidate with good record and five sponsors, but added an additional two years when sponsors were too few. (KMPY,1043/10; HCP,144,8b–9b.)

3. Obscurity and Freedom from Factional Ties

The requirements of experience, which we have just seen, ruled out as sponsorship candidate the untried newcomer in the service. In contrast with these, a different set of requirements sought to rule out also the man whose friendships or abilities had already ensured him notice. At least three considerations focussed the attention of sponsorship on the man without influential connections and in a relatively obscure position. First, much of the unique value of recommendation lay in its potential effectiveness in discovering able men who might otherwise be overlooked. Second, personal considerations, whether through connection of the sponsored with the sponsor or with any other party, might impede objective recommendation on the basis of merit. Third, there was constant awareness of the lurking danger that a faction in temporary ascendency might achieve a perpetual power monopoly, using recommendation as a tool.

One consideration rather notable for its absence from this list was that of economic status. Such a concept did not fit the patterns of Sung thought. The civil service recruited men from differing occupational backgrounds, and of varying resources, as we saw earlier. Toward descendants of merchant families there may have been some lingering feeling of condescension. But in the sources I have used I have found no hint that either favor or discrimination based on differences of wealth or family background entered into the discussions of sponsorship. When there was complaint of favor, it was of that shown scions of those momentarily in power. When need to aid the able but obscure scholar was expressed, it was implied that indigence might be a factor in his failure to make his talents known, but not that it had been a source of prejudice.

Another consideration that did not enter directly into discussions of sponsorship was the possibility of bias through local prejudice. We have, however, indirect evidence that this danger may have existed in some degree. The complaint of Ssu-ma Kuang that the doctoral examinations favored unfairly the candidates from the southeast has already been noted. It appears that during the first half century, the northern founders of the new state (both rulers and officials) looked with disfavor on the admission of the lately foreign southeasterners to the most important posts.[34] The south-

[34] As late as 993, T'ai-tsung remarked that the men of Chiang-tung won advancement not for virtuous conduct but through their scholarship (*HCP*,34,11b). A decade

easterners soon assumed a leading role, nevertheless, but traces of regional feeling may have remained to become a factor in the development of partisan groups.

The importance attached to the discovery of overlooked ability was clearly expressed now and again. A proclamation of T'ai-tsung was prefaced with the remark, "We are concerned that bosoms clothed in coarse fabrics may carry qualities of jade, and the fact remain unknown." Another said, "We are anxious lest there still remain neglected ability in low positions. Those who may be already known by name and have now been commissioned are certainly not unnoticed. For what reason should they benefit by singling out and introduction?" [35] A proclamation of Chen-tsung, beginning with almost the same words, goes on to say, "If some have perhaps been long in local offices, and have had no chance to signal themselves, combine to send up memorials of recommendation, faithfully assisting the advancement of complete justice. As for those who have already come to court [there is already adequate provision] . . . Why complicate it with extraordinary encouragements [for these]?" [36] We sense the importance attached to objectivity and party diversity, in the reiterated disquiet that factionalism and sycophancy continued to motivate recommendations. Found as early as 987, references to these abuses recurred under T'ai-tsung, Chen-tsung, and Jen-tsung.[37]

---

or so later, WANG Tan argued against promotion of WANG Ch'in-jo to chief councilor on the ground that the first rulers had never placed a southerner in such a position, but admitted that if a man were really worthy it might be permissible (SS,282,13a–b).

[35] Texts 12 and 21 (982, 992).

[36] Text 59 (1012).

[37] A proclamation of 987 deplores the fact that recommendations from various places often instance factionalism (ch'in tang 親黨), injuring justice and opening the door to undeserved good fortune (text 15). In 993, it was said, factionalism (p'eng-tang pi-chou 朋黨比周) was openly discussed without fear (text 27). In 1002, to forestall it, the heads of the Censorate and High Court of Justice were omitted from the sponsors for certain posts in those offices (text 41), and in 1018 circuit intendant sponsors were admonished not to give advance notice of recommendations, in order to discourage personal favors (ssu en 私恩). (Text 87.) Sycophancy in seeking recommendations was mentioned frequently: in 993, it was said, the begging was carried on publicly (text 27); in 998 the Emperor feared such begging was carried on in prefectures (text 30); in 1021 it was noted especially among men who, though recommended, had failed to secure promotion to titular capital rank, and begged for further sponsors (text 91). In 1024 the potential sponsors were redefined in order to discourage men with less than the required number of sponsors

Apart from public admonition, repeated attempts were made to favor the obscure and independent in concrete ways. On a number of occasions sponsors were forbidden to recommend men in certain specific high or conspicuous positions. Under Jen-tsung candidates holding commissions of circuit intendant or higher were disqualified by rule from 1053.[38] Special advantages in seeking promotion might not be limited to important officials. Men in humbler positions might also have special access to potential sponsors, as we are reminded by an interesting measure discouraging the ambitions of "technician officials"—perhaps artists, physicians, or craftsmen—who sought to exploit their connections with members of the Imperial family or other important persons.[39] The rules of recommendation called for an explicit statement of facts which might imply the presence of improper favor, particularly the family connections and native place of a candidate.[40] In at least individual instances the recommenda-

from begging recommendations. They had, it seems, importuned even men just commissioned but not yet at their new posts (text 97). (In 1055 similar action was taken with respect to military officials, as seen in text 135). In 1045 a major reason for abolishing the semimandatory sponsorship for promotion was said to be the toadyism of men seeking promotions (text 123). The same reason dictated in 1053 a rule that men might not elect to serve in the place where they were at the time of recommendation (text 134). See also text 82.

[38] The rule of 1053 barred judicial intendant or higher (text 133). In recommendations for fiscal intendant, those already holding this post or that of its assistant were barred in 992 and 998 (texts 20, 30). Those employed in the Finance Commission were also barred on these occasions, and on another when recommendation for promotion to court rank was in question (992, text 21). In 992 and 1059 men holding institute assignment were barred (texts 21, 142), and in the former year also those employed in the Bureau of Judicial Investigation or holding offices in princely households (text 20). Similar bars to the recommendation of higher military officials appeared in three proclamations of 1016 (texts 75, 76, 77) and in one of 1028 (text 106). See also previous note.

[39] A proclamation of 1023 directed that technician officials who begged recommendations or sought favors in such quarters should be sentenced to the punishment for violation of regulations (*HCP*,101,8a).

[40] The requirement of information on native place was made a rule as early as 993 (text 27). In 1016 (recommending men for military commission, but with civil experience), sponsors were called on to state openly if their candidates had influential relations, by blood or otherwise (text 75), and in 1026 the statement of such relationship to officials at Court was made a rule (text 102). In an instance of 1028 (for military command) in addition to such information, the statement of any relationship or even long-standing friendship between candidate and sponsor was required (text 106).

tion of men related to the sponsor or to high officials was altogether forbidden, though it does not seem that this became an established rule.[41] Other devices, which seem intended to gain the same ends indirectly, will be discussed in later chapters. They included a long and finally fruitful effort to discourage sponsorship by officials in the capital and sporadic attempts to bar in particular that by the highest officials. They included also rules defining the sponsors' official relation to their candidates and the separation of sponsor and candidate in their subsequent work. The motivation was not always expressed, but when we consider the collective implication of these measures, there can be little doubt that they were intended to favor the obscure and factionally independent man.

But we must not assume that there was a complete agreement on the evil of factionalism. While it is clear from the practical measures invoked that many policy makers recognized it as a genuine threat to the system, it is also clear that some were quite willing to tolerate it and to turn it to profitable use.

Factionalism was growing in political significance during the reigns of Chen-tsung and Jen-tsung. The tendency to condone it was not entirely confined to the political opportunists, nor was ostensible opposition to it necessarily a sign of political disinterestedness. As early as the first half of Jen-tsung's reign, those who had themselves used political patronage freely in the attempts to entrench their faction in power, assuming the role of virtue's defend-

---

[41] The normative proclamation of 1010, in providing a special category for otherwise neglected executory-class officials, stipulates that it shall not be used to benefit "sons and younger brothers of influential families" (text 55). The instance of 1028 mentioned in the note above excludes as candidates any relatives of officials in the Secretariat or Bureau of Military Affairs. One of 1029, seeking men for difficult commissions, excludes as candidates relatives both of the sponsor and of councilors of state (text 108). Relatives of the sponsor were excluded when men were sought from the lower local officials in another case of 1029 (text 109) and in 1059 (text 142). The latter apparently excluded also relatives of Secretariat and Bureau of Military Affairs officials. The general feeling that sponsoring relatives was at least inappropriate was suggested by a proclamation of 962 which expressly *permitted* the practice (text 1). No hint of the reason for this unusual expression was given; perhaps the urgent need for men at the time explains it. If intended to facilitate personal favor, it would be rather barefaced. A similar express permission to sponsor relatives or members of important families is found in 1066, when, in an attempt to improve the calibre of those assigned to the institutes, the civil councilors of state were directed to recommend unusual men (*HCP*,208,16b; *SCSS*,9,148).

ers, hurled the charge of factionalism at their opponents.[42] Under the circumstances, it is not too surprising that the latter, animated by a crusading zeal and an intense conviction of their own rightness, accepted the designation of faction and drew the battle line rather in a distinction between beneficial and detrimental factions. This position was taken by such respected men as OU-YANG Hsiu and FAN Chung-yen.[43] The tacit indulgence in factionalism by the one party and its open espousal by the other seem to explain at least partially why measures to eliminate the effect of personal ties in recommendation stopped short of the utmost severity. We have noted that the ban on recommending relatives of powerful officials or of the sponsor seems not to have become a permanent rule. We shall see later that the councilors of state were not consistently excluded from the sponsoring groups. Perhaps more important, we shall see that the principle of singling out men to be sponsors on the basis of moral qualifications, though advocated with apparent sincerity, tended in practice to promote factionalism. The lack of unanimity in opposing this danger was perhaps one of the most serious weaknesses in the institution of sponsorship.

4. Sponsorship and Morale

Although sponsorship was primarily a device to recruit men for more important positions in the civil service, as the evidence we have examined indicates, this was not its sole concern. It is evident

[42] LÜ Yi-chien, in 1036 chief councilor, had, we are told, packed the high offices with his adherents. But he used the charge of factionalism effectively against the reforming group of FAN Chung-yen (HCP,118,9b; SCKY,5,8b; KMPY,1036/5).

[43] During the party struggle of 1044, the Emperor Jen-tsung had remarked "From of old, men of low character frequently formed factions. Can it be that there are also factions of superior men?" FAN Chung-yen (who had now come to power) replied "When I was on the border, I saw that the good fighters formed into factions; the cowards did so as well. As for these at Court, the factions of the crooked and the straight are also thus. . . . If, through friendship, men work good for the state, what is the harm?" (HCP,148,6a.)

OU-YANG Hsiu expatiated on this theme in his "Discussion on Factions," presenting historical and supposedly historical examples in which factions of good officials had benefited the state or suffered persecution at the hands of those who eventually destroyed the state (OYWC, Chü-shih-chi, 17,6b–8a; HCP,148,6b). This is all the more remarkable when we remember that Confucius was held to have said "The superior man . . . while sociable, does not identify himself with a faction" (Analects, XV,21). In all these instances, the word for "faction" is the same, tang 黨.

that the system was designed also to encourage better performance in the service as a whole. This aim was to be reached through affording fairer treatment to the individual who might otherwise be slighted unjustly. It offered greater hope of a successful career to the man who, while able and conscientious as an administrator, lacked the scholarly talents needed to take and pass the special examinations for promotion. It gave the supervisory official a means of rewarding good performance more concretely than through merit ratings, which as we have seen were not in practice too effective. The wording of a number of proclamations makes it quite clear that the reassurance of the average official was among the important motivating considerations.[44] It was clearly seen that the rapid advancement of some and the retarded progress of others could not but damage the service morale unless these things were clearly dictated by justice. In the words of a renowned official who lived at the end of this period, if the proper sponsorship policies are followed, "Those who advance will know encouragement; those who retrogress will know trepidation. . . . Nothing comes before this."[45]

[44] A proclamation of 982 remarked that "the worthy men of the many villages yet feared it was difficult to arrive" (text 12). In 993 we read, "Hitherto it has been ordered to encourage by recommending, thinking to stimulate those who were obstructed and submerged" (text 27). A concern with equity is suggested by a remark of 1022: "We are somewhat anxious lest executory officials experience hindrance because of a small private offense" (text 93), and in one of 1045: "We worry lest honest scholars may, [because of required sponsorship for promotion], be unable to advance themselves" (text 123). In 1066, a method of reducing the number of officials on the waiting lists was advocated partly because "there would be no cause for disappointment for the human feelings" (text 153).

[45] Pao Ch'eng. *PHSKTY*,3,47a.

VIII

THE PROCEDURES OF SPONSORSHIP

In order to find men of the kind and quality desired for positions so many and so varied, it was obviously necessary to construct an elaborate apparatus to administer the sponsorship process. In the adaptation to institutional use, the simple act of recommendation was transformed into a complex series of procedures. Rules governed each step, from the decision to employ sponsorship for a given purpose, and the sponsor's writing and submittal of a recommendation, to the final appointment of the candidate to a new position and the enforcement of guaranty thereafter. To bring these rules to the attention of the officials who were to be governed by them was the responsibility of the Censorate.[1]

An act of sponsorship was undertaken either at the direction or the permission of a governmental order, issued with Imperial approval. It might occur under one of three circumstances: it might be made at any time during the year under a regular annual quota allowed to an official according to his office; or it might be made by an official returning at the expiration of a local commission; or it might be made at a time indicated by a special Imperial directive.[2] For a time not only the compliance with special orders to recommend, but the full use of allotted annual quotas became mandatory. The offices transmitting recommendations coöperated with the Censorate in checking on conformity with the rule, and the Censorate

[1] Texts 21, 92, 122.

[2] The distinction between these three kinds of sponsorship becomes clear in 1015 and thereafter (cf. texts 68, 91, 107, 122). Before this, there is no clear indication that recommendations were made except in compliance with enabling proclamations repeated on each occasion. The normative proclamation of 1010 (text 55) seems to be the first clear reference to annual quotas. General rules found before 1010 might imply that sponsorship was already practiced on occasion without enabling proclamation, or might be interpreted as rules to guide the drafting and implementation of such enabling proclamations (e.g., texts 26, 27, 46).

lodged complaints against violators, who were liable to a fine.[3] But as it soon appeared, officials were only too willing to become sponsors, and compulsion became superfluous.

Whether because he had been expressly directed, then, or on his own volition, the prospective sponsor, having selected a candidate, prepared a letter of recommendation in conformity with established forms. He was required to include the official rank and legal residence of the candidate; to provide an itemized report of the achievements and faults of the candidate's entire previous career, and an estimate of his character and efficiency; to state whether the candidate was known to the sponsor personally or highly recommended by others.[4] There was also required a statement of the kind of position for which the candidate was fitted.[5] Only one candidate might be recommended in a single form, and it might include only recommendation by a single sponsor.[6] Finally, an elaborate procedure for sealing the recommendation provided authentication.[7]

The form thus prepared was then deposited, if the sponsor were in the capital, at the Palace Postern Office.[8] If stationed away from the capital, he would forward it via the General Memorial Acceptance Bureau.[9] Regular annual recommendations were to be deposited before the end of the year, except those from outside the capital, which should be received by the twenty-fifth day of the second month.[10] The time allowed for the reception of directed recommendations varied from as much as two months to as little as five days.[11]

[3] The Censorate was specifically instructed to note and remind dilatory sponsors in an instance of 990 (text 17). Other provisions were fixed by rule in 1010 (text 55).

[4] Requirement of rank and residence, rule of 993 (text 27). Character and career, texts 19, 26, 27, 31, 40, 42, 44, 51, 55 (showing slight variation in detail). Personal knowledge, text 55 (1010).

[5] Text 55.

[6] Texts 110 (1029) and 118 (1041). These rules were probably not regularly observed before then; both provisions were specific only in cases of promotion to the administrative class.

[7] Rule of 1030 (text 111). The details are interesting; this also applies to promotion to administrative class.

[8] Rules of 1010, 1030 (texts 55, 111).

[9] Text 55. In 991, local sponsors are to send the form by government post (text 18).

[10] Text 55.

[11] An instance of 1000 allowed five days, at a time when men were needed for border service (text 37); instances of 1014 and 1020 allowed ten days (texts 65, 90);

The information from the recommendations was then entered in a register in the Secretariat, where it was combined with past and current information on candidates derived from merit rating reports and other sources. Note was made of the number and names of each candidate's sponsors. A copy of this register was forwarded to the Palace on the first of the fifth month each year.[12] The personnel offices would check on the sponsor's record, watching also for any evidence that the recommendation had been influenced by ulterior considerations.[13]

At the appropriate time each case would be taken up by the cognizant personnel agency. The Bureau of Executory Personnel (after 993) had charge of all sponsored executory officials, whether for executory class positions or for promotion to the administrative class; administrative class officials fell to the Bureau of Administrative Personnel. Action was begun when the number of sponsors and the period of service satisfied requirements. If the candidate had not been recommended in response to an immediate need, the procedure of the time might require that action be deferred until he had been relieved at his current post.[14] With candidates for institute assignment, action was in later years postponed until a post should be vacant.[15]

The first step to be taken by the personnel agency was the case review of the candidate: a careful scrutiny of all information bearing on his character and ability. If all were in order, a proposal for promotion would be drawn up, and submitted for the approval of the Secretariat and the Imperial assent. The dossier on each case would include the record of the candidate, including length of service in his present office, and perhaps that of the sponsor.[16] The final

---

instances of 999 and 1059, one month (texts 34, 142); one of 990, two months (text 17); and in 1029 it was permitted to defer a choice if there were at the moment no adequate candidates (text 109).

[12] Text 55. See also Chapter V, Note 30.

[13] In 1011, it was ordered that the Ministry of Justice should be prompt in answering requests from the Bureau of Administrative Personnel for information on sponsors records (text 56). In 962 a reward was offered for information on recommendations obtained through bribery (text 2).

[14] Thus texts 64, 67, 83. But text 89 says act immediately. (All these refer to action on executory class candidates.)

[15] Text 152a.

[16] Data on candidate and sponsor required in a case of 1012 (text 58); on candidate, by a rule of 1015 (text 66); both were specific only for administrative class candidates.

approval by the Emperor and Council might, it seems, be some-thing more than a mere formality, and the proposals of the personnel agencies were not necessarily accepted without modification.[17] For men being newly promoted to the administrative class, a presenta-tion at Court was also a necessary part of the procedure.

If an executory class official, having been replaced in office and recommended for the administrative class, for any reason failed to secure his administrative class appointment, he was given an execu-tory position according to his normal seniority. He could not be considered again for sponsored promotion until the expiration of another term of service.[18]

Men who were sponsored for positions in the institutes, or the Directorate of Education, or for certain other specialized functions would have to pass a qualifying examination, which might be given under the joint auspices of the Secretariat and another appropriate agency.[19]

The time required by these long processes apparently differed considerably. Clearly in some cases two or three years would inter-vene between a given recommendation and the promotion toward which it was directed. In the case of a prefectural judge who in 1006 was promoted from the executory to the administrative class and appointed an auxiliary lecturer in the Directorate of Education, the entire process, including an examination, occupied five or six months.[20] In two promotions within the administrative class a little later, on the other hand, while there seems to have been no special urgency, the new appointments came only thirty-three days after a recommendation. It should be noted, however, that one of the men involved had received fifteen earlier recommendations.[21]

When sooner or later the candidate received his appointment, the name of his sponsors would once more be recorded, that their re-sponsibility as sureties for his conduct be evident.[22] It now became the duty of the Censorate to keep special watch over the conduct of the sponsored official, and to lodge an immediate accusation if he should prove delinquent in any respect.[23] The Secretariat, too, took

[17] Cf. text 66.

[18] Text 91 (1021). For data on procedure after the receipt of recommendations, see, in addition to sources cited above, texts 69, 92, 117.

[19] Cf. texts 48, 141, p. 97 above, and p. 163 below.

[20] Texts 47–48.   [22] Cases of 964 and 967 (texts 5, 6).

[21] Texts 65–66.   [23] Text 133 (1053). For details, see below, pp. 180–181.

a special interest in his case, and if he performed well he received special consideration for rapid advancement at the end of his term.[24] Whether he did well or badly, his sponsors would now also share in the rewards and penalties.[25]

One is impressed with the quantity of paper that must have been consumed in the process of promoting one man and checking on the results of the promotion; yet the elaborate process was no doubt necessary if the twin dangers of blind routine and bias were to be avoided. But could the mass of information be measured by standards both fair and effective? Could the individual judgment that gave recommendation its real value be preserved in an undertaking of these proportions, or would human intelligence and character be somehow lost in the maze of forms and rules? These problems the Sung government soon faced.

[24] See Chapter XI.
[25] See Chapter X, 2. Disciplinary methods.

IX

THE POLICIES OF SPONSORSHIP: THE
SELECTION OF THE SPONSOR

We have seen that the documents concerning sponsorship defined its objectives and procedures explicitly and in detail. The procedures outlined in the previous chapter provided, however, only the framework of the system. The policies which should govern their application raised a number of problems to which the answer was by no means obvious, and the attempts to reach a solution were necessarily experimental. It was not until the reign of Chen-tsung that the policies began to follow a fairly uniform pattern. Objectives were formulated; supervisory machinery was erected; consistent policies were developed for encouraging the candidate to perform well after promotion and—perhaps still more important—for selecting and controlling the sponsor so as to improve the quality of the candidates recommended.

The sponsor, carefully selected and controlled, might give valuable assistance to the central personnel agencies. If he accepted voluntarily the moral obligations of sponsorship and the hazard of suretyship, he might act with greater objectivity and care than when he merely rated the merits of his subordinates as a routine part of his supervisory duties. Thus the effective reach of central personnel supervision would be greatly increased.

1. Considerations in Selecting the Sponsor

The memorials and proclamations which provided us rather generously with discussions of the principles and objectives behind specific policies also help us often with many observations on the practical considerations that shaped the form of action. But many of these considerations we can only infer from the actions themselves and from their apparent relation to announced objectives. In the following discussion I shall try to make clear the distinction between considerations expressly stated and those revealed only indirectly.

Perhaps the first of all considerations was that of the sponsor's personal qualities. These received a degree of emphasis that was characteristically Confucian, being considered by many statesmen far more important than the institutional restraints which to us might seem more reliable. Only the selection of excellent sponsors could hope to bring about the recommendation of first class men, it was held. Legal checks on the sponsor offered only a tardy and incomplete protection against the worst abuses. "Rewards and punishments," said a proclamation of Chen-tsung, "are carried out after the recommending has already been done. In recommending for office, the act of selecting should precede the exercise of recommendation. Only the straight know the straight. . . ." [1]

The most important of the sponsor's qualities was his moral character, since "only the straight know the straight." As moral qualities were the primary consideration in the candidate, they were necessarily so in the sponsor. And a good sponsor might, at least, act with greater freedom from partisanship. But how could moral qualities be ascertained? The perception of the highest worth was clearly a matter of subjective judgment not susceptible to rules. Rules could merely protect against the worst mistakes. One might consider the factors of past merit ratings, clearly demonstrable achievements, past legal offenses, or the previous requirement of discipline. The records of men previously recommended by a potential sponsor might be appraised according to criteria of varying objectivity. But all these tests yielded at best uncertain results. For positive assurance, it was necessary that the sponsors be selected as individuals and by individuals. [2]

It was of course realized that moral worth by itself did not guarantee the ability to discern character. As WANG An-shih once wrote, he who could detect the specious man was indeed sage. [3] Such perspicacity was recognized to be a rather rare quality, and those who

---

[1] Proclamation of 1009 (*SHY:CK*,42,58b). Cf. also proclamation of 998: "One should first select the sponsor in order to seek men of the same kind" (*ibid.*, 58a). Also *KMPY*,1042/4.

[2] In 998, for instance, the repeated report of misbehavior of sponsored men was the stated reason for the personal selection of sponsors (*HCP*,43,5b).

[3] *Che* 哲.

LCHSWC,69,11a–b. (Translated in WILLIAMSON, II,366.)

possessed it left lasting reputations.[4] Sponsors with this quality, again, were to be obtained only through personal and individual selection.

The measures that were tried imply an awareness that the sponsors should be men of ability and experience, no doubt both in order to understand the qualities demanded by the service and to recognize these qualities in the candidate. This awareness appears frequently in the concern that sponsors should have direct experience in local administration. Less frequently it is manifested in the selection of sponsors who, by education or employment, have a more specialized knowledge in the field for which a candidate might be recommended. The average of ability might be raised by selecting sponsors who had won high office; experience would be most pertinent if the sponsor were still employed in the past or future field of the candidate.

Other factors affecting the sponsor's sense of responsibility may also have come under consideration. As WANG An-shih remarked, any man, even one without a special sense of integrity, is apt to be more trustworthy when charged with a serious responsibility.[5] A man who valued his position, moreover, would hesitate to endanger it by guaranteeing a candidate of uncertain character. A sponsor of high office might, therefore, be more responsible.

The sponsor's knowledge of the candidate's qualities would be a natural consideration. The administrative relation of a sponsor to the man he recommended, therefore, became of consequence. The candidate who had served under the sponsor's jurisdiction—not necessarily immediate—had greater difficulty in concealing his true character. Few potential candidates would be so well known to the man holding a sinecure or out of active service, temporarily or permanently.

The need that the candidate be impartially and justly selected, on the other hand, might in some ways suggest policies quite opposed to those which would promote the sponsor's knowledge of the man's qualities. The chances of impartiality might be somewhat greater in the case of a sponsor who had retired from active service, and selection might be less often motivated by personal preference when a sponsor was not formerly or prospectively in the same administra-

[4] For a collection of stories concerning such discerning sponsors, see *HCLY*,57.
[5] *LCHSWC*,69,9b–11a. (Translated in WILLIAMSON, II,368.)

tive unit as his protégé. If the sponsor were not the immediate superior of the candidate and not too close in rank, the chances either of personal friendship or rivalry might be lessened. If those empowered to sponsor were equitably distributed among the several branches of the central government and the numerous local units, the opportunities of the potential candidates would be more nearly equalized. (The potential candidate stationed in the capital of course enjoyed an initial advantage in the competition for promotion, and the man in a distant city or town depended on sponsorship to a much greater degree.) The distribution of recommendations might be more equitable also if each sponsor recommended only within his own jurisdiction. The larger the number of sponsors, the greater was the likelihood that personal prejudices would cancel out. The danger of factional power monopoly suggested in particular that the sponsors should not be limited to those who held the highest governmental posts, or to their friends, as Sung statesmen did not fail to point out. The personal selection of sponsors by the highest officials, according to subjective criteria, was for this reason clearly a hazardous practice.

2. *The Processes of Selecting the Sponsor*

When we consider the conflicting demands of the above desiderata in selecting the sponsor, it is not difficult to guess that unsatisfactory compromises and vacillating policies often emerged from the attempt to reconcile them. Objective criteria were applied very widely, and a considerable diversity of devices resulted. But under T'ai-tsung and Chen-tsung particularly, the quest for true worthies to ensure recommendations of similar worth also took the more subjective form of personal selection.

Personal Selection

We are told that T'ai-tsung in his moments of leisure examined the registers of the Secretariat-Chancellery, the Han-lin academicians, the Secretariat special drafting officials, and the censors, seeking out those of good reputation whom he would then call to be sponsors.[6] Chen-tsung did similarly in 1007, when he personally selected fifty men known for their justness.[7] In more of the recorded instances, however, such personal selection of sponsors was placed

[6] Text 25.   [7] Text 51.

in the hands of a limited group of the highest officials.[8] These cases were not only concerned with recommendation for such important posts as fiscal intendant; they were also for officials of prefectures and subprefectures.

It is difficult to say how often men were selected in this way to make recommendations. The *Sung-hui-yao chi-kao* documents on sponsorship supply a number of instances clearly suggesting the use of the practice. Those before the normative proclamation of 1010 number perhaps ten, about half as many as the instances in which the sponsors seem defined rather in terms of rank or function groups. After 1010, the growth of regular annual recommendations, permitted according to rank and office, seems to have relegated personally selected sponsors to a secondary role.[9] The idea none the less retained its attractiveness to those who hoped to purify the Sung officialdom, and half a century later it found distinguished advocates in two men eventually to become political enemies, CHANG Fang-p'ing and WANG An-shih.[10]

A variation of the principle of selecting sponsors personally was the perhaps more objective practice which may be described as chain recommendation. By this practice, men who had been recommended and guaranteed in turn recommended others for promotion.

[8] As in 998 (*SHY:*CK,42,58a; *HCP,*43,5b; *KMPY,*998/6), and in 999 (text 35). In the latter, the sponsors were to be men respected for their incorruption, without numerical limitation. PAO Ch'eng (999–1062) in a memorial of uncertain date refers to a recent order directing the Secretariat and the Bureau of Military Affairs to select twenty sponsors (*PHSKTY,*2,41a).

[9] At least seven documents, ranging in date from 993 to 1027, list by name sponsors whose offices do not seem to fall into any clearly formulated rank or functional groups, and whom we may therefore assume to have been selected as individuals. (Texts 25, 47, 63, 65, 90, 101, 104.) In another group of some eleven documents (dating 964 to 1028) the sponsor list has been abbreviated to a formula such as one of 1007 (text 51): "the Han-lin Academician CHAO Chiung and others, fifty men." Still others read merely, as one of 1041, "the Han-lin Academician for the Transmission of Directives TING Tu and down." In such cases the definition may have referred to selected individuals, or may have been a more general one.

[10] CHANG in 1048 would entrust the selection to the councilors of state (*TK,*39,41b). WANG refers to the principle in his "Myriad Word Memorial" of 1058 (*LCHSWC,*39,5b and 12a. Translated in WILLIAMSON, I, 58 and 70; FRANKE, *Bericht,* 25 and 36). SU Shen advocates the idea in a memorial of uncertain date, perhaps about 1040 (*SS,* 294,4b). It is interesting that he suggests it as a means of *preventing* the exercise of improper influence.

An example of this, seemingly an impromptu afterthought, occurred in 1001, when five men recommended to administer large prefectures were each directed to recommend three others to administer subprefectures.[11] Although this precedent apparently remained an isolated example at this time, the idea was urged by such reformers as FAN Chung-yen and HAN Ch'i over forty years later. It is not clear to what extent their proposals were actually carried out.[12] Certainly, if the selection of the first sponsors were left in the hands of a few high officials only, the danger of factional monopoly would remain. On the whole, whether through fear of factional monopoly or simply because the personal selection of sponsors in any form became more cumbersome as the number of recommendations increased, the trend in practice seems to have been rather toward the selection of sponsors through more objective criteria.

Objective Checks on Character

Since the sponsor's character was not generally to be warranted through personal selection, the need for devices to eliminate at least the most undesirable became apparent. There were, however, reasons for applying such devices with some caution. As WANG An-shih held, at least in theory, when men were made strictly accountable for small missteps, they would not put forth their fullest efforts in working toward more important objectives.[13] Mechanical disqualifications for minor faults might easily, too, be unjust in individual instances. During the first half century of the Sung, relatively few moral restrictions were applied to the sponsors. Even when a circuit intendant had for some misstep been demoted in

---

[11] Text 39.

[12] The proposal of HAN Ch'i and FAN Chung-yen in 1043 entrusted the selection of sponsors to the Secretariat and the Bureau of Military Affairs. (FAN was at the time a high official of the latter.) (Text 120.) The short version in *SHY* indicates that some parts of the proposal were adopted in the fifth month of that year, but does not mention the selection of sponsors. In the tenth month effect seems to have been given to another proposal of FAN's, this time jointly with FU Pi, constituting a chain of selections: by the Secretariat-Chancellery and Bureau of Military Affairs for fiscal intendants; by these for prefectural administrators; and by these in turn for subprefectural administrators. The terminology employed, however, seems to suggest a simple act of choosing their subordinates rather than that of guaranteed sponsorship (*HCP*,144,5a–b; *KMPY*,1043/10).

[13] *LCHSWC*,69,9a–b.

function, he retained his former right to recommend.[14] T'ai-tsung at least on one occasion selected as a sponsor a man one of whose previous recommendations had proven very poor, in order that he might redeem his error.[15] The past of the sponsor soon came under closer scrutiny, however. In 1011 we find an order urging the Ministry of Justice to greater promptness in answering requests by the Bureau of Administrative Personnel for data on sponsors' records, and the following year such information was requested to be sent to the palace after recommendations had been made.[16] These actions were followed by a more definite step in 1017, when officials who for some offense were demoted to the post of service agent (the lowest in the administrative class) were regularly forbidden to make recommendations.[17] Measures of gradually increasing severity followed later in Jen-tsung's reign, barring first those guilty of any offense involving corruption, and finally those convicted of any private offense punishable by more than the light rod, the least of the five punishments.[18] These provisions also banned automatically some who had recommended badly on previous occasions, since as we shall see later the sponsor of an offender incurred a penalty related to that of the offender himself. Beyond this point, it would seem, the attempt to measure character by a fixed yardstick did not go.

Selection on Grounds of Rank, Function, and Experience

To seek sponsors with desirable qualities other than moral, the Sung administrators could use objective methods with somewhat better prospect of success. They could place their selection on the basis of official rank, function, and experience.

[14] *YYY*,2,2b.

[15] An incident of 993. The sponsor, Lü Yu-chih, had been demoted for a poor recommendation, which will be discussed below. He had previously served in important posts, and later rose to Han-lin academician. At this time he was named to sponsor two men for promotion to capital official (text 25).

[16] Texts 56, 58.

[17] Text 80. In the earlier period, apparently such men actually retained the sponsorship privilege of their former office. There had been reports of recklessness and questionable motives in recommendations by such men, not surprisingly (text 79).

[18] A proclamation of 1044 bars those guilty of corruption, but only in connection with a single group within the classified list of sponsors, who were also required to have doctoral degrees (text 121). The more severe provisions are found in proclamations of 1055 and 1056 (texts 136, 137). For the private offense and the five punishments, see below, pages 170–172.

In setting desirable qualifications of this kind for the prospective sponsor, the principal difficulties appear to have lain in the need to reconcile the requirements of antifactionalism and justice with other conflicting considerations. To counterbalance the possible partiality of sponsors representing the faction in power, and to make sponsorship equally available to deserving and capable men in all parts of the service, it was desirable that the recommending power be spread widely and among officials of comparatively low rank. High officials ought not to be the sole sponsors, and perhaps should not be sponsors at all, since the administration of the system lay in their hands. This consideration also suggested the elimination from among the sponsors of those specially charged with personnel administration. But there were many arguments for the contrary policy of favoring higher officials: the desirability of choosing sponsors with greater experience, responsibility, and demonstrated ability, and very possibly that of avoiding personal friendship or rivalry as potential sources of bias.[19] Another practical motive also entered in: the most expedient way of reducing the number of promotions through recommendation, as we shall see below, seemed to be the restriction or the simple elimination of the lowest groups of sponsors, who were the most numerous.

The qualifications actually applied represented an intermediate course. Sponsors were drawn in general from the upper group of the administrative class, the court officials.[20] While this group from the beginning numbered hundreds, and later passed the thousand mark, it constituted only perhaps a fifth to a tenth of the whole civil service. Since, however, the major factional divisions were represented within this group, and found their chief spokesmen there, its recommendations would not promote any single clique so long as the power was widely distributed within the group. The parts played by different strata of the court officials varied from time to time. On the whole, the trend was to reduce or eliminate recommendations by the lower ranks of the group and to favor those by local administrative officials rather than by men in the central government.

Before 1010, we do not find any clear statement of rules governing the rank of sponsors, and the intentions of policy must be conjectured

[19] Cf. *OYWC*,107,2b–5b.

[20] Capital officials are mentioned as possible sponsors of candidates for promotion to the civil aide group in 1060 (text 144).

from the sum of individual actions. These show a rather impartial distribution, from the highest to the lowest ranks of the court officials, but with a strong tendency to favor the intermediate ranks (especially List: J to L). Although the members of the Council of State were at this time included among sponsors named, they appear in barely a third of the cases recorded. There seem to be no clear instances in which recommendation was entrusted to them alone.[21] On at least one occasion, a chief councilor (Lü Meng-cheng) protested against his inclusion at all, because of his position as head of the government, but he was overruled by the Emperor.[22] The Chief Councilor Wang Tan apparently had no such scruples, and was known to have recommended a large number.[23] But in nearly a third of the recorded cases during this period, the group of sponsors included none higher in rank than junior lord of a court (List: J), and in a few cases none higher than a chancellery Imperial recorder (List: L). At the lower extreme, on the other hand, while about a third of the clear cases included sponsors no lower than the general rank range of special drafting official (List: G) and another sixth no lower than that of policy critic (List: L), about half seem to have included officials down to the lowest court ranks. On a few occasions, the privilege was extended to all court officials, but usually only to members of designated categories. When the numbers of sponsors are indicated, they vary widely: sometimes fifty or more, and once over one hundred, but also on occasion four or five.[24] During this earlier period, each sponsor was occasionally directed to recommend two men, but more usually one, and on occasion they were directed to pair, each two recommending one.[25] Sometimes no quota is recorded. Already we find in two scattered instances distinction in quota according to the relative rank of the sponsor, such as become more common later on.[26] The first of these cases involves military officers as sponsors; in the second, the distinction is between sponsors who are censors of miscellaneous affairs (List: L) or higher, and

[21] One unclear instance of 999 is a possible exception (text 36).

[22] Text 28 (994). Held post 988–991 and 993–995.

[23] HCP,83,10b. Held post 1006–1017.

[24] 103 in 993 (text 25). In examples showing a very small number, no councilors of state are included.

[25] As in 990 (text 17) and in 1004 (text 43).

[26] 967 (text 7), 1000 (text 37).

those below. In both instances, the higher group recommends two, the lower, one. Functionally, the sponsors seem to have come from all parts of the government, those from the Secretariat-Chancellery and the academies and institutes being especially noticeable.[27] There seems, however, to be no reference to officials connected with the personnel agencies, except as they might be included in groups selected on the basis of general rank.

With the codifying proclamation of 1010, the selection of sponsors was subject to more regular definition. All court officials, possibly excluding some of the highest, had both the privilege and the obligation to recommend one man each year, but not more than one, whether in response to a special enabling proclamation, applying to a single occasion only, or on return from a commission, or else by the end of the year. All officials holding provincial commissions higher than that of prefectural vice-administrator, however, might recommend as many as they saw fit.[28] The subsequent evolution of the restrictions, as they became more refined and complicated, is somewhat beclouded by ambiguities and gaps in the documents as we now possess them. There was soon evidence that the original restriction was suffering wholesale violation, and those who hoped to correct this offered diametrically opposite remedies: the elimination of recommendations by all but local officials, on the one hand, and on the other the increase of central government quotas. The latter course seems to have prevailed at first. In 1023 court officials without local commission were permitted to sponsor three men a year.

The sponsorship of executory officials for promotion to the administrative class evidently received special attention, and most of the measures extant deal with that. In 1027, if not earlier, higher central government officials were each permitted to recommend five

[27] Other central offices mentioned, apart from the Council of State, were the Department of Ministries, the Finance Commission, the Censorate, and the Directorate of Education.

[28] The provision for recommendation at the end of the year, without any special direction, first appears in the codifying proclamation of 1010 (text 55). This is specifically addressed to court officials from the Han-lin academicians down (List: E, but then apparently somewhat lower in the protocol list. See *SHY:*YC,3,1a–10a). Subsequent proclamations, however, refer to court officials without reservation. The mutual exclusiveness of the three kinds of recommendation was made explicit in a proclamation of 1015 (text 68).

of these, other central officials of court rank three. Sometime between 1029 and 1041, however, the trend was reversed and the number of recommendations decreased; the higher group was restricted to three each, and the lower court officials, treated as two groups, to two or one. In 1041, the upper two of the three groups were restricted to two recommendations and the lowest deprived of the recommending privilege. In 1066, finally, the privilege of recommending for promotion to capital rank was lost by all central government officials.[29]

Concerning the number of men central government officials might sponsor from among administrative class officials, we have little indication for the half century after 1010. Scattered instances show sponsors directed to recommend one to three men each; a rule of the year 1044 allowed the annual recommendation of three men from among court officials, by higher court officials, and two by lower.[30]

[29] It was reported in 1017 that some officials had sponsored over ten men in a single year (text 79). It was proposed in 1016 to deprive central government officials of all sponsorship rights, and in 1017 of the right to sponsor men for capital rank, but apparently without effect (texts 74, 80). A statement found in a 1029 document (text 110) ascribes to 1017/5 a rule permitting higher Secretariat-Chancellery officials to recommend five men annually, and other court officials three. *CYTC* and *YH* ascribe the same rule to this date, and characterize it as the first limitation on recommendations. *SHY:*HC and *HCP,* however, show no such document under this date, and other circumstances suggest the five-to-three quota came a little later, while limitations, as we have seen, existed already in 1015. An order of 1023 limited all (central) court officials to three recommendations, seemingly for any post or purpose, in response to enabling proclamation (text 94), to be followed in 1027 by an order permitting the higher Secretariat-Chancellery officials to recommend five executory officials, presumably for capital rank (text 103). This seems the more probable origin of the five-to-three quota. In 1028 it was reiterated that quotas for year-end and enabling-proclamation recommendations might not be combined (text 107). In 1029 the five-to-three rule was still in force (text 110), but a measure of 1041 (text 118) shows that a three-two-one rule was then in force, and changes it to two-two-zero for civil, and two-zero-zero for military sponsors. (But a remark of 1045 suggests higher officials then had three. Cf. *OYWC,*107,3b–4a.) The group divisions at this time are roughly List: A–G, G–L, and L–O for civil sponsors, and B–G, G–K, and K–L for military. The rule of 1066 (text 153) was intended to be temporary until the glut of administrative class officials was reduced. (*SHY* places this rule in 1067.)

[30] See instances of 1020 (text 90), 1026 (text 101), 1027 (text 104), and 1029 (text 108). The rule of 1044 (text 121) defined an upper group extending down to List: H, and a lower group including titular officials List: I–L and certain functional officials of varying rank. (See Table 6.)

The total number of recommendations coming yearly from each group according to rank was of course determined by the number of officials in the group as well as by the quota allowed each sponsor within the group. Since the numbers of officials naturally decreased as the rank ascended, the numbers of the lower sponsors tended to counterbalance the larger quotas of the higher. Our incomplete evidence on the numbers of officials by rank and period does not permit even an approximate estimate of the resulting volume of recommendations. Such information as we have does, however, suggest three tentative inferences. The first is that the successive changes in the rules of sponsorship for promotion to capital rank after 1027 reduced the number of recommendations radically each time, despite the gradual increase in the number of court officials. The second is that successive changes after 1023 always resulted in an increase in the proportion of the total recommendations coming from the highest court group, and a decrease in the proportion from the lowest court group. The third is that the proportion from the middle court group rose after 1027 even more than that from the highest group, and came to represent a considerable majority of the total recommendations made at the capital.

The loss by central government officials of the right to recommend men for promotion to the administrative classes in 1066, was in fact merely a final step in the policy of favoring sponsors with local government commissions. In 1010, as we have seen, local sponsors, from the post of circuit intendant down to prefectural vice-administrator, were entirely free from the numerical limitation which bound the recommendations of other officials. While this freedom was gradually modified in the case of the prefectural administrators and vice-administrators, the circuit officials preserved their privilege intact until 1050, and even thereafter retained far higher quotas than other functionaries. The emphasis on local sponsors was shown not only by the numbers of recommendations allowed them, but by the provision, to be discussed later, requiring that certain local officials be included among the sponsors of a given candidate before action could be taken on his case.[31]

As sponsors, the circuit officials included the fiscal intendants and their assistants, the judicial intendants, the intendants of exchange and their assistants, and the supervisory officials of the fiscal and ex-

[31] See below, pp. 165–166.

change intendancies. The fiscal intendants, assistant intendants, and the judicial intendants, find regular mention in the documents, and their freedom from restriction down to 1050 is clear. Such freedom may be assumed with some confidence in the case of the intendants of exchange and their assistants, at the times when such officials were appointed, and evidence exists that the supervisory officials of the fiscal and exchange intendancies enjoyed the free privilege during certain times and circumstances at least.[32]

The restriction of 1050 resulted from a case which came to the Emperor's attention in which a judicial intendant a day before the expiration of his term recommended sixteen men for the post of sub-prefect. Recommendation for this critical office was, it seemed, being used to gratify friendship or to win favor, and restrictions were promptly imposed on sponsorship for the post in question. (Other kinds of sponsorship were apparently not affected.) The resulting quotas, interesting for their detail, are shown in Table 4. We see here a distribution of the recommending power in a way reflecting very roughly the numbers of subprefectures in the different regions. In 1066 a personnel administrator proposed the extension of this principle to control the rising flood of officials qualified and ready for promotion to the capital official class, and escape the increasing embarrassment as they waited longer and longer without appointment. He asked a reduction of 30 to 50 per cent in the numbers recommended, to be apportioned according to the number of officials on the staff of each administrative unit. But while other measures to curtail the number of candidates were adopted at this time, the proposal to limit sponsorship by the circuit officials appears to have been without result. With officials at the capital no longer making

[32] The freedom of fiscal and judicial intendants and the formers' assistants was frequently repeated, and in 1025 it was stated explicitly that any official charged with the functions of judicial intendant, regardless of his titular rank, might recommend (text 99). The intendants of exchange and their assistants were often listed as sponsors together with other circuit intendants; a proclamation of 1029 mentions their past freedom from quotas and continues it (text 110). The two kinds of intendancy supervisory official were permitted unlimited recommendation in a measure of 1044 regulating recommendation from among court officials (text 121), and the fiscal supervisory officials were listed along with other circuit officials as potential sponsors (no mention of quota) in 1061 (text 145). Beyond this, we can only say that there is no explicit mention of any time when they had *less* freedom to recommend than the other circuit officials.

TABLE 4

ANNUALLY ALLOWED RECOMMENDATIONS FOR PROMOTION
TO SUBPREFECT, 1050

Post of Sponsor / Governmental units	Intendant			Assistant Intendant		Administrators	Total recommendations by area or administrative level
	Fiscal	Exchange	Judicial	Fiscal	Exchange		
Circuits *							
K'ai-feng-fu area			3				
Ho-pei	12		6	12			
Shensi	12		6	12			
Ho-tung	10		5	10			
Ching-tung	10		5	10			
Ching-hsi	10		5	10			
Huai-nan	10		5	10			163
Liang-che	4		4	4			
Chiang-nan-tung	4		4	4			
Chiang-nan-hsi	4		4	4			
Fu-chien	4		4	4			
Ching-hu-nan	4		4	4			
Ching-hu-pei	4		4	4			
Kuang-nan-tung	4		4	4			
Kuang-nan-hsi	4		4	4			
Yi	4		4	4			
Li	4		4	4			
Tzu	4		4	4			
K'uei-chou	4		3†	4			143
"Six Circuits"‡		6			6		12
Total for all Circuits	112	6	82	112	6		318
Prefectures §							
Superior						11	
Ordinary						254	
Military						46	
Industrial						3	
Total for all Prefectures						314	314
Total	112	6	82	112	6	314	632

Source: Based on text 127a.

　* Assuming that each circuit had one official of each kind, except for intendancy of exchange as noted, and K'ai-feng, which while not properly a circuit at this time had a judicial intendant.

　† Following *HCP. YYY* says 2.

　‡ One intendancy of exchange had jurisdiction over the six circuits of Huai-nan, Liang-che, Ching-hu-nan, Ching-hu-pei, Chiang-nan-tung, and Chiang-nan-hsi.

　§ These numbers represent one recommendation to each administrator of a unit of prefectural rank. The estimated numbers of administrators in 1050 are my computation, based on various data presented in NCC:FCCC.

recommendations for the capital class, the circuit officials predominated still more among sponsors.[33]

The lower local officials who in 1010 and later received special preference as sponsors were all top officials in units of prefectural rank. They included the administrators of ordinary and military prefectures, and prefectural vice-administrators. Those of superior and industrial prefectures, named only rather rarely, and then to sponsor men to be subprefects, pose a problem. While it is not difficult to conceive that administrators of industrial prefectures, usually of small area, normally enjoyed no special quotas to recommend for higher office, it is much harder to explain or believe that this was true of the administrators of superior prefectures. The latter were, however, relatively few and would usually enjoy in any case quotas as higher court officials.[34]

The favor of unlimited recommendation accorded the prefectural officials in 1010 was short-lived, and a proclamation of 1015 appears to reduce them to the same level with central government officials of similar rank. For some time thereafter, their status seems to have remained thus, although the recurrent proposals to eliminate the central officials provided for preserving the recommending rights of the local administrators. In 1041, however, when the central government officials were restricted to two recommendations or none for promotion to capital rank, prefectural administrators and vice-administrators of court rank were permitted three.[35] Three years later, in the select list of those permitted to recommend from among court officials, prefectural administrators were allowed a quota of two

---

[33] The measure adopted in 1066 to drop sponsors in the central government was a part of the same proposal (text 153). The proposal would have limited the lower local officials as well as the circuit officials, had it been adopted in full. There had already been an order some twelve days before, reducing radically the number of promotions to capital rank through sponsorship (text 152). For number of subprefectures per circuit, see CHJ:HKP.

[34] Prefectural vice-administrators are conspicuously absent only from the lists of 1044 (for court rank) and 1029 and 1050 (for subprefect). Specific references to sponsorship by administrators of military prefectures occur irregularly but repeatedly: in at least seven measures of 1010 or later, others earlier. Superior prefectures are mentioned directly only in 1029, 1040, and 1050 (texts 110, 117, 127a), and industrial prefectures then and in 993 and 1029 (texts 23, 109). Except for 993 and 1029, all these instances concerned recommendation for subprefect.

[35] Text 118.

annually (along with such officials as assistant finance commissioners or administrators of the Bureau of Policy Criticism).[36] In recommendation for subprefect, they had been allowed one candidate in a rule of 1029, and again in 1050 as seen in Table 4.[37] In 1066 they, like the circuit officials, retained the right of recommendation when officials at the capital lost it.[38]

Although local officials lower than prefectural administrator or vice-administrator had in general no right of recommendation apart from what they might derive from their court rank, an exception was made at least as early as 1041 in the case of the prefectural judges and staff supervisors of the capital, K'ai-feng; these in certain cases received the same quotas as prefectural administrators.[39]

Taken as a whole, the lower local officials of court rank, by virtue of their numbers, as well as their special sponsorship privileges, must have played even before 1066 a more important role as sponsors than the aggregate of capital officialdom.[40] And as Table 4 demonstrates, when the circuit officials were held to any quota, even a large one, the prefectural officials practically counterbalanced these also in numbers of recommendations.

The emphasis on recommendation by circuit and prefectural officials served a double purpose. It was valuable not only as a way of distributing selections more widely in the civil service; it also gained as sponsors men experienced in local administration, familiar with the qualities of the average subordinate official in the prefectures and subprefectures. A proclamation of 1024 serves as evidence that the latter factor was indeed a consideration. This measure denied to most central government officials without previous local service the right of sponsoring executory officials for capital rank.[41]

---

[36] Text 121.   [37] Text 109.   [38] Text 153.

[39] For sponsorship for capital rank in 1041 (text 118), and of court officials in 1044 (text 121). Strangely, they are listed among sponsors affected by the penal record rule of 1055, while the prefectural administrators themselves are not (text 136). It was seemingly proposed in 1016, and explicitly in 1017, apparently without effect, that officials of court rank serving as local service agents or subprefectural administrators should lose the right altogether (texts 74, 80). The *YH* version of text 97 (1024) interprets it as excluding from sponsors all officials lower than prefectural vice-administrator.

[40] Note that the total number of court rank officials, both civil and military, was only somewhat over 1000 in 1023 (*YH*,119,30b; *SCSS*,9,139).

[41] Text 97. Experience in local posts of prefectural vice-administrator or higher was required. Only the highest group of sponsors was exempted from the ruling. A

Aimed (as we shall see below) primarily at the elimination of sycophancy, the rule may not have affected greatly the number of recommendations from the central government group. But it gives us a clue to the importance which was attached to this factor of local experience.

In considering the criteria of rank and function applied in selecting sponsors, we should note also that military officers were permitted to recommend men for civilian office on terms which often corresponded to those governing recommendation by civil officials of similar rank. In this connection, it must be remembered that military officials in the central government were by no means isolated from the civil officials, but came into regular contact with them in the transaction of governmental business. In the discharge of their duties outside the capital, military officers often had concomitant responsibilities for civil administration in a given area, and in such capacity were placed over civil officials. They often served as judicial intendants, and sometimes in other civil posts. For all of these reasons, the ends of fairness were served by permitting them to act as sponsors in the civil service.

Policy in this respect was not at all uniform throughout the period we are considering, however. During the reigns of T'ai-tsu and T'ai-tsung, when the government was concerned with limiting the war lord power, and under Chen-tsung as well, proclamations clearly asking the military to sponsor civil officials were relatively few. But during the latter part of Chen-tsung's reign and under Jen-tsung their inclusion among the sponsors became the rule rather than the exception.[42] The normative proclamation of 1010 empowered military officials to sponsor along with the civil (though not among the specially privileged local officials) and they appear thereafter to have participated in the normal recommending privileges according to their rank groups.[43] In addition to the rights they might derive from

proclamation of 962 (text 1) had required that court officials who then sponsored men for higher executory class positions should have served in that class themselves.

[42] Down to 1021, we find some seven proclamations in which military are clearly included, out of twenty-three; after that date they appear in at least twelve out of fifteen. In addition, there are a large number of inconclusive cases in the earlier period, and a few in the later.

[43] Often no special distinction of civil or military sponsors is indicated. Sometimes the rank requirements differ slightly, being slightly higher for a military officer than for a civil sponsor with similar quota (cf. instances of 1041, 1055, 1066; texts 118, 136, 153).

acting as officials in a civil circuit or in a prefectural administration, military officers even without civil commissions soon came to participate in the special privileges of local sponsors. Eventually, the military intendants came to enjoy the privilege of unlimited recommendation accorded the intendants of civil circuits.[44]

During the reign of Jen-tsung, the question of the sponsorship rights of the official not in active service drew some attention. Such an official might be supposed to be capable of greater impartiality, particularly if he were in permanent retirement. But the prevailing opinion seems to have held that the immediate contact that an active official had with potential candidates was the paramount necessity, and inactive officials were gradually barred from recommending. The first sponsors to be eliminated in this way were local officials who had not yet taken up the duties of the post to which they had been appointed; later (at least for some kinds of recommendation) both retired and sinecure officials were similarly eliminated.[45] An exception was made, however, in the case of retired officials who had held posts of particular distinction. These seem to have retained a rather broad privilege of recommendation.[46]

[44] The proposal of 1016 (text 74) would include certain military officers among the local sponsors whose right would be preserved. Their privilege is affirmed in 1024 (text 97). The sponsorship right of military officers acting as judicial intendant is clearly stated in 1025 (text 99), and of those in prefectural administrations in 1040 and 1041 (texts 117, 118) and later. Military intendants were permitted in 1004 to recommend court officials without limit (text 121), and in 1061 the existing rule allowed them the same privilege in recommending for subprefect or for capital rank (text 153).

[45] The requirement of present service was applied to the military service as early as 1016 (text 74). Measures of 1031 and 1034 forbade local civil officials not yet at their posts, first to sponsor for capital rank and then generally, naming specifically prefectural administrator and circuit intendant sponsors (texts 113, 114). The ban on retired and sinecure officials referred specifically to sponsorship of candidates for subprefect and executive inspector (text 137 in 1056).

[46] In 1059 officials formerly in the Secretariat-Chancellery and the Bureau of Military Affairs were requested to make recommendations without qualification of kind or number (text 142); in 1064, to recommend two civil officials for unspecified purpose (text 149). Li Hsin-ch'uan says that under the early Sung rulers—"the ancestors"— former councilors of state might annually recommend five candidates for capital rank (CYTC,II,14,15b). The exact date to which he refers is, however, not clear, and our evidence as a whole is rather slender on the subject.

X

THE POLICIES OF SPONSORSHIP: THE CONTROL
OF THE SPONSOR

Once the sponsors were selected, if they were all men of true worth, the act of recommendation could be left safely to their judgment, and the men they recommended could be confidently invested with responsible office. This was the ideal toward which the system aimed; but as we have already seen, it was tacitly recognized by most that the ideal was not fully realizable in practice, since one dealt not with individuals but thousands. Because the selection of sponsors of uniformly high quality could not be ensured, it was necessary to encourage those selected to make proper use of their recommending authority, and punish them for the misuse of it.

1. Measures of Encouragement and Assistance

Government by persuasion was a primary tenet of Confucian political philosophy. It applied both to the relationship between government and governed, and that between upper and lower within the government. In essence it included the approaches to the disciplinary problem which today we sometimes call promotional methods. In dealing with the average man, it stressed the fact that education and a favorable economic condition must pave the way for other appeals, if they were to be fully effective. Its strongest compulsions were perhaps the force of example and of public opinion based on a commonly accepted code of behavior.

The early Sung personnel administrators applied these forces to sponsorship in the typically Confucian form of exhortations and appeals to principle, and also through rewards and commendations. To create favorable conditions for the conscientious exercise of the sponsoring power, they endeavored to avoid situations that might lead an average official to misuse it: they adjusted the official relationships between sponsor and candidate, and defined the number and kind of sponsors a candidate should have. In drafting these measures, they attempted to achieve as much flexibility as they could without sacrificing effectiveness.

Exhortation and Guidance

The statements and reiterations of the ultimate objectives of sponsorship which, as we have seen in earlier chapters, occur liberally in the proclamations even in their present abridged versions, naturally helped to remind the sponsors of the considerations which should govern their actions. Further guidance was provided in the repeated stipulations of the qualities candidates should possess, and in the announcements of posts for which candidates were needed. As we have seen, sponsors were admonished to avoid recommending men as a personal or party favor. They were cautioned not to make full use of their recommendation quotas unless they had genuinely suitable candidates.[1]

Appealing to historical and Confucian precedents, these exhortations probably had in that day a compelling force greater than one might now imagine. The impartial recommendation of good men became, for the conscientious official, a matter of personal pride. An early eleventh century official, we learn, once recommended a subordinate who had reason to expect quite different treatment, having disciplined severely a relative of the sponsor's some time before.[2] The Second Privy Councilor SUN Pien, when Executive Censor, recommended for the Censorate two men with whom he was personally unacquainted. These later achieved high repute, and SUN is said to have remarked in his later years, "What did I accomplish as Councilor of State? But I need not be ashamed of the two censors I recommended."[3]

---

[1] Texts 150, 151 (1065). The filling of the quotas had been optional at least since 1029 (see below).

[2] *HCLY*,57,3b. The uncle, related by marriage to Ts'AO Li-yung, then a titular chancellor (see below, Note 81), had become the terror of the subprefecture where he lived. CHANG Tai-wen, registrar of the place, finally brought the uncle to court, where he was sentenced to the heavy rod. The nephew, LU Shih-lun, to everyone's amazement, congratulated CHANG on having caused the uncle to change his ways, and recommended CHANG.

[3] *Ibid*. SUN Pien (996–1064) was an executive censor under Jen-tsung. Recorded at the end of the eleventh century, these stories throw a light on attitudes of the time that is quite independent of their authenticity (of which we cannot of course be certain). Other examples may be found in CML, p. 29.

Rewards and Commendation

References to recognition to be given a sponsor of good candidates recur in a number of proclamations, particularly during the reign of Chen-tsung. They are, however, vague in their phrasing, and it does not seem that any consistent system emerged for the application of such encouragements. The measures to be taken are most often described merely as "requitement and commendation," [4] with occasional indication that the exact nature is to be discussed in each instance. In 1010 it was provided that the action should be initiated by the Secretariat, after examining the performance records of the candidates in their new posts.[5]

The ways of determining eligibility for recognition were also rather undefined. A rule of 1009 based such action on the candidates' performance in the new posts over a period of one or two terms aggregating five years, during which time they were to be without deficiencies, and achieve accomplishment with efficiency. How these qualities were to be measured, we are not told.[6] With the codification of 1010, superior performance by three candidates became the criterion for recognition. If the men recommended included both outstandingly good and outstandingly bad choices, however, the good choices would be used instead to balance the bad and cancel out the discipline otherwise incurred for the latter.[7]

Restrictions on the Relational Scope of Sponsorship

Some of the considerations affecting the selection of sponsors on the basis of rank and function were mentioned in the preceding chapter. One of these was the official relationship to a prospective candidate which a sponsor's office would give him: a relationship which

---

[4] *Ch'ou-chiang* 酬獎.

[5] Text 55. A military official of about this time, a certain LIU Wen-chih, was given a promotion from Imperial officer in attendance (group O) to assistant commandant of the Western Capital Workshops (group M) in recognition of eight good recommendations he had made (*SS*,160,2b–3a).

[6] Text 53. A special enabling proclamation of 985 provides recognition if the candidate prove "strong, intelligent, and pure," and one of 999 if after three terms he have governmental accomplishments (texts 14, 34). A special enabling proclamation of 1015 refers to two terms of specially efficient service by the candidate before action (text 69), but thereafter it is not clear whether the rule was continued.

[7] Text 55. The later history of this provision is again obscure. A similar idea is embodied in a proposal of SUNG Ch'i in 1041–1048 (*SCWC*,28,10b), and also in one by SU Shen about the same period (*SS*,294,4b).

might affect the objectivity and discernment of his recommendation. While the relationship was in part influenced by the allocation of the sponsoring power, it was possible to regulate it further by restricting the sponsor in his exercise of that power. His choice could be restricted to a rank group bearing a certain relationship to his own, or to men bearing a certain professional or jurisdictional relationship to him. In the course of time, all of these expedients were used.

In the matter of rank relationship, it seems from the first to have been accepted that the rank and function of the man recommended would always be lower than those of the sponsor. Beyond this, it seems that the candidates prospective rank as well was commonly lower than that of the sponsor, though in many instances our information is insufficient for complete certainty on this point. As one might expect, when candidates for positions of several different ranks were required, the higher ranking sponsor would be directed to recommend the men for the higher posts.[8] A similar relationship appeared when sponsors were selected on the basis of local commission. The circuit intendants recommended officials holding commissions as high as prefectural administrator.[9] Administrators of prefectures of various kinds and vice-administrators recommended men with positions as high as civil aide. Until 1031 administrators of ordinary prefectures (and presumably superior prefectures) apparently had the privilege of recommending also those who were vice-administrators, but in that year the practice was forbidden. (See Table 5.)[10]

[8] A common relationship is shown by a proclamation of 990, which divides the sponsors, all court officials, in two groups. The higher recommend men to be fiscal intendants or assistant intendants, the lower recommend men to be prefectural administrators or vice-administrators (text 17). A case of 1025 illustrates the practice clearly: sponsors, including a titular senior lord of the Court of Imperial Banquets (List: H) with the commission of prefectural administrator, recommend a candidate who is a staff supervisor in a militia command prefecture (List: R), and who is then promoted to titular under-secretary of the heir apparent in the Left Secretariat (List: O), an office of court rank (text 98).

[9] The assistant intendants and the fiscal intendancy supervisory official seem to have shared this privilege (texts 122, 145, et passim).

[10] Text 112, et passim. While there are examples to show that the candidates named by each kind of sponsor reached ranks at least as high as here stated, the assumption that they ranked no higher rests on negative evidence, except for the rule of 1031 affecting the administrator-vice-administrator relationship.

TABLE 5

RELATIONSHIP OF SPONSORS AND CANDIDATES ACCORDING
TO THE NORMATIVE PROCLAMATION OF 1010

Sponsors Who Are	May Recommend Candidates Who Are
Central officials:	*Central officials:*
Finance commissioner	Court rank
Assistant finance commissioner	Capital rank
Court rank, Han-lin academician and down	
Military officials from commandants of the several offices to Imperial warder of the Inner Hall	
Local officials:	*Local officials:*
Fiscal intendant	Fiscal intendant?
Assistant fiscal intendant	Assistant fiscal intendant?
Judicial intendant	Judicial intendant?
Administrator of:	Administrator of:
superior prefecture?	superior prefecture?
ordinary prefecture	ordinary prefecture
military prefecture	military prefecture
industrial prefecture?	industrial prefecture?
Prefectural vice-administrator	Prefectural vice-administrator
	Subprefectural administrator
	Civil aide
	Other executory officials

The proclamation does not specify how high a rank or commission a candidate may have; this interpretation is based on the practice shown in other sources. Local officials may recommend only those under their jurisdiction.

———————— Unlimited recommendations
- - - - - - - - - One recommendation annually

With a proclamation of 1044, a clearer pattern of relationships was worked out for those candidates who were of court rank. The rank relation of each candidate to his sponsor was now precisely defined. The position of the candidate was determined in terms of his titular office, while that of the sponsor was defined in terms of titular offices, assignments, or commissions. The resulting pattern may be seen in Table 6. In this scheme, there emerges more clearly the tendency to select the candidates from the group not immediately below the sponsor in rank, but a step still lower. An exception to this appears in the case of the lower ranking censors and policy-criticism officials, whose prestige exceeded their rank. It is noticeable also that comparatively few officials in the list play the dual role

TABLE 6. THE RELATIONSHIP IN RANK AND FUNCTION BETWEEN
SPONSORS AND COURT RANK CANDIDATES ACCORDING TO THE RULE OF 1044

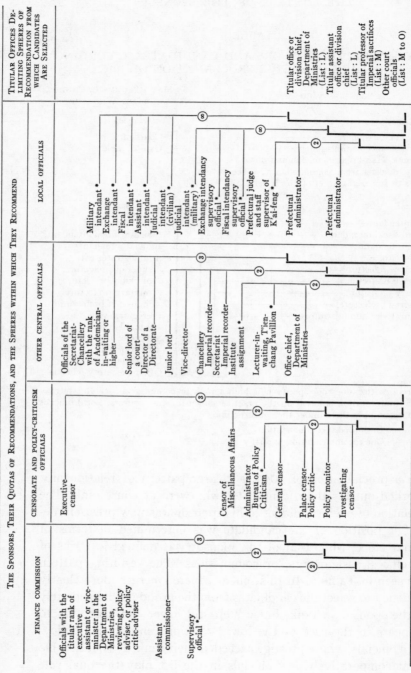

The Sponsors, Their Quotas of Recommendations, and the Spheres within which They Recommend

| FINANCE COMMISSION | CENSORATE AND POLICY-CRITICISM OFFICIALS | OTHER CENTRAL OFFICIALS | LOCAL OFFICIALS | TITULAR OFFICES DELIMITING SPHERES OF RECOMMENDATION FROM WHICH CANDIDATES ARE SELECTED |

Officials with the titular rank of executive assistant or vice-minister in the Department of Ministries, reviewing policy adviser, or policy critic-adviser

Executive censor

Officials of the Secretariat-Chancellery with the rank of Academician-in-waiting or higher

Military intendant *
Exchange intendant *
Fiscal intendant *
Assistant intendant *
Judicial intendant (civilian) *

Assistant commissioner

Censor of Miscellaneous Affairs

Senior lord of a court
Director of a Directorate

Supervisory official *

Administrator, Bureau of Policy Criticism *

Junior lord
Vice-director

General censor

Judicial intendant (military) *
Exchange intendancy supervisory official *
Fiscal intendancy supervisory official *

Chancellery
Imperial recorder
Secretariat
Imperial recorder
Institute assignment *

Palace censor
Policy critic

Lecturer-in-waiting, T'ien-chang Pavillion *

Prefectural judge and staff supervisor of K'ai-feng *

Policy monitor

Investigating censor

Office chief, Department of Ministries

Prefectural administrator

Prefectural administrator

Titular office or division chief, Department of Ministries (List : L)
Titular assistant office or division chief (List : L)
Titular professor of Imperial sacrifices (List : M)
Other court officials (List : M to O)

② Two annual recommendations permitted to each sponsor.
③ Three annual recommendations permitted to each sponsor.
∞ Recommendations unlimited, but from sponsor's jurisdiction only.

Source: Text 121
* Vertical placing of sponsors indicates their place in the Protocol List, except for those posts indicated by asterisk (*) which have no place in the List. Any sponsor (except local sponsors, as noted) may recommend any official within the indicated rank range.

of potential sponsor and potential candidate for recommendation.[11]

It appears that sponsors in the central government were free to recommend officials employed outside the capital, subject to the rank and functional qualifications imposed on sponsor and sponsored.[12] Sponsors serving in local posts, however, from 1010 if not earlier, seem to have been confined in their recommendations to men serving under their jurisdiction.[13] This provision helped to reserve the advantages of sponsorship for the candidate outside the capital; but its primary purpose was rather to ensure the sponsor's knowledge of the candidate. It was reinforced by added stipulations that the locally employed sponsor might not employ his power to recommend before he had actually entered on the duties of his local post, and that he might recommend only a candidate who had served under him for at least a year.[14] In the case of an executory class candidate at least, it was necessary that the relationship should not have ended before the recommendation.[15] A rule of 1021, however, permitted a circuit intendant to recommend an executory official from another circuit if, when specially called upon to recommend, he had no suitable candidate in his own.[16]

The element of personal familiarity, emphasized by these jurisdictional requirements, received still greater stress in a rule which

[11] Text 121. The absence of a number of titular and functional officials from the sponsors in this list, including some comparable in importance with those found, is difficult to explain.

[12] And in some cases if they had local experience (see p. 152). The normative proclamation of 1010, in fact, does not seem to give many of them the right to recommend officials at the capital (text 55).

[13] *YH*,118,19b says this was not always the case, but the stipulation appears in documents of 993 and 1004 (texts 23, 42); it is found in the normative proclamation of 1010 and in others of 1024, 1044, etc. (texts 55, 97, 122).

[14] The first stipulation appears in text 114 (1034). The second is said to have followed an incident of uncertain date under Jen-tsung: a prefectural administrator recommended for promotion a prefectural judge who had served with him barely a month. The action was challenged by a censor as one obviously motivated by considerations other than the good of the service (*TK*,38,12a).

[15] A rule of 1024 (text 97). This rule does not seem to have been followed in cases of specially enabled sponsorship, especially of administrative class candidates (texts 90, 142, 149).

[16] In this case, he was to state on the form of recommendation the lack of suitable men in his own circuit (text 91).

made recommendation by at least one jurisdictional superior mandatory before sponsorship became effective. This rule will be discussed below.

A somewhat different problem arose in using sponsorship to find men for certain specialized offices, such as the Censorate, the schools and institutes, and the legal and financial organs. To some extent the problem was the same for all. For all these offices the character of the candidate was a factor scarcely secondary to his intellectual qualifications; whether the duties in question required above all moral courage, intellectual integrity, devotion to justice, or merely financial honesty. The professional qualifications of the candidates could be adequately judged only by officials of the offices in question, who were presumed to be the best qualified men in their specialties. But lest on occasion the opinions of these specialists be swayed in some degree by personal motives, particularly since the candidates might become future colleagues in their own offices, a need for some effective outside check was felt.[17]

Having these problems in common, the several organs also had special difficulties of their own. The Censorate was of them all most fundamental to the proper functioning of the state. The quality of its staff—both intellectual and moral—was critically important, and recommendation for its positions could not be lightly delegated. But the most responsible officials of the state—the members of the Council—must not exercise influence over the Censorate. In the words of Jen-tsung, "If the Chief Councilors themselves employ the censors, there will be none who dare to speak the faults and errors of the Chief Councilors."[18] Yet if the members of the Council should not recommend, who could be entrusted with the responsibility?

The practices actually adopted with respect to the several organs were rather variable. In general, the sponsors tended to include both the appropriate specialists and men from other fields, though cases occur in which the sponsors were exclusively specialists or exclusively nonspecialists. In recommendation for nonacademic posts, the outsiders were frequently represented by academicians, draft-

[17] See, for instance, a case in the Censorate of 1039 (*SHY:*CK,17,6b). The possibility of bias was adduced as a reason for choosing nonspecialist sponsors for Censorate and High Court of Justice candidates in 1002 (text 41).

[18] *HCP*,113,14b; *KMPY*,1033/12.

ing officials, and policy-criticism officials, all men who were carefully selected and supposedly characterized by a special sense of responsibility. The councilors of state appear among the sponsors with
fair frequency; but the expansive tendency of their power, particularly toward the Censorate, kept the defenders of the traditional
checks and balances on their guard. In 1033 it was made mandatory
that the two chief Censorate officials participate in sponsoring men
for that organ, and in 1044 the participation of the civil councilors
of state in such action was forbidden. The procedure devised at
this time seems well adapted to solve the problem. When a vacancy
occured, two candidates were recommended by a group of sponsors
in which the heads of the Censorate were included, and the Emperor personally selected one of these for the position.[19] The
professional standards of the legal offices and the institutes had protection also in the examinations which were given the men recommended, under the auspices of the offices in question.[20]

Mandatory Sponsors

An important development in the evolution of sponsorship, and a
necessary concomitant of the multiplying recommendations, was the
determination of how many sponsors should qualify a candidate for
promotion, and what weight should be given to recommendations by
different sponsors. This development began soon after 1010, when
a mandatory number of sponsors was prescribed for certain promotions through sponsorship, and led before long to the requirement
that certain superiors be included in this number.

Some of the advantages of these requirements are easy to see. If

[19] The action of 1033 followed an action of a chief councilor in appointing two
censors on his own authority (*HCP*,113,14b; *KMPY*,1033/12). For the ban of chief
councilors and the subsequent system, see *SHY*:CK,17,7a; 7b; *CYTC*,I,9,15a; *HCP*,
189,17b; *SCKY*,6,11b; *KMPY*,1059/5. The ban remained in force until 1059. For
deliberating and reviewing officials of the Bureau of Judicial Investigation and the
High Court of Justice, a rule of 1061 arranged for sponsorship by the Censorate, the
academicians, and the Bureau of Drafting Officials, as well as by the judicial organs in
question (*HCP*,194,23a).

[20] Early in Jen-tsung's reign a military councilor of state sought an academic position for his son, causing the Emperor to reiterate that the institute examination would
be the sole way of access to such places (*LPC*,2,10a). This was repeated in 1043
(*KMPY*,1043/11), and in 1057 (text 141). But see p. 97 above. For the legal examinations, see *HCP*,91,5a (1018).

each candidate were to be judged by several sponsors, the discernments of the individual sponsors would supplement each other and achieve a more reliable appraisal. After promotion the candidate would be free from a special bond of obligation to a particular sponsor; but he would, through his obligations to several, be under increased moral pressure to do well. These considerations played a part in motivating the use of mandatory sponsors. But another consideration also was clearly present: the need to dam the rising flood of effective recommendations and diminish the effluent stream of automatic promotions.

As noted in an earlier chapter, the numbers in the civil service were growing throughout this period. The ranks of the administrative class grew with the service as a whole, expanding by some 40 per cent during Jen-tsung's reign.[21] As early as 1036, the Bureau of Administrative Personnel was perplexed with the problem of placing ninety-two officials for whom it had no vacancies.[22] When a limitation was placed on the number of officials who could enter the administrative class annually, there was soon an accumulation of men properly sponsored, given case review, but unable to have the Imperial audience which would confirm formally their new status. Numbering sixty or seventy about 1050, fifteen years later they were reported as 250 or 350. It was noted in 1066 that at the current rate of one hundred men annually, it would require two and a half years for these men to be absorbed. At the same time new men were being added to those already waiting: some nineteen hundred recommendations were being processed yearly. And meanwhile, the number of civil aides, from whom the excess numbers in the administrative class had been promoted, was falling short of the demand. In 1060 the shortage amounted to eighty or ninety men.[23]

More than once the sponsors were urged not to use their full quotas of recommendations unless they had candidates of real worth; but a single circuit intendant, such as the generous CHIANG T'ang, might recommend as many as two hundred subordinates in a single year.[24]

[21] YH,119,30b–31a.

[22] HCP,118,4b; SHY:CK,11,3b. The solution at this time was to distribute the unemployment by accelerating the rotation of posts.

[23] Texts 144, 151, 153; YH, loc. cit.

[24] Texts 150, 151; HCP,107,3a; SS,298,15a. See also below, Note 92.

How could the promotions be diminished without damage to the morale of the service? As we have seen, the recommendations allowed to certain sponsors were diminished partly with this end in view. But reductions drastic enough to curtail the promotions effectively would make the system inflexible, since a rigid rationing of recommendations would ignore local inequalities in ability among lower officials. The alternative was to make the mandatory number and kind of sponsors so exacting that, given the existing number of recommendations per sponsor, fewer candidates could hope to qualify.

For these several reasons, the establishment of a minimum sponsor requirement followed closely the first radical expansion of the system. The use of sponsorship in promotion to the administrative class, where, as we saw, the problem of oversupply was particularly acute, seems to have engaged special attention from the first. In 1012, sponsors in the central government were directed to pair in recommending for this purpose, and two years later we find the mandatory sponsors (of any kind) set at five.[25] Before a decade had passed, however, this number of sponsors was found unduly onerous. Deserving but inconspicuous men found it hard to meet the requirement, and those eager for promotion were led to beg for recommendation.[26] The mandatory number was therefore modified, in certain cases at least. Promotion was allowed when a candidate could secure recommendations from two of his direct superiors—circuit intendants, prefectural administrator, or vice-administrator—or one of these and two other officials.[27] The inclusion of the latter alternative serves to

[25] Texts 59, 64. The requirement of five was reiterated in 1019; while the order of 1014 appears in both *SHY* and *HCP, YH* and *CYTC* seem to overlook it in dating the requirement from the later year (text 88).

[26] Text 97.

[27] This seems to me the best interpretation of a confusing passage in a measure of 1024. (See text 97 for further discussion.) The principle had been applied in at least two earlier measures. In 1022, an arrangement was made permitting the recommendation of men who had once committed a private offense of lesser importance, punishable by the heavy rod or less (see below, Table 7). They would need seven sponsors, or else a circuit intendant and two others, or two circuit intendants (text 93). In a case of 1023, a candidate having as sponsor only a fiscal intendant was rejected, but it was announced that with two additional sponsors such a case could be processed (text 95). Lacking the recommendation of any direct superior, it must have remained possible to obtain a promotion with five other sponsors, as the case below of Lı Chih-ts'ai seems to indicate. It is also suggested by a statement of Su Shen, around the middle of Jen-

remind us that the central government sponsor filled an important function; his help remained a recourse for the executory official undeservedly overlooked or discriminated against by his direct superiors. This is illustrated by an interesting letter of YIN Chu describing the plight of the candidate LI Chih-ts'ai, who later was to be noted for having taught the philosopher SHAO Yung. LI, despite his ability, was a man who did not thrust himself forward, and though already in his thirty-ninth year, was little known. He was then the judicial inspector of a prefecture. His term was about to expire; he had only four of the five recommendations necessary for action on his promotion to the administrative class and had no friends at court. YIN Chu addressed the letter to his friend at the capital YEH Ch'ing-ch'en, who on the strength of YIN's testimony supplied the needed recommendation and secured the promotion.[28] When in 1066, however, central officials were forbidden to recommend local candidates, such a recourse for a neglected candidate was no doubt eliminated.

In sponsorship for appointments other than for promotion to the administrative class, the rules concerning mandatory sponsors came rather later and seem never to have been so severe. It is not until 1029 that we find a rule requiring men sponsored for subprefect to have two recommendations.[29] At first they were permitted, if they did well, to advance to civil-aide positions or even to the administrative class on the strength of the same two recommendations; but later separate sponsors were required for each of these steps.[30] In 1040 it was required that one of the sponsors be a directly superior circuit intendant or prefectural administrator; with the general tightening of recommendations for subprefect toward the end of the reign, both the administrator and one intendant as well were made mandatory, and the minimum number of sponsors was raised

---

tsung's reign, that for promotion to capital office, five sponsors were necessary, instead of the three of older rules (*YH*,118,19b; *SS*,294,4b). *TK*,38,11a mentions an increase from *four* to five sponsors, though the date in question is unclear. It adds, however, that without the recommendation of a directly superior circuit intendant, sponsorship was *not* permitted, even when other recommendations were many.

[28] This letter was written some time after LI's achievement of the doctoral degree (1030); both he and YIN died about 1046. See text 97a.

[29] Text 109.

[30] *YYY*,5,10a; *TK*,38,11b.

to three.[31] The sponsors for promotion to civil aide were also raised to three at this time.[32]

For officials already in the administrative class, mandatory sponsors were less important on the whole. But numbers still played a part. We hear, for instance, of an official who received an unusual promotion because, in addition to other qualifications, he had no less than sixteen sponsors.[33] Experiments were tried reducing the normal time in a commission or titular office for those who had five or more sponsors. They were not, however, long-lived. Here, too, the practice was found to promote sycophancy.[34] "Men without stability," a censor noted, "frequent the doors of the influential. This is not the way to nourish the honesty and scruples of the literati." [35]

It is not surprising that when the need to restrain promotions became critical under Ying-tsung, the personnel administrators turned not to stricter sponsor requirements, though these were proposed, but to the more radical restriction on the recommending power which

[31] Text 117; *CKFC*,42,9b; *KMPY*,1050/6; *TK*,38,12b.

[32] Texts 144, 152 (1060 and 1066). According to the latter, the same three sponsors, or three new ones (thus *SHY*, but *HCP* says two) would suffice for the further promotion to capital rank.

[33] Text 66 (1015). Together with a promotion in titular office, his commission was to be raised from prefectural administrator to fiscal intendant or assistant intendant.

[34] At the beginning of 1028, it was ordered that cases with many sponsors should receive special consideration (*SHY*:CK,11,2b), and later the same year it was determined that candidates with five sponsors would be eligible for promotion one term sooner (*HCP*,106,18a; *YYY*,3,7a). The ruling was revoked, however, in 1030, and such privilege extended only on the ground of merit ratings (*SCKY*,5,5a; *HCP*, 109,9a). PAO Ch'eng proposed a practice under which men with five sponsors and no private offense would receive first priority in the allocation of posts, to be followed by those with three or less and similar record, and then by others. He stated that at the time posts were actually distributed on the basis of seniority. There is no indication that the proposal was adopted (*PHSKTY*,3,47a). In 1043, a plan was introduced by which men with five sponsors would become eligible two years earlier for promotion at several steps of the ladder of titular offices: promotion to assistant office or division chief (List: L), to office or division chief (List: L), and to junior lord or vice-director (List: J). At higher levels, there were no fixed time requirements (*KMPY*, 1043/10; *HCP*,144,8b–9b). This plan was dropped after two years (text 123). A still more drastic rule was proposed in 1062, requiring for promotion to titular junior lord or vice-director or higher office at least five sponsors, including three who were circuit intendants, or higher officials of the Secretariat-Chancellery. It is not clear this was adopted (*HCP*,208,10b–11a).

[35] Text 123.

was noted in the previous chapter. The experience with sycophancy was no doubt a contributing motive, although the reason expressed was that a restriction on recommendations was less discouraging to the "feelings of men"—presumably those of the hopeful candidates whose advancement was to be retarded.[36] Even the restriction of recommendations was not adopted without misgivings. The censor CHIA Yen held that the imposition of fixed maximum quotas had awakened in many an urge to fill them. Speculating on the situation nearly a century later, the scholar-statesman YEH Meng-te, also, thought that sponsors had recommended more carefully and soberly in earlier years, when they had been unrestricted in their numbers. Restrictions had added to the evil they sought to correct, until it was too late to turn back.[37] Was this mere nostalgia for the days of the great dynastic founders, or did it contain a measure of truth?

2. Disciplinary Methods

While the Confucian ideal stressed promotional methods as the only means that could win the fullest administrative responsibility in the long run, it of course acknowledged the necessary place of punishments in the practical scheme of administration. Early Sung legislation reduced considerably the severity of T'ang punishments, which themselves were far more lenient than those of earlier periods. But in terms of modern concepts Sung laws were still severe.

This severity was apparent in the legal responsibility which attached to the act of sponsorship. This responsibility in a sense made the sponsor one with the man he recommended. If the candidate offended, the sponsor, even without will to offend or knowledge of the offense, became a participant in the same offense.

The Nature of the Sponsor's Legal Responsibility

Such a concept of joint responsibility was common in governmental practices of the time. By means of it the government could make constructive use of the peculiarly strong social bonds that controlled the relationships of individuals and families: bonds of kinship, of friendship, of beneficiary and benefactor, enforced by the sanction of the ethical code and of public opinion. Where a man might venture to risk punishment for himself, he could not do so for another to whom he owed an obligation.

[36] Text 153.   [37] Texts 150, 151; *TK*,38,16a.

Joint responsibility appeared in the relationship which bound the members of an administrative unit. If one of these were guilty of misconduct, his associates in office shared the responsibility and the punishment, in degree varying according to official relation and circumstances.[38] In such cases, the implication of the associated officials in the offense stemmed perhaps in part from their failure to prevent or discover the misconduct, in part from a concept of single, shared responsibility within a governmental unit.[39] The concept of guaranty also played a very important role in the economic life of the time in connection with financial obligations.[40]

The legal responsibility of the sponsor resembled that of the financial surety in the fact that the responsibility was voluntarily accepted. The general laws on sponsorship for office and the special enabling proclamations required it, and the sponsor himself acknowledged his liability in the form of the recommendation which he submitted.[41] The word for guaranty used in the civil service context [42] was the same as that used in business contracts. But the Chinese concept of guaranty, particularly in governmental matters, involved certain connotations quite foreign to normal modern Occidental usage. To begin with, the sponsor as surety did not merely guarantee to produce the person of his candidate—the principal—in case of legal prosecution, nor did he guarantee the performance of any other single act: he guaranteed the official actions of the principal as a whole. The punishment of the principal for an offense did not end the legal responsibility of the surety: the latter was still liable to punishment, having himself become an offender. And finally, the surety did not simply risk liability to a single foreknown penalty, whether as a forfeit or in some other form: the penalties he might incur were governed by fixed rules, but they varied widely according to the nature of the principal's offense and other circumstances.

While one who sponsored a malefactor might incidentally violate

[38] This was governed by a special section of the Sung code: see *Hsing-t'ung*, 5, 7b–10a.

[39] For this problem in T'añg law, cf. Ou, *La Peine*, 20. The Sung code followed the T'ang in most essentials.

[40] See NIIDA, *Tōsō hōritsu*, 296–329.

[41] Cf. examples in *WYHC*,15,15a–b; 16,2b–3a.

[42] *Pao* 保.

other laws with separate penalties, the primary penalty he might incur was defined in terms of that incurred by the principal. The sentence of the sponsor as surety would be the same as that of the principal, or lighter by a designated degree, as the legal circumstances indicated. Penalties so defined may for the sake of convenience be called linked penalties.

Pertinent Features of Sung Law

The gravity of the offense committed by the principal, and the responsibility of the sponsor as surety, were calculated in terms of the five traditional punishments, each of which was subdivided into several degrees of severity. The punishments and their degrees were considered to form a single continuous scale of graduated severity, from the lightest penalty, ten strokes of the light rod, to the heaviest, death by decapitation. The punishments and their degrees are shown in Table 7. Normally the sponsor's offense was defined as one less grave than the principal's by one or two degrees according to this list: if the principal, for example, committed an offense nominally punishable by fifty strokes of the light rod, the sponsor as surety might be considered guilty of a forty- or thirty-stroke offense.[43]

The penalties listed were theoretical rather than actual, however, and the punishment actually administered differed in at least two major respects. In the first place, when a culprit was sentenced to one of the listed penalties, its execution was automatically modified in conformity with the dictates of supplementary legislation. In the second place, while the laws made each kind of offense punishable under normal circumstances by one of the listed penalties, it was provided that certain factors should cause variations in the exact sentence. These factors included the circumstances surrounding the commission of the offense, confession of the defendant before apprehension, the official status of the defendant, the relation of the defendant to the party injured, and a number of others. The defendant might, through the operation of these factors, be permitted to commute his penalty to the payment of a fine, which was graded according to the degree of the penalty he might otherwise suffer.

---

[43] On the identity of the degree measuring implication in offense with the degree as a subdivision of the five punishments, see BÜNGER, *Quellen,* 85, nn. 35 and 36. Cf. also *Hsing-t'ung,* 19,10a, for an example of its application.

TABLE 7

THE FIVE PUNISHMENTS ACCORDING TO
THE SUNG CODE *

Punishment	Degree	Commutation (in catties [i] of copper)
Death [a]	decapitation [f]	120
	strangulation [g]	120
Deportation [b]	3000 li [h] distance	100
	2500 " "	90
	2000 " "	80
Forced labor [c]	3 years	60
	2½ "	50
	2 "	40
	1½ "	30
	1 year	20
Heavy rod [d]	100 strokes	10
	90 "	9
	80 "	8
	70 "	7
	60 "	6
Light rod [e]	50 "	5
	40 "	4
	30 "	3
	20 "	2
	10 "	1

* Hsing-t'ung, 1, 1a–3b. The provisions here shown were identical with those of the T'ang code.

[a] 死   [b] 流   [c] 徒   [d] 杖   [e] 笞   [f] 斬   [g] 絞   [h] 里   [i] 斤

(These fines afford an interesting clue to the relative seriousness attributed to the offenses subject to the several penalties.) Or, in the case of an official, the penalty might take the form of demotion in rank, transfer to a border post, or expulsion from the service.[44]

The sentence finally given was affected also by another factor, particularly important as it affected the civil servants with whom we are now concerned. This was the distinction between an administrative delinquency and a private offense. The administrative

[44] On the factors modifying penalties in T'ang law, see Ou, *La Peine, passim;* and Bünger, *Quellen,* pp. 86–88, etc.

delinquency[45] was a punishable shortcoming, through oversight or negligence, of which an official might be guilty in his official capacity. A private offense [46] was one he might commit in his private capacity, for the sake of personal or family advantage. Since any form of corruption or in fact any intentional violation of the law was most probably for the sake of private advantage, offenses of these categories were classified as private offenses even though committed in the administration of public affairs. In view of this construction, it is not surprising that the rules of justice dealt more severely with private offenses, and alleviation of punishment was more difficult to obtain in cases involving them.[47] The divergent treatments of administrative delinquency and private offense affected the punishment of a surety as well as that of a man he guaranteed.

The Evolution of the Sponsor's Liability

How far linked penalties applied to sponsorship during the opening years of the Sung is not altogether clear. Two questions arise: did such penalties apply to offenses of all kinds which the principal might commit? And did they apply to all cases of sponsorship?

Early proclamations specify a number of offenses in which, if the principal committed them, the sponsor would be legally implicated.[48] The use of this term implies the application of linked penalties.[49] But the offenses covered by the provision in the earlier usage vary from proclamation to proclamation, and the terms describing the offenses are neither uniform nor precise. Sponsors are to be legally

---

[45] *Kung-tsui* 公罪.

[46] *Ssu-tsui* 私罪.

[47] Cf. *Hsing-t'ung*, 2,11a; Ou, *La Peine*, p. 68.

[48] *Lien-tso* 連坐.

[49] The same term was used for the linked penalties applied in other cases, including that of officials jointly responsible for an offense of a fellow official (see note 38). The ambiguous and changeable terminology used for the act of recommendation or sponsorship creates a special and constant problem in interpreting the sources. The act of recommendation is sometimes expressed by the term *chien-chü* 薦舉 , "to select for formal presentation," or by *chien*, "to present formally," alone. More commonly it is expressed simply by *chü*, "to select." These terms have a number of uses quite distinct from that of sponsorship in the sense we are here considering. Except in the instances where they are preceded by expressions indicating guaranty, such as *lien-tso, pao, pao-jen,* or *t'ung-tsui* (see below) we rely entirely on the context to discover whether or not formal sponsorship for office is in question.

responsible for such offenses of the principal as being sullied with greed, unfair, apprehensive and soft, inert, neglecting duties, errant in verdicts, crooked in dealings, or merely guilty of offense.[50] Are these expressions perhaps merely warnings of prosecution which would take place under the terms of more comprehensive and precise legislation, covering all such contingencies and other as well? We do have one section in the existing fragments of the Sung code which provides a general rule on the implication of sureties in the principal's offense. Since this section was taken without change from a section of the T'ang code, it was presumably valid from the beginning of the dynasty.[51] It seems intended to apply to guaranty for office; it does not specify the exact offenses which are governed by its provisions, and thus may be evidence that guaranty from the first applied to all offenses within a given range of gravity.

But the early proclamations are inconsistent not only in the offenses covered by the guaranty clause; many lack such clauses entirely, although otherwise similar to those having them. Was guaranty implied in such cases? It is possible that the historians have dropped guaranty clauses from the documents in their editing, or that general legislation provided for guaranty even without such specific reference.[52] But two proclamations of 998 and one of 1007, clarifying the situation then and thenceforth, at the same time suggest that the previous policy may have been ambiguous. These measures successively extended the guaranty rule to all recommendations by prefectural administrators and vice-administrators, then to all those by fiscal intendants and assistant intendants, and finally established guaranty regulations covering all cases of sponsorship.[53]

The exact gradation of the responsibility assumed by the sponsor as surety in the earliest period is also not entirely clear. If the article of the Sung code concerning guaranty, mentioned earlier, was applicable to guaranty for office, it appears that the offense imputed to the surety was regularly two degrees less than that of the

[50] See texts 1, 6, 8, etc.

[51] *Hsing-t'ung,* 25,18b; cf. *T'ang-lü shu-yi,* 25,29b.

[52] A thirteenth-century historian describes the punishment of a sponsor in 961 and the inclusion of guaranty clauses in 962 and 964 proclamations as "making severe the law of implication in offense for sponsors" (*KMPY,*962/2). This would seem to imply that the T'ang law mentioned above was supplemented in some way at this time, or else that it had been in abeyance.

[53] Texts 31, 33, 50.

principal, and in cases of rapacity the surety would be charged with not more than the offense he would be charged with if the principal committed larceny.[54] A proclamation of 982, clearly applying to sponsorship for office, places us on firmer ground. If the principal committed offense, the relation of the surety's offense to that of the principal was now to vary according to the character of the principal's infringement. If the original offense were an administrative delinquency, that of the surety would be less by two degrees. But if it were a private offense, that of the surety would be less by one degree only.[55] Here we see already a movement to single out corruption, the chief private offense of an official, for special attack.

This rule appears to have remained unchanged during the following quarter century. There were, however, intimations that a need was felt for measures which would stimulate sponsors to still greater caution in selecting candidates who would be free from offenses of rapacity.[56] These eventuated, in the latter part of Chen-tsung's reign, in a series of measures revising the system in important respects. The chief innovations came between 1009 and 1016. The penalty for sponsoring a corrupt man was again reinforced: if the principal profited directly from corruption, the offense of the surety was to be identical with that of the principal. If, however, the offense of the principal were punishable by one of the death penalties, that of the surety would be fixed at one degree less than death. The rule for other offenses apparently remained as before, except for two adjustments designed to eliminate inequities of the law and sharpen the concentration on the more important objectives. In administrative delinquencies of the principal liable to penalties less than forced labor, the implication of the surety was suspended pending special

---

[54] *Ch'ieh-tao* 竊盜.

Hsing-t'ung, 25,18b. The punishment for larceny varied according to the amount taken, and might reach the most severe degree of deportation with added forced labor (*Hsing-t'ung*, 19,10a).

[55] Text 12. The expression for administrative delinquency in this instance is *kung fa* 公罰.

[56] At least five proclamations in the years 998 to 1004 stressed the surety's implication if the principal offended through rapacity (texts 30, 32, 34, 43, 44). The word here translated as "rapacity," 賊 *tsang*, was used to cover not only official venality, presumably its primary meaning here, but theft, robbery, and the loot acquired by such means. BÜNGER (*Quellen*, p. 198) therefore translates it as *"unrechtes Gut," "Beute,"* and *"Bereicherungsdelikten."*

government decision, and eventually implication was abolished altogether, even in private offenses of these degrees, so long as they did not involve rapacity. The surety's implication was abolished also in cases where the principal unintentionally committed an offense technically classed as private.[57] Special provision was made to ensure a strict application of the laws on offenses of rapacity. In cases involving these, it was provided that sentences of the surety less drastic than loss of titular office and termination of current employ must be referred to the Bureau of Judicial Investigation for deliberation and confirmed by the higher authorities.[58]

These were the essential features of the linked penalty system. Supplementing them, there developed also a body of laws defining their application more closely, and eliminating some of their ambiguities. What, for instance, was the responsibility of the sponsor if the recommendation did not bring the anticipated promotion or

[57] A proclamation of 1009 provided equality of offense (*t'ung-tsui* 同罪) in cases of personal rapacity offenses (*ju chi tsang* 入 己 贓). It also called for special instructions in administrative delinquencies, heavy rod or less; this probably ended implication in such cases, in practice, for the subject does not recur in later documents. The proclamation applied expressly only to recommendations by circuit intendants and assistant intendants (text 53). According to one version of the 1010 codifying proclamation, the equal offense clause was extended to all kinds of sponsorship there treated (text 55, note 3). Proclamations of 1014 include it in enabling measures (texts 64, 65), and one of 1015 states explicitly that all sponsors are bound by the clause in all cases of sponsorship (text 68). The exception for cases liable to death penalty was made in 1011 (text 57). The need for this is evident in view of the extreme severity of the laws on official rapacity, which, for instance, set the penalty of death by strangulation for the receipt of loot exceeding a certain amount (*Hsing-t'ung*, 11,5b–6a). The exception for cases of unintentional private offense dated from 1012 (text 61), and probably stems from a case two months before its promulgation. A prefectural administrator was fined ten catties of copper for submitting an inaccurate report. Although this was a private offense, the sponsors and others legally implicated remained unpunished. On a request by the Bureau of Judicial Investigation, the Emperor ruled that since the principal's fault was only subject to the heavy rod, and the sponsors and others therefore subject only to the light rod (*?sic*), further action would cause trouble without being effective in promoting morale. He ordered that henceforth such cases should be decided by special directives (*HCP*,78,4b). The rule removing the surety's liability in private offenses without rapacity, heavy rod or less, is variously dated 1017 and 1018 (text 85).

[58] Embodied in a proclamation of 1016 (text 70). The alternatives which might be considered were demotion in titular office, demotion in commission (less severe), or pardon (see the provision for confession, below).

TABLE 8

THE SPONSOR'S LIABILITY AS SURETY ABOUT 1020 *

Character of Principal's Offense	If Principal's Offense Liable to Penalty of:	Surety's Offense Will be Liable to Penalty of:
Private offense: personal rapacity	Death	One degree less than death
personal rapacity	Less than death	Same as principal
other, intentional	More than heavy rod	Less than principal by one degree
other, intentional	Heavy rod or less	None
other unintentional	Any	None
Administrative delinquency:	More than heavy rod	Less than principal by two degrees
	Heavy rod or less	None

* Based on sources indicated in the discussion above, of varying date. Their incompleteness leaves some interpretations tentative. Note that the penalities were rarely carried out in the form here shown, but normally commuted in some way.

assignment? If the recommendation did not result in a transfer of the candidate, or if the ensuing transfer was of a sort which would have taken place without recommendation, the provisions of linked penalty presumably did not come into full effect, but there is some indication that they may not have been entirely waived.[59]

And did the sponsor become responsible for all the principal's conduct, extending into the past and into the indefinite future? The time span of the principal's conduct guaranteed under the linked penalty provisions is quite clear in some respects, but not in all. It seems to have been uniformly accepted that the guaranty applied to the principal's conduct during a period after the act of sponsorship.[60]

[59] A puzzling proclamation of 1030, which I have found only in *HCP*,109,1a, provides that if a candidate recommended for promotion to capital official class receives actually only a civil aide position or his ordinary seniority advancement, and "later may commit offense," the sponsors shall be judged "less than equal offense by one degree." Perhaps the text should have read "later may commit offense of rapacity," in which case the liability of the surety would be one degree lower than if the recommended promotion had been given.

[60] At least as early as 970 (text 8). There is no evidence of variation in this down through 1067.

Most measures agree in applying the guaranty to the period beginning with his appointment to the new post for which he was sponsored.[61] This limitation was announced as a general rule in a proclamation of 1023, when sponsors were specifically relieved of implication in an offense during the period intervening between recommendation and transfer of post.[62] (For previous misconduct on the part of the principal, unreported in the recommendation, the sponsor was liable to penalties of other kinds, as we shall see below.)

On the duration of the surety's responsibility for the principal's conduct after the latter entered the position for which he was guaranteed, the available documents have little to say. By the rule of 1007, when men were recommended only for commission, the liability of the surety ended with the expiration of the term following the recommendation. In other kinds of recommendation, however, there seems at this time no definite termination of the guaranty, and some half century later Su Shih deplores the unfair policy of holding sureties responsible "ten years and more afterward." [63]

What recourse had the sponsor if he discovered, long after the recommendation, that his judgment of a candidate's character had been in error? As Su Shih argued, "Today a man may do good, tomorrow he may do wickedness. If one cannot guarantee him to this extent, what of ten years and more afterward? Those who were young are already mature; those who were mature are already old; but still holding the sponsor to his word once spoken, we make him share the offense. Is this not too much? When he has not yet realized the ambitions of his career, no man of the empire will fail to do good with his utmost energy, seeking recommendation. But having achieved his promotion already, he has no concern and thus feels a vast freedom to do as he likes. When the man was in a prefecture or subprefecture, his official superior beheld personally the integrity of his frugality, industry, and application to work; how could he but be recommended? But how could that superior know what he would do in the long run, indeed! So that is why I say the present

---

[61] This provision was incorporated into rules of 993 and 998 (texts 26, 31), as well as various enabling proclamations.

[62] *HCP*,101,4a.

[63] For the rule of 1007, see text 50. Su Shih's comment is found in *STPCC*, Yingchao, 2,11b; quoted also in *TK*,38,14b.

laws charge men with that which is beyond their [the sponsors'] powers."[64]

To mitigate in some degree the injustice of this situation, the sponsors during most of the period of our concern were permitted to make use of the general legal principle absolving them from implication if they confessed an offense of the principal before it had come to light.[65] The words of SU Shih were strikingly similar to the preamble of the earliest extant measure extending this right to sponsors, a legislation of 993.[66] But justice was not the sole consideration; at a time when such confession was not permitted, there were complaints that fear of possible implication prevented the recommendation of many deserving but unrecognized officials.[67] Although the motive was not stated, it is obvious also that the possibility of confession would gain the assistance of the surety in discovering a principal's misconduct. In theory at least the benefit of confession was limited to cases in which the principal, exemplary in his conduct before the recommendation, had altered his ways afterward.[68] For a certain period, at least, sponsors who had recommended men of demonstrably exceptional past merit were freed from implication even without confession, if their candidates should later turn dishonest: a provision of surprising liberality which may have been soon reversed.[69]

In redressing an injustice, however, the right of confession at the same time weakened the sponsor's compulsion toward care in selecting his candidates, as personnel administrators early recognized. In 1016 it was directed that all cases of prosecution in which sureties might receive light sentences or none should be submitted by the Bureau of Judical Investigation to the higher authorities for final

[64] *STPCC, loc. cit.*

[65] For the general rule on confession, see *Hsing-t'ung*, 5, 10a. This applied only to cases in which restitution was possible. For the rule in T'ang law see KENNEDY, *Geständniss.*

[66] Text 22.

[67] Text 98 (1024).

[68] The stipulation that the principal be blameless at the time of recommendation was repeated in 993, 1004, and 1024 (texts 22, 45, 98). In 1025, nevertheless, a sponsor, immediately after the promotion had been granted, confessed a fault his candidate presumably committed before recommendation. The candidate's new rank was withdrawn, and one infers that the sponsor escaped punishment (text 98). The confession of the surety did not, according to rule, relieve the principal from punishment (cf. text 45).   [69] A provision of 1007 (text 50).

confirmation.[70] Some time before 1024, the right seems to have been suspended altogether, but in that year it was restored after deliberation by the three highest judicial bodies to remain in force thenceforth until its abolition once more in 1057. The considerations which prompted the last decision are left to our conjecture.[71]

Separate Penalties for Poor Recommendations

Thus far we have considered only the linked penalties and their application. The separate penalties played a role of much less importance, and comprise a relatively small part of the legislation on personal guaranty. They fall into two general categories: penalties for misstatements of fact in connection with sponsorship, and measures of discipline for recommendations of poor quality. Both kinds were intended to cover cases of careless recommendation beyond the reach of the linked penalty provisions, since the latter could naturally apply only when the principal committed a legally punishable offense.

The clauses on misstatements applied principally to the information provided on the forms of recommendation, concerning such subjects as the candidate's character, the details of his past record, his abilities, his relationship to the sponsor, and suitable future employment for him. Although as early as 992 allusions are made to punishment for such misstatements, its exact nature is not made clear except in a special enabling proclamation of 1044, which stipulates it shall be the penalty regularly prescribed for any erroneous report.[72] Punishment, again of unspecified nature, was also prescribed for the sponsor who, to avoid possible implication in an offense, made accusations against the principal which could not be substantiated.[73]

[70] Text 70. The measure concludes by saying "Henceforth, let [sponsors] manifest just recommendations, with ever earnest care selecting the honest and able; they will not again be among those confessing."

[71] A proclamation later in 1057 made it clear that the right of a superior official to avoid by confession his implication as an associated official was not impaired (text 139).

[72] 992 and 993 proclamations merely refer to punishment for the sponsor (texts 19, 26), while that of 1007 refers to the "court institutions" (*ch'ao tien* 朝典). All three make it clear that the penalty is distinguished from that of implication in the principal's offense. For provision of 1044, see text 122.

[73] Text 98 (1024).

Disciplinary measures for recommending men who proved un-satisfactory but not necessarily vicious, mentioned in 1001, were stipulated in 1010 for those who had recommended as many as three men guilty of minor offenses. The exact discipline, which might involve demotion, was left for separate decision in individual cases. Some time after 1040 SUNG Ch'i proposed a scheme by which the principal's merit ratings would affect the sponsor, but this may not have been accepted, and the details of the proposal are not clear.[74]

Evidence on the Enforcement of Guaranty in Practice

On paper these measures to implement guaranty in various ways add up to a fairly complete system. To what extent were they en-forced in practice? Evidence preserved shows many cases of prose-cution and punishment under the guaranty laws. We find at an early date directions to speed the answers by the Ministry of Justice when the Bureau of Administrative Personnel enquires concerning spon-sors' offenses.[75] At a later time we hear the Censorate instructed to investigate the recommendations and make accusations where proper at the beginning of each year.[76] These instructions stipulate that the punishment of offending sponsors "should begin with high quarters" and the records show a fair number of cases in which relatively prominent sponsors were penalized. These included men with posts as high as that of academician.[77] In many of these in-stances (to judge from the samples at hand) the punishments given were comparatively severe.[78] These things tell us that the law was

[74] *HCP*,48,2a & *KMPY*,1001/1; text 55; *SCWC*,28,10a–b.

[75] Text 56 (1011).

[76] Text 133 (1053, 1061).

[77] E.g., in 1043 a Han-lin academician (text 120f) ; in 1019 an auxiliary academician of the Lung-t'u pavilion (text 87a): both these group E. In 1020 and 1024, reviewing policy advisers (texts 90a, 96a) ; special drafting officials of the Secretariat about 990, and in 1029 (two) (texts 25, 107c) ; a policy critic-adviser in 1028 (text 107a): all of these group G. These men held in addition responsible posts such as doctoral examination administrator and administrator of the Bureau of Administrative Per-sonnel.

[78] In 1020, for instance, it involved for one official titular demotion from reviewing policy adviser (G) to assistant regional commandant (P) combined with a func-tional transfer from administrator of a superior prefecture to a prefectural military post without civil governmental authority. In 1028, for one official it involved titular demotion from policy critic-adviser (G) to junior lord of Imperial sacrifices (J) com-bined with a functional transfer from provisional supervisor of the Bureau of Execu-

enforced; but they do not reveal how many sponsors may have evaded punishment for their poor recommendations. Su Shih complained that through the combined effect of oversevere laws and the natural tendency of the officials to mutual protection, there were in fact always some who went unpunished.[79]

A few instances of punishments under the guaranty laws may give a clearer idea of how the rules were translated into action, after commutation and other factors had been taken into account. Taken at random from various sources, and often incomplete in data, they serve as illustrations rather than as a basis for generalization. They are scattered in date between 961 and 1055, and tell of the sentencing of more than thirty-one sponsors for the offenses of fourteen different principals. The sentences of the sponsors on which we have information seem limited to four general forms of penalty: reduction in titular office, reduction in assignment, reduction in other central or local functional office, or the payment of fines. Most often the punishment consists in one of these penalties or some combination of two of them, but in two cases a sponsor receives three forms of penalty simultaneously. Each form of penalty assumes varying severity in different instances.

Often a case seems to involve only a single sponsor. But sometimes several sponsors of the same principal are sentenced on a single occasion—perhaps by a single action. On one occasion there were eleven. In such instances, the several sponsors might or might not receive the same penalty.

From the material at hand, it is difficult to perceive a clear relation between the severity of the sponsor's punishment and either the principal's punishment or the nature of his offense. Some relationships, however, suggest themselves. Penalties as severe as demotion in titular office seem normally given to sponsors in cases originating in the principal's rapacity, perversion of justice, or fraud and rebellion; while sponsors received rather less drastic punishments under extenuating circumstances, or in cases involving the few other offenses clearly identifiable.

---

tory Personnel to administrator of a prefecture. In one instance the discipline was somewhat less, and in others the data are incomplete.

[79] *STPCC,* Ying-chao, 2, 12b. He advocates that sponsors exchange the severe penalties of sponsorship for the lighter ones visited on officials who fail in the supervision of their subordinates, and vice versa.

Rapacity accounted for four cases involving sixteen sponsors. (In three at least, personal rapacity seems implied.) In two of these cases a sponsor received a demotion in titular rank, although in at least one of them the principal received a death sentence. The circumstances affecting the treatment of the sponsor are not indicated.[80] Both other cases involved extenuating circumstances. In the first of these, the principal, a notoriously corrupt official named Ts'Ao Li-she, was expelled from the civil service and sentenced to the rod in addition. Although he had been sponsored at different times by eleven men, it was clear that his advancement had really come through the good offices of his brother, a powerful official whose indiscretions brought him also to grief at this time. But it was felt that sponsors who could recommend such a man did not deserve to escape entirely, and the eleven were accordingly fined thirty catties of copper each.[81] In the second case, a corrupt official confessed his offense knowing that he was about to be accused of it, and had his punishment (nominally strangulation reduced by one degree) reduced to two years of forced labor (commutable to a fine of forty catties of copper). Of his three sponsors, however, two lost assignments and important functional posts, and one was given the lowest administrative class commission, that of service agent in a small place. All three in addition were fined ten catties.[82]

Two cases arose from judicial abuses of the principal. In the first, the principal lost his titular office, and the sponsor suffered a considerable titular demotion, a reduction of his assignment, and apparently of an important functional office.[83] In the second, the offense seemingly took place before the act of guaranty, and the several sponsors received fines.[84]

This second case contrasts with another also involving an of-

---

[80] In both cases, the demotion was one from titular office or division chief of a ministry to assistant chief (both group L). The principal who received the death penalty (in 981) was a titular executive censor who turned the public funds of the prefecture he administered to his own profit. The sponsor, a censor of miscellaneous affairs, retained that office (text 11a). In the other case (in 1019), the sponsor retained his assignment. The sentence of the principal is not reported (text 87a).

[81] Text 107b (1029). The brother, Ts'Ao Li-yung, had been a commissioner of military affairs.

[82] Text 107c (1029).

[83] Text 25 (case of about 990).

[84] Text 30a (about 997).

fense before recommendation, but treated more severely. The principal had been guilty of lack of filial piety. Recommended to be a censor and actually appointed, he was demoted again to prefectural vice-administrator on the protest of Ou-YANG Hsiu, then a policy-criticism official. The sponsor, Su Shen, was reduced in assignment and sent from the capital to administer a prefecture. The severity of this penalty is interesting when we note that just previously Su Shen had delivered a veiled attack on Ou-YANG Hsiu and his fellow policy-criticism official, whose expressions of opinion annoyed him. Was this episode in part an expression of the party antagonisms which were at this time (1043) bitter? [85]

The case of fraud and rebellion involved a major political scandal at the end of Chen-tsung's reign. The principal had connived in a scheme to play upon the Emperor's now obviously unsettled mind by the discovery of a new auspicious "heavenly missive," and forcibly resisted arrest when the scheme collapsed. Five sponsors suffered titular demotions of differing degree (some severe), and all underwent great reductions in function.[86]

In four cases, whose original offense is unstated, a total of five sponsors received demotions in titular office, and three of these reductions in functional post.[87]

On the other hand, in a case of flagrant maladministration, in which the just Pao Ch'eng said that the principal merited a death penalty (whether rhetorically or literally is not clear), a sponsor, to Pao's great disgust, was merely fined forty catties of copper.[88] And finally, in one case of technical private offense, for which the principal was fined ten catties, the sponsor or sponsors were pardoned.[89]

What kind of men were the sponsors who suffered penalty? Did their poor recommendations result from disregard for character in making their recommendation, from carelessness, or from undeserved bad luck? There seem to be cases which fall in each of these cate-

[85] A political ally of Ou-YANG, the reformer FAN Chung-yen, had also recommended the principal earlier, but for a different post, and thus escaped legal implication by sheer good luck.. The offense of the principal was failure to protect his mother from an apparently justified legal punishment, but he may have had a bad record apart from this (text 120f).

[86] Text 90a (1020).

[87] Texts 1a, 96a, 107a, 136a (961, 1024, 1028, 1055).

[88] Text 115a (a case probably between 1030 and 1040).

[89] Text 61 (1012).

gories. In the above case of Ts'ao Li-she, it is difficult to believe that the sponsors made their recommendations in entire ignorance of the principal's character: perhaps the political influence of Ts'ao's brother was an instrumental factor.

In another case, personal factors played a part: Lü Yu-chih, the offending sponsor, had recommended a relative of his wife; the principal was one of those guilty of judicial abuses.[90] In this case, despite the temporary setback, the sponsor eventually continued a successful career, holding a number of important posts and rising to the titular office of a vice-minister.

Still another interesting type was that of the sponsor Li Chung-jung. He is said in his biography to have been easygoing, a lover of wine; a man who in social conversation avoided discussions of political expediency, and one who in his official life did not insist on maintaining a point. He was one of those who learned of the offense of his candidate too late to confess.[91]

A man of different stamp was CHIANG T'ang, whose act of sponsorship so outraged PAO Ch'eng. CHIANG T'ang left a reputation for exceptional honesty, courage, stoicism, and even in poverty generosity to those in need. Having a bent for scholarship and the writing of poetry, he was also an indefatigable worker. But as a sponsor his generosity was excessive. When cautioned about his superabundant recommendations, which invited trouble, he is quoted as saying that if in ten recommendations two or three turned out well, that benefit to the State justified the risk.[92] A final example was PAO Ch'eng himself, famous for his equity in judicial decisions. In 1055, late in his career, he suffered demotion in titular office and transfer from the administration of a larger prefecture to a smaller one because of an act of sponsorship. The circumstances are not clear; the recommendation had been made when he was fiscal intendant of Shensi, a post he may have held as early as 1040 or even before. The year after the case he was restored to his former rank and rose to posts of increasing importance thereafter.[93]

[90] Text 25.

[91] Text 107c.

[92] Text 115a. As a subprefectural administrator he brought to justice a wealthy local lawbreaker with whom other officials had been unable to cope. As an executive censor, he dared to defend the Empress Kuo from the Emperor's displeasure.

[93] Text 136a.

The varied treatment accorded in these cases seems to exemplify one aspect of Chinese law: the flexibility with which it was applied under differing circumstances. We see in practice the legal axiom that the judge must reach his decision not only by applying the letter of the law, but by considering the entire nature of the case—the *ch'ing* [94]—as well. It involves a deliberate preference for the risk of the judge's human fallibility rather than the alternative risk of injustice through legal rigidity. But it does not seem, when we consider these few cases as a group, to have resulted in extreme lenity.

[94] 情.

XI

THE POLICIES OF SPONSORSHIP: THE ROLE
OF THE PRINCIPAL

In the aspects of sponsorship that we have considered thus far, the role of the man sponsored has been in general a passive one: he was selected because of qualities he possessed, for the sake of performance which might reasonably be expected from him in the future on the basis of past showing. If he failed to fulfill the requirements of his new post, the blame was placed on his sponsor and perhaps on sponsorship methods through which he was selected.

Obviously, however, the performance of the sponsored man was not solely a matter of his ability and character. His effectiveness, like that of all members of the civil service, was influenced by pressures both aiding and inhibiting his desire to act in the government's interest, and by conditions which affected his morale both positively and negatively. Demands of family and friendship could conflict with those of the state. His enthusiasm could be affected by pay, working conditions, recognition, and hope of advancement. But the fact that he had been sponsored set him somewhat apart in the service, as a man in whom higher morale was to be expected. The requirement that candidates for the administrative class be men with doctoral degrees, and the preference for such men in other cases, meant not only that the candidate would be better educated but that he would be more intensively subjected to Confucian indoctrination. Sponsorship had given him not only recognition and promotion, but the anticipation of further success in the future. The quality of his work, good or bad, was now under closer observation. If he proved efficient and scrupulous, the rules of sponsorship provided that after a term of service his case would receive special consideration for further rapid advancement.[1] If he failed, on the

---

[1] A rule of 981 and a case of 1023 stipulate such consideration at the end of three years of service, while the rule of 1010 says after one term (text 10; *SHY*:CK,48,25b;

other hand, the ignominy of transfer to "a distant, rustic, and lethargic place" was not a pleasant prospect.[2] He had every reason to exert himself.

The sponsored candidate had a special position in another respect also. His obligation to the men who sponsored him placed him under pressures which might be both beneficial and noxious. If by misconduct he involved his sponsors in trouble, he certainly would face social disapproval and could have little hope for recommendations from others in the future. But obligation to a sponsor could also bind him to a political faction. As we have seen, the desire for recommendation might make a candidate cultivate the good graces of a higher official even before the act of sponsorship; this was a reason for the dropping of compulsory recommendation.[3] But while the state might hope to avoid prior factional ties and their damage to objective recommendation, it was almost inevitable that the act of recommendation would itself create new ties which might be factional. The man recommended would subsequently find it hard to be fully objective and impartial in his official relationships with the sponsor. (The fact that in later periods he had a number of sponsors might, of course, neutralize the factional tie if the sponsors were factionally divided.)

The strength of the tie of principal and sponsor is impressively shown by one fact. Although there was no law of reciprocal guaranty, making a principal responsible for the conduct of his sponsor, principals did in fact more than once share in a sponsor's punishment or disgrace. The downfall of Ts'AO Li-yung in 1029, for ex-

---

text 55). A rule of 1009 requires one or two terms amounting to five years; cases of 1015 and 1029 say merely "when replaced" (texts 53, 69, 109). The rule of 981 distinguishes between recognition to be given for satisfactory service and special promotion for merit; the rule of 1010 and cases of 1015, 1023, and 1029 each mention special promotion. The rules of 1009 and 1010 seem to apply to men sponsored for all positions, while the others mentioned above and a rule of 1061 (text 145) apply variously to those given positions of subprefect, subprefectural or prefectural administrator, and prefectural vice-administrator.

[2] Text 55. The discipline was not to extend to deprival of titular office. A rule of 993 provides for the principal an unspecified punishment for the failure to live up to the recommendation (text 26).

[3] Another measure to discourage begging was a rule of 1021 making executory officials ineligible for recommendation during the interval between their replacement at one post and their appointment to another (text 91).

ample, brought demotions to four men at least whom he had recommended.[4] In cases when the sponsor's fall was primarily an incident of party strife, also, the men he sponsored might suffer. This happened in 1036 after one of the eclipses of the reformer FAN Chung-yen. One of his supporters, YIN Chu, vaunting the fact that FAN had recommended him, said that he shared any culpability of FAN's and asked to share FAN's demotion. YIN's wish was quickly granted.[5]

In all these cases, whether the sponsor was guilty of real criminality or merely defeated politically, the reason for the principal's implication was clearly more than that of being sponsored by him: the sponsorship relation was an important part of the charge, but subsequent association played an important part also. The fact of sponsorship might not always by itself involve the principal in a sponsor's difficulties, as we may see from the same episode in FAN Chung-yen's career. Disavowing completely any factional connection with the fallen statesman, another of FAN's recommendees succeeded in preserving a position in the Council of State.[6] On another

---

[4] Those so involved included the former Chief Councilor CHANG Shih-hsün (*KMPY*, 1029/2), the Stud Supervisor HAN Chü (*HCP*,107,6a), the Assistant Finance Commissioner in Charge of Census WANG Tsung (*SHY*:CK,64,30a), and the Prefectural Judge of K'ai-feng LI Chao-shu, son of the prominent LI Tsung-o (*HCP*,107,14b). All were sent from the capital to less desirable commissions, and WANG was also demoted in titular office. For TS'AO Li-yung, see p. 182. A military officer recommended by the rebel CHU Neng (see p. 183) was even sentenced in 1020 to the heavy rod on the back, branding, and exile (*HCP*,96,12a–b).

[5] FAN was charged with violating the newly conceived and quite un-Confucian dictum that one might not "discuss affairs beyond his purview." He was deprived of the assignment of academician-in-waiting of the T'ien-chang pavilion and his commission of provisional administrator of K'ai-feng, and sent to administer an outer prefecture (*HCP*,118,9b). YIN Chu's action was nine days later; he was demoted from titular under-secretary of the Heir Apparent in the Left Secretariat (List: O) and from the assignment of revising editor of the institutes and archives, and made prefectural general secretary (List: R) in charge of a prefecture's wine revenues (*HCP*, 118,12a).

[6] The man was the Associate Administrator of the Bureau of Military Affairs HAN Yi. FAN had rather recently recommended him confidentially to the Emperor, while criticizing the partiality of appointments by the Chief Councilor LÜ Yi-chien. Informed of this, HAN said: "I . . . have never been involved in a trace of factionalism. I am on good terms with everyone. Even less am I related with Chung-yen, nor am I an old crony of his. . . . As for Chung-yen recommending me through motives of public interest, I have always been free from seeking favors. . . ." HAN retained his

occasion, a son of WANG Tan was selected as an administrator of
the Bureau of Policy Criticism, although his sponsor had been degraded: a fact his biographer found worthy of mention.[7] But the
apparently unusual nature of these cases still further emphasizes the
principal's common participation in his sponsor's fortune.

The bond of sponsor and sponsored being as strong as these examples show, it is not surprising that the rule of avoidance was
eventually applied to men thus associated. A proclamation of 1053,
explicitly to prevent undue favor, forbade the principal thenceforth
to elect a position under his sponsor.[8] The relationship was thus
acknowledged to be in a way similar to the kinship tie to which
avoidance normally applied. But while nature held the number of
a man's kin within certain bounds, the number he might sponsor
in a few years (even after the tightening of quotas) was far more
extensive. And the administrative problem posed by such a relationship grew with the number.

Seen as a whole, while the obligations and liabilities which the
sponsor assumed were more conspicuous, often resting as they did
on legal sanctions, the obligations and liabilities of the principal
were no less real. In many aspects these influences were beneficial,
and such aspects the government tried to reinforce. But these
benefits may have been in some degree counterbalanced by a contribution to the ties of factionalism.

---

post until the following year, when he became Second Privy Councilor under LÜ Yi-
chien and WANG Tseng and their successors WANG Sui and CH'EN Yao-tso (HCP,
118,10b–11a; SS,315,3a; NYSSP,34,7a; SCKY,4,3b. SS,211,3a–b seems to err in saying
he was made Finance Commissioner the following year).

[7] SS,320,6a. The son was WANG Su. This event was some time after the death of
WANG TAN. The sponsor, K'UNG Tao-fu, a noted censor, several times came into disfavor for his frankness.

[8] Text 134.

XII

CONCLUSION

In the preceding chapters we have considered the ways in which the objectives of sponsorship, its procedures, and its polices evolved. Each of these, as we have seen, developed and changed in its several aspects over a considerable period of time. When we bring these varying phases of sponsorship together in a single chronological sequence, we see a long and interlocking series of developments, stretching from the very beginning of the dynasty to the very end of the period we have taken for consideration. Clearly the system was not the product of any single mind, any single generation, or any single political situation.

A certain pattern does, nevertheless, appear in the rapidity with which the system developed. It seems possible to distinguish three general stages in the process: first an opening period of somewhat under fifty years, during which the changes, beginning slowly, gradually acquire greater momentum; second, a period of a quarter century during which the developments follow in rapid sequence; third, a period of some thirty-five years during which the development continues fairly steadily, but at a rather slackened pace.

The three periods resemble closely, though they are not identical with, the three periods into which early Sung history was divided, on other grounds, in Chapter II. The first period lasted from 960 until about 1006. While producing comparatively few generalized statements of policy, it did show several significant steps. Early in T'ai-tsu's reign the use of sponsorship was extended from its earlier use for lower local offices to appointments both for Court rank and for commission. In the reign of T'ai-tsung and early in that of Chen-tsung the sponsor (at least if he held a local post) was required specifically to guarantee his candidate, and a scale was established graduating his legal responsibility according to the kind of infraction; his right to confess the offense of a sponsored man was also recognized.

The second period lasted from about 1007 until around 1031. It began with a group of important measures which by 1011 made the outlines of the system quite clear. The normative proclamation of 1010 defined the rules for regular annual recommendation, and established the quota distinction between central and local sponsors. It fixed procedures for making the recommendation, and for the subsequent handling of each case; it established rewards and penalties for the sponsor based on the candidate's future performance. The same proclamation, and others made just before and after it definitely universalized the guaranty clause, limited the responsibility period in recommendations for commission, and in corruption cases established equal penalties for the sponsor, short of death.

The aspects of the system not covered by these proclamations were practically all regulated by measures adopted in the following two decades. The steps of promotion through sponsorship were prescribed, as were the experience requirements. Doctoral degrees became, according to the case, either necessary or advantageous qualifications for the candidate. Mandatory numbers of sponsors, including specific direct superiors, were established for promotion by this method. The jurisdictional relationship between sponsor and candidate was circumscribed by a number of detailed rules, and several measures discouraged the recommendation of candidates influentially connected.

During the third period, which extended from about 1032 until 1067, most of the enactments—not all—were extensions or modifications of practices that had already been introduced; but while innovation was not so frequent, there was not a decade which lacked important change of some sort in the system. Except in recommendations for the administrative class by local sponsors, quotas were, for most purposes, reduced. Men with more important posts were excluded as candidates. The experiment of making sponsorship compulsory for all promotions at certain ranks was tried and abandoned.[1]

---

[1] It is interesting to compare the chronological distribution of important measures with the total numbers of documents on sponsorship preserved for corresponding periods. There is a certain parallel tendency; for the second period here discussed the average number of documents per annum in *SHY* and *TK* is more than twice that for the first or third periods. It is not impossible, therefore, that the seemingly unequal distribution of important measures represents to some extent an accident of

Is there anything in the conditions of the time that will explain this pattern of growth? I think that at least five factors may have helped to determine the sequence of events: the growth of the governmental structure, the evolution of other personnel practices, the demands of war and financial problems, accidents of dominant political personality, and the natural evolution of the sponsorship system itself.

By the early eleventh century most of the administrative organs of the government were abandoning their earlier variable makeshift character, and one by one assumed the general form and duties which would be theirs during the following sixty or seventy years. As the governmental structure took permanent shape, the body of officials was already well started on the path of expansion which was eventually to present such a problem. The number of Court officials at the accession of T'ai-tsung had doubled by the accession of Chen-tsung, and quintupled by the beginning of Jen-tsung's reign.

Meanwhile, the Peace of Shan-yüan in 1004 had brought a respite from the recurrent wars and skirmishes that had been the lot of the Sung dynasty since its foundation. Except for an occasional border fracas on a limited scale, the period of tranquillity was to last for thirty years. The time immediately after Shan-yüan saw a remarkable number of new measures affecting governmental organization and practice. As a consequence and as a necessary part of the new organizational development, personnel administration attracted increasing attention. In 1006 and 1009 we find the first steps toward the provision of public education outside the capital schools. The numbers recruited through the doctoral examinations had reached a peak of 1,548 for the year 1000, and in 1005 attained the still very considerable number of 817. In 1007 the system of candidates' anonymity was extended to the departmental examinations, and the Bureau of Examination Copyists was established less than a decade later. The increase of the numbers in the service

---

transmission; but it is equally possible that the inequality in number of documents results from a deliberate weeding out of less significant documents by official historians. The parallel between documents and measures is less exact when we compare their quantities over shorter periods. The key years 1007–1011, for instance, actually show many fewer documents annually than the period 1012–1031, or even than 992–1001.

and the rapid recruitment through examination obviously called for more efficient methods of promotion, particularly since a greater number of the incoming men were qualified by training to compete for higher offices. To meet this need no method of promotion but sponsorship gave promise of adequacy, as we have seen: merit ratings constantly tended to become routine, and promotion examinations, eventually to be abandoned except as tests for special qualification, were already in 1004 found to be ineffective as a general method. The recourse to the extension of sponsorship was a logical experiment under the circumstances.

Thus the stage was set for the rapid evolution of the sponsorship system, which reached a climax in the years 1007–1011. But one enigma remains. In the case of the most important document of all, the normative proclamation of 1010, we have no evidence of the discussions that preceded the measure, no direct indication of the special reasons for such action at this time, no reference to the proposer or proposers of the measure. We can only suspect that the impulse came from the dominating personality in the government during this period: WANG Tan.

Less than two years after the Peace of Shan-yüan, he had been elevated from Assisting Civil Councilor of State to Chief Councilor. During the following six years, since no fellow chief councilor was appointed, he held great power. WANG has left in history a somewhat dubious reputation because of his willingness to countenance such absurdities of the unfortunate Chen-tsung as the Heavenly Letter hoaxes. His biography pictures a man not too finical about niceties of form or conduct, and preoccupied rather with the fewer matters that he conceived to be of lasting consequence; none the less a man of basic integrity and much ability. Like some of his predecessors as chief councilor, he felt the recommending of able men to be a special function of his office, and he did it frequently and apparently well. His interest in personnel administration must have been the keener because of his earlier experience as a personnel administrator. He had served at different times as doctoral examination administrator (twice), as associate supervisor of the Bureau of Executory Personnel, and as administrator of the Bureau of Merit Ratings and the Bureau of Administrative Personnel.[2] WANG's

[2] SS,282,7a–18a.

presence on the scene at this time may well have supplied the impetus and the imagination needed for the final step that transformed a useful custom into a system.

The period of continued rapid development corresponds roughly with the era of relative peace following the Shan-yüan agreement. But with the renewal of the ominous and persistent Tangut raids on the western border in 1034, growing to a full-scale war and further complicated by the threat of Khitan intervention, the government was spared little time for long-term administrative experiments. With the gradual termination of the war in 1044, attention was turned to dealing with border raids in the South, disaffections in the conscripted Sung armies, and economic problems greatly aggravated by the war. The focus was still on the immediate situation rather than long range policies. But had it not been so, perhaps the development of sponsorship would have slackened all the same, as the obvious policy variants were tested one by one, and incorporated or rejected. In many respects, the trial of alternative policies had reached what seemed the most workable compromise. When in later years the curtailment of promotions through recommendation became the immediate concern, the need to reconcile this with the requirements of morale placed the personnel administrator in a quandary. And when the venture of making sponsorship a compulsory step for promotion proved unsuccessful, a further limit seemed to impose itself on the scope of the practice. For the time, at least, sponsorship appeared to have reached a natural pause in its evolution.

What had been its real significance? Certainly it had been a remarkable and unique endeavor to increase responsibility in the civil service: responsibility in the act of appointing and promoting officials, and responsible conduct on the part of the officials appointed and promoted. The play of personal influence had been brought into the open, and subjected to rules and standards. The Chinese had long recognized not only that patronage was inevitable, but that it offered actual advantages when practiced with the interests of the state in mind. Long before the Sung that concept had been incorporated into political institutions; the task of the Sung was to expand and develop it further into a vital part of the civil service system. In the running argument between the partisans of a government of laws and those of a government of men, it afforded a ground of compromise, providing a place for both personal judgment and impersonal equity.

The method of competitive examination offered a way of testing abstract reasoning powers and skills that could be formally taught, but it could not foretell how a man would meet the practical challenges that faced an official. Merit ratings attempted to measure energy, zeal, and ability in the actual performance of duties, but were almost inevitably deficient in objectivity. Sponsorship, however, gave greater emphasis to the act of appraising merit, and strengthened the incentives to perform it objectively and responsibly. Thus sponsorship seemed particularly suited to supply the deficiencies of the examination method.

It seems in fact, as we consider the various methods of appointment and promotion described in Chapter V, that, apart from considerations of seniority, the major role was assigned to examinations and sponsorship, in differing forms and combinations. By the middle of the eleventh century, as OU-YANG Hsiu tells us, sponsorship was in actual use for practically all important commissions, great and small, and 80 or 90 per cent of the officials, whatever their rank, had at some time been recommended. Practically all who were permitted to recommend had at some time exercised the privilege.[3]

We have seen the labyrinthine structure of regulations and sanctions with which the sponsoring act was surrounded. No doubt such a structure was needed as a safeguard against abuses. But we may conjecture that the real value of the practice lay simply in the publicity of the act, which appealed to the sponsor's pride and made it possible to create a standard and tradition of good sponsorship. This was strengthened by Confucian precedent, and further assisted by considerations of self-interest, inasmuch as helping an able man won both personal gratitude and public reputation.

The impartiality and honesty with which the system was administered was of course crucial. The extent to which this condition was fulfilled must be judged, unfortunately, almost entirely on the basis of negative evidence. There seems very little complaint that partiality was shown to particular sponsors in processing recommendations, though this must at times have been a factor.[4] Evidence

[3] *OYWC*,107,2b–5a (a discussion of 1045).

[4] The exertion of influence in appointments apart from those through sponsorship occasionally caused preventive action. In addition to cases already mentioned, cf.

of corruption in obtaining recommendations is also rather conspicuously absent.[5] The chief defect in administration of which we have evidence was a passive one: the tendency, mentioned earlier, to overlook at times the enforcement of the guaranty clause.

How should we evaluate the practical success of sponsorship in attaining its objectives? Even after a much more thorough exploration of the political life of this period than has here been possible, one could scarcely hope to isolate the influence of sponsorship from that of other factors and conditions affecting the civil service. But it is at least clear that among these various influences sponsorship was one of the more important and had much to do with the outcome.

Among the most conspicuous complaints concerning officials of this period were low morale and venality, particularly in the lower ranks, traceable in large measure to inadequate pay. Were sponsored men freerer than the average from these defects, as they should have been? We find no answer. As always, contemporary observers were voluble about abuses and shortcomings that affected them adversely; but when or if the system gave a reasonable degree of satisfaction they found no cause for comment.

We have noted the relation between sponsorship and the problem of factionalism at several points in the preceding chapters. The evidence already quoted seems sufficient to establish the fact that sponsorship did in some ways promote factionalism. The effects, however, were discernably of two quite distinct kinds: the effect on the growth of factional groupings in general, and that on the balance of influence between the different factions.

On the one hand, it seems unlikely that the attempts to make recommendations factionally impartial were ever completely successful, and if a candidate were chiefly sponsored by a given faction, his ties to it would be further strengthened. On the other hand, the fairly wide distribution of the recommending power would tend to spread the benefits among different factions, and the favor shown to local sponsors, often men out of favor at the capital, might

---

HCP,106,2a–b; *LPC*,2,10a. On the other hand, we have an instance in which a man sponsored by FAN Chung-yen while a councilor of state failed to receive the suggested promotion because an associate felt the man to be inadequate (*HCP*,144,7a).

[5] Isolated measures against bribery of sponsors (in 962) and falsification of recommendations (1030) have been mentioned above. See Chapter VIII, Notes 7 and 13.

even weigh the balance against the stronger faction. To the extent that appointments to office were automatically governed by fixed numbers of sponsors, sponsorship would inhibit the tendency of the party in power to extend its share of the higher offices. It is conceivable that sponsorship helped to postpone the era of single party dominance until after 1067, though this suggestion can only be offered tentatively.

There remains a final influence of sponsorship that can be stated more confidently: the influence on the quality of the higher government circles. In the histories of the mid-eleventh century, when the government halls of K'ai-feng were notably supplied with able and vigorous men,[6] it is not often that one reads an important official's biography without learning that at some key point in his career he received recognition and advancement through sponsorship. The most famous of these men were not, in general, from families of great prominence. Yet through the combined action of the examination and sponsorship system, many of them reached important positions at a relatively early age.[7]

The qualities of these men reflect the system through which they rose. Nearly all the great statesmen were also famous as writers and scholars. They were men in the humanist tradition, whose interests extended to the whole culture of their time. Practically none of them were really specialists in a single narrow aspect of government activity, such as finance or water control. In this attainment, and this limitation, they displayed not merely the influence of the examination system, but the generally accepted values of the time, which guided the operation of sponsorship as well.

Equally noteworthy was the remarkable number of influential officials that in the mid-eleventh century showed a zeal for the im-

---

[6] It is true that WANG An-shih once said officials had never been more deficient in ability than in his time (1058) (*LCHSWC*,39,2b). This was no doubt partly a rhetorical exaggeration; but seen in the perspective of later times it also exemplifies remarkably the difficulty of judging one's own age.

[7] WANG An-shih became a judicial intendant about the age of thirty-six (TSH:*WCK*, 5,10b), having previously refused several promotions for which he was recommended. HAN Ch'i, of an illustrious family, became a policy-criticism official at about twenty-eight (*AYC*, Chia-chuan, 1,2a). OU-YANG Hsiu, after several reverses in fortune because of his political opinions, became an administrator of the Bureau of Policy Criticism at about thirty-six (*OYWC*:Nien-p'u,7b). See also above, Chapter IV, Notes 18–19; Chapter V, Notes 59–60.

provement of government according to the Confucian standards, and a dedication to their task that often courted political eclipse and adversity rather than yield a principle. We need only to think of men such as FAN Chung-yen, PAO Ch'eng, OU-YANG Hsiu, HAN Ch'i, SSU-MA Kuang, WANG An-shih, or (somewhat later) SU Shih. These men differed and sometimes conflicted, but rather through temperament and in questions of immediate method than through any basic disagreement in their ultimate objectives. Their character was of the kind that the advocates of sponsorship had proposed to encourage, and their attainment of influence was perhaps the chief evidence that sponsorship had not entirely failed in its purpose.

TEXTS ON SPONSORSHIP

TEXTS ON SPONSORSHIP

960 – 1067

The following section presents source references for documents on sponsorship more frequently cited in the previous discussions, and certain selected documents in full and annotated translation.

All the proclamations, memorials, and other documents to be found in *SHY:*HC,27 and 28, for the first five Sung reigns are listed, including, for the sake of completeness, a few dealing only with the sponsorship of military officials. References to location in *SHY* are supplemented by references to variant versions in other sources. Text numbers followed by letters indicate documents not found in the two *chüan* of *SHY* just mentioned. Such documents are included here, however, only when frequently cited in the foregoing discussions. Otherwise they have been fully identified in footnotes at the points of citation.

The texts presented in translation have been selected to illustrate early Sung administrative methods and the character of the sources on which the preceding interpretations have been based. By examining such documents directly or in translation, it is hoped that the reader will more fully sense the manner in which personnel problems were handled, the tone of the measures and discussions, and the varying degree of explicitness and precision in the measures as they have been preserved. For this purpose the reading of text 55 is particularly recommended. The translations may also, by exemplifying the kind of material on which we must base our conclusions, make clearer the limits that bound the attainable certainty of our understanding in this field. In selecting the texts for translation, those already discussed or quoted at length have for the most part been avoided.

Unless otherwise stated, the translation follows the first source cited for a given text. Portions of the translation in square brackets supply interpretation or additional material from other sources, as indicated.

1. *Proclamation of Chien-lung 3rd year* [*962*], *2nd month,* [*2nd day*][1]

Sources: *SHY:*HC,27,1a; *HCP,*3,2a; *TK,*38,4a; *YH,*118,21b; *KMPY,* 962/2; *SCKY,*1,7b; *CYTC,*II,14,7a; *SS,*160,1a-b.

Translation: Han-lin academicians and civil court officials[2] who have formerly served as civil aides or as [lesser] officials in the prefectures or subprefectures shall each recommend one man suitable to be a civil aide, subprefect, or executive inspector.[3] If [the sponsor] have near relatives [who are suitable] selection may also be made from among them. Then set forth all [pertinent facts] in a form of recommendation. On the day of appointment [of a recommended man], further set forth the name and surname of the sponsor. If in office [the recommended man] should prove greedy and sullied, unfair, apprehensive and soft, inert, neglectful of duties, [or] errant in his legal verdicts and evasive, then, weighing the gravity of the case, implicate [the sponsor] in the offense.[4]

Notes: 1. Day supplied by *HCP* and *SCKY*. *YH* and *CYTC* place it in 961, but others agree on 962. 2'. *Ch'ang-ts'an kuan.* Cf. above, Chapter V, note 12. 3. *YH* and *CYTC* observe that this was the first case of sponsorship for these positions (under the Sung, presumably). 4. According to *TK*, implication resulted from the principal's offense or failure to bear out the recommendation.

1a. *Punishment of a Sponsor, Chien-lung 2nd year* [961], *1st month, 13th day*
Sources: *HCP*,2,1a; *KMPY*,962/2.

2. *Adopted Proposal of Kao Hsi,* [962], *8th month,* [10th day][1]
Sources: *SHY:*HC,27,1a; *HCP*,3,9b; *TK*,38,4a; *SS*,160,1b.

Translation: The Left Policy Monitor [2] and Special Drafting Official of the Secretariat KAO Hsi said: Recently there was a proclamation that the officials of the court should each recommend men they know. Apprehensive lest some obtain recommendations by bribery, [your servant] requests that people be permitted to lodge accusations. If they accuse falsely, let them be punished. If their accusation is found to be true, give office to accusers not in the civil service; [3] as to those who have office, I beg that they be liberally encouraged in their appointment; to slaves, neighbors, or relatives who combine to make an accusation, if they are not officials by vocation,[4] give a reward of 500,000 cash. Approved.

Notes: 1. Day supplied by *HCP*. 2. *Tso shih-yi* 左拾遺 . This title became in 988 *tso cheng-yen*. 3. *Pai-shen* 白身 . 4. *Fei shih-huan che* 非仕宦者.

3. *Proclamation of* [*Chien-lung*] *4th year* [963]
Sources: *SHY:*HC,1a; *HCP*,5,12a; *TK*,38,4b; 62,25a.

Note: *HCP* dates this Ch'ien-te 2nd year (964), 7th month, 19th day. The latter *TK* version also places it in 964, while the former agrees with *SHY*.

4. *Proclamation* [*of same date as above?*]
Sources: *SHY:*HC,27,1a; *TK*,38,4b.

5. *Proclamation of Ch'ien-te 2nd year* [964], *7th month,* [21st day]
Sources: *SHY:*HC,27,1b; *HCP*,5,12a; *TK*,38,4b; *CYTC*,II,14,7b.

Note: *HCP* gives day. *TK* gives what seem to be two variant versions, all of whose elements appear in *SHY*. *SHY* gives 45 sponsors, *HCP* 43, and *TK* 42. *CYTC* seems to be a version of the same, but dates it 6th month, and describes rank of sponsors.

6. *Proclamation of [Ch'ien-te] 5th year [967], 3rd month, [15th day]*
   Sources: *SHY:*HC,27,1b; *HCP,*8,5b.
7. *Proclamation [of the same month?]*
   Sources: *SHY:*HC,27,1b; *SS,*160,1b.
8. *Proclamation of K'ai-pao 3rd year [970], 4th month, [24th day]*
   Sources: *SHY:*HC,27,2a; *HCP,*11,5b; *CYTC,*II,14,7b.

Note: Day in *HCP. CYTC* comments that this was the first instance of use for promoting executory officials in titular office (to administrative class?).

9. *Proclamation of [K'ai-pao] 6th year [973], 11th month, [3rd day]*
   Sources: *SHY:*HC,27,2b; *HCP,*14,13b.
10. *Proclamation of T'ai-p'ing-hsing-kuo 6th year [981], 1st month, 6th day*
    Sources: *SHY:*HC,27,2b; *HCP,*22,1a; *TK,*38,6a; *SS,*160,2a.

Note: According to *HCP* this was in response to a memorial of Lü Yüan, who requested that the Emperor should see the candidates in person before appointing them, in view of the importance of their duties.

11. *Proclamation of [981, 1st month], 28th day*
    Sources: *SHY:*HC,27,3a; *HCP,*22,1b; *SS,*160,1b.
11a. *Punishment of a Sponsor, [981], 11th month, 3rd day*
    Sources: *SHY:*CK,64,2a; *HCP,*22,14b; *SS,*276,3b.
12. *Proclamation of [T'ai-p'ing-hsing-kuo] 7th year [982], 6th month, [7th day]*
    Sources: *SHY:*HC,27,3a; *HCP,*23,9b.

Note: The version of *HCP* seems to have an important lacuna after *"ssu-tsui,"* and a misreading of *ssu* 死 for *ssu* 私.

13. *Proclamation of [982], 8th month, 19th day*
    Sources: *SHY:*HC,27,3a and 3b; *HCP,*23,11b.

Note: The text appears twice in *SHY,* with slight variation. The date of the second appearance agrees with that in *HCP,* which also names an additional sponsor.

14. *Proclamation of Yung-hsi 2nd year [985], 1st month, [9th day]*
    Sources: *SHY:*HC,27,3b; *TTHTSL,*32,1a; *TK,*38,6b; *SS,*160,2a.

Note: Day in *TTHTSL,* which also gives the preamble, not found elsewhere.

15. *Proclamation of [Yung-hsi] 4th year [987], 8th month, [5th day]*
    Sources: *SHY:*HC,27,4a; *HCP,*28,7b; *TTHTSL,*41,10b; *TK,*38,6b.
16. *Proclamation of Tuan-kung 2nd year [989], 8th month*
    Source: *SHY:*HC,27,4a.

17. *Proclamation of Shun-hua 1st year [990], 4th month, [9th day]*
   Sources: *SHY*:HC,27,4b; *HCP*,31,4a.
18. *Proclamation of [Shun-hua] 2nd year [991], 9th month*
   Source: *SHY*:HC,27,4b.
19. *Proclamation of [Shun-hua] 3rd year [992], 1st month, [10th day]*
   Sources: *SHY*:HC,27,5a; *HCP*,33,1a.
20. *Proclamation of [992], 2nd month, 3rd day*
   Sources: *SHY*:HC,27,5a; *HCP*,33,1a; *TK*,38,7a.

Note: *TK* differs from both others in dating Tuan-kung 3rd year, but that period had only two years. The versions differ in defining the sponsors.

21. *Proclamation of [992], 4th month*
   Sources: *SHY*:HC,27,5a; *HCP*,33,1a; *TK*,38,7b; *SS*,160,2a.

Note: *HCP* mentions that one source places this in 2nd month, 8th day.

22. *Proclamation of [Shun-hua] 4th year [993], 5th month, 1st day*
   Sources: *SHY*:HC,27,5b; *TK*,38,7b; *SS*,160,2b.

Note: *Wu* 無 presumably a mistake for *wei* 位.

23. *Proclamation of [993], 7th month*
   Sources: *SHY*:HC,27,5b; *HCP*,34,4a.

Note: *HCP* dates this 5th month, 7th *day*.

24. *Proclamation of [993], 8th month [23rd day]*
   Sources: *SHY*:HC,27,5b; *HCP*,34,7b.
25. *Proclamation of [993], 9th month, [21st day], with Commentary on the Case of the Sponsor Lü Yu-chih*
   Sources: *SHY*:HC,27,6a; *HCP*,34,8a; *TK*,38,7b; *SS*,160,2b; 296,15b.
26. *Proclamation of [993], intercalary 10th month, 2nd day*
   Source: *SHY*:HC,27,6a.
27. *Proclamation of [993, intercalary 10th month], 4th day*
   Sources: *SHY*:HC,27,6b; *TK*,38,7a; *SS*,160,2b.

Translation: The way of ruling a state is simply to give its men of excellence their due; the establishment of a sound reputation rests, after all, on the word of those who really know one. Hitherto orders have directed encouragement through recommending, thinking to stimulate those who were obstructed and submerged, but measures of restraint were regarded with disfavor. Men publicly indulge in importuning and make a practice of sycophancy. In former times men were even punished with demotion for factionalism; today men do not tremble to recount it publicly. It is fitting to issue special restrictions so that this may gradually be purified. Henceforth in all recommendations by officials in the capital or elsewhere, there must be set forth the rank and village of the official recommended, as well as the merits and demerits of his official career. Submit this information in detail. Let there be no concealment.

28. *Proclamation of [Shun-hua] 5th year [994], 11th month, [18th day]*
Sources: *SHY*:HC,27,6b; *HCP*,36,16b; *KMPY*,994/11.

Note: Date supplied by *HCP*.

29. *Report of Finance Commission and Proclamation, Chih-tao, 2nd year [996], intercalary 7th month, [2nd day]*
Sources: *SHY*:HC,27,7a; *HCP*,40,6b; *TTHTSL*,78,10b; *CYTC*,II,14,7b.

Note: Day supplied by *HCP* and *TTHTSL*.

30. *Proclamation of Hsien-p'ing, 1st year [998], 6th month, 4th day*
Sources: *SHY*:HC,27,7a; *HCP*,43,5b; *KMPY*,998/6.

Note: *HCP* and *KMPY* add data lacking in *SHY*.

30a. *Proclamation of about 997*
Source: *SS*,199,16a.

31. *Proclamation of [998, 6th month], 8th day*
Sources: *SHY*:HC,27,7a; *HCP*,43,6a.

32. *Proclamation of [998], 12th month*
Sources: *SHY*:HC,27,7a; *KMPY*,998/12.

33. *Proclamation of [998, 12th month], 23rd day*
Source: *SHY*:HC,27,7b.

34. *Proclamation of [Hsien-p'ing] 2nd year [999], 1st month, [10th day]*
Sources: *SHY*:HC,27,7b; *HCP*,44,1a.

Note: Day supplied by *HCP*, which varies slightly in details.

35. *Proclamation of [999], 6th month*
Source: *SHY*:HC,27,7b.

36. *Proclamation of [999], 9th month*
Source: *SHY*:HC,27,7b.

37. *Proclamation of [Hsien-p'ing] 3rd year [1000], 2nd month, [13th day]*
Sources: *SHY*:HC,27,8a; *HCP*,46,8b.

Note: Day supplied by *HCP*.

37a. *Adopted Proposal of Ch'a Tao, [1001, 1st month], 26th day*
Sources: *HCP*,48,2a; *KMPY*,1001/1.

38. *Proclamation of [Hsien-p'ing] 4th year [1001], 3rd month, 4th day*
Sources: *SHY*:HC,27,8a; *HCP*,48,9a.

Note: *HCP* places this on the 3rd day.

39. *Adopted proposal of the Censor of Miscellaneous Affairs Fan Cheng-tz'u, [1001, 3rd month], 11th day*
Sources: *SHY*:HC,27,8a; *HCP*,48,9b.

40. *Proclamation of [1001], 6th month, [14th day]*
Sources: *SHY*:HC,27,8a; *HCP*,49,2a.

41. *Proclamation of [Hsien-p'ing] 5th year [1002], 4th month, [8th day]*
Sources: *SHY*:HC,27,8b; *HCP*,51,16b.

42. *Proclamation of Ching-te 1st year [1004], 7th month*
Source: *SHY*:HC,27,8b.

43. *Proclamation of [1004], 8th month, [17th day]*
Sources: *SHY*:HC,27,8b; *HCP*,57,2b; *CYTC*,II,14,7b.

44. *Proclamation of [1004], 9th month, 9th day*
Sources: *SHY*:HC,27,8b; *HCP*,57,4b.

Note: *SHY* says 72 sponsors, *HCP* says 70.

45. *Proclamation of [1004, 9th month], 28th day*
Sources: *SHY*:HC,27,8b; *TK*,38,8b.

46. *Proclamation of [Ching-te] 2nd year [1005], 11th month, 18th day*
Sources: *SHY*:HC,27,9a; *HCP*,61,21a.

Note: *HCP* places it same day of 12th month.

47. *Proclamation of [1005], 11th month, [4th day]*
Sources: *SHY*:CK,28,1b; *SHY*:HC,27,9a; *HCP*,61,15b.

Note: Second version in *SHY* gives 12th month. Day given by *HCP*.

48. *Case of T'ien Hang, [Ching-te] 3rd year [1006], 5th month*
Source: *SHY*:HC,27,9a.
Translation: The Prefectural Judge of Ning-chou, T'IEN Hang, is made [titular] Executive Assistant of the Court of Imperial Banquets, filling the post of Auxiliary Lecturer in the Directorate of Education.

The Han-lin Lecturer-in-Waiting HSING Ping and others received a proclamation to recommend academic officials. They said that [T'IEN] Hang was fond of study, had good principles of conduct, and was suitable for this selection. He was therefore summoned to the Capital, and the Bureau of Academicians and the Secretariat were ordered to examine him in lecturing on the Three Commentaries [of the Spring and Autumn Annals]. The description of him was confirmed in all respects. Hence this order.

49. *Proclamation of [Ching-te] 4th year [1007], 6th month*
Source: *SHY*:HC,27,9b.

50. *Proclamation of [1007], 7th month, [5th day]*
Sources: *SHY*:HC,27,9b; *HCP*,66,2a; *TK*,38,8b.

51. *Proclamation of* [*1007*], *10th month,* [*12th day*]
    Sources: *SHY:*HC,27,10a; *HCP,*67,3a; *KMPY,* 1007/10.
52. *Proclamation of Ta-chung-hsiang-fu 2nd year* [*1009*], *4th month,*
    2nd day
    Sources: *SHY:*HC,27,10a; *HCP,*71,11a; *TK,*38,8b.

Note: *HCP* and *TK* add important details.

53. *Proclamation of* [*1009, 4th month*], *18th day*
    Sources: *SHY:*HC,27,10a; *SHY:*CK,42,58a; *HCP,*71,15a; *KMPY,*
    1009/4; *SCKY,*3,14a.
54. *Proclamation of* [*Ta-chung-hsiang-fu*] *3rd year* [*1010*], *1st month,*
    [*26th day*]
    Sources: *SHY:*HC,27,10a; *HCP,*73,3a; *YH,*118,21b; *CYTC,*II,14,8a.

Note: Day in *HCP. YH* and *CYTC* say this was the first term of service requirement for sponsorship. But cf. text 52.

55. *Proclamation of* [*1010*], *4th month,* [*9th day*] [1]
    Sources: *SHY:*HC,27,10a; *HCP,*73,12b; *TK,*38,8b; *KMPY,*1010/4;
    *SS,*160,3b.
    Translation: Considering the [difficulties imposed by] geographic
extent and administrative complexity,[2] and pondering how to gain the
assistance of available talents in promoting the welfare of the state, We
wish for the coöperation of all officials in the careful choice of the proper
course of action. Legal measures have not yet been put completely in
force. If we broaden the path of sponsorship, then wrangling [for patron-
age] will be ever increasing; if we sever the sponsorship provision, then
outstanding men will easily be lost. Therefore we must consider an intermediate policy, in order to achieve a suitable system. Let all plan together
that future excesses may be prevented.
    Henceforth at the end of each year let the court officials of the rank of
Han-lin academician and lower sponsor, [accepting equality of offense],
one man each from among the capital and court officials employed elsewhere than in the capital, the military officials of the three echelons, the
civil aides, or the [lower] prefectural and subprefectural officials.[3] [Let the
sponsor] state clearly the [past] administrative conduct [of the candidate],
for what employment he is fitted, and whether he is well known to the
sponsor himself or highly praised by others in general.
    At the proper time let the Palace Postern Office and the Censorate take
note and urge [any delinquent sponsor to make his recommendation]. If
at the end of the year there are any who have not presented their forms
of recommendation, report the facts in a memorial. Fines should be
imposed. If within the period of twelve months [an official required to

recommend] is sent from the capital on a commission, he must first recommend an official, after which he may be allowed to have his parting audience.

[The high military officials] from commandants of the several offices to Imperial warders of the inner hall, who have formerly served as *ch'ien-hsia* or general administrative officials in Ho-pei, Ho-tung, Shàn-hsi, [the Hsi-]ch'uan [circuits], or [the two] Kuang [circuits], shall also [recommend] in conformity with this ruling.

Fiscal intendants and their assistants, judicial intendants, administrators of ordinary and military prefectures and vice-administrators are to recommend, accepting implication in offense, officials within their jurisdiction without numerical limitation. Let them state clearly the administrative accomplishments [of the candidate]. If there are no men worthy of recommendation, or if there are manifest transgressors, that also must be pointed out. It is not permissible to overlook them for any reason. [The report] must reach the capital before the 25th day of the 2nd month of the following year. If there are any who disregard this limit, the General Memorial Acceptance Bureau is instructed to report them by name. The punishment shall be determined according to the "Regulation on non-transmission of annual merit rating lists."

The commissioners and assistant commissioners of finance [may] recommend, accepting implication in offense, capital, court, or military officials occupied with business in the capital.

It is also ordered that the Secretariat shall establish registers. Set forth first the name and title of the man recommended; next the achievements and faults of his official career, the names and surnames of his sponsors, and the number of recommendations [received]. Let one copy [of this register] remain in the Secretariat; one copy shall regularly be sent to the palace on the first day of the fifth month. The following year, record in the registers the faults and achievements [of the candidate] in the meanwhile, and the number of further recommendations. In the case of military officials, the registers shall be kept by the Bureau of Military Affairs.

Whenever those sent out on commission return to the capital, the officials of the Secretariat, Chancellery, Department of Ministries, and Censorate shall inquire concerning good and bad in the administrative work of all officials in the places where they have been or near which they have passed. This should be reported. Whenever fiscal intendants or assistant intendants, judicial intendants, prefectural administrators or vice-administrators come to audience, let each of them prepare a statement of the administrative work, whether able or incompetent, of officials employed under his jurisdiction during his past term. If he has found out any excellence or evil of officials in neighboring prefectures or subprefectures, or those which he has passed, he may add this to his memorial.[4] He shall first deposit it at the Palace Postern Office, after which he may enter for audience.

When the court is in need of men for employment, or there is a disordered prefecture or sub-prefecture with business difficult to [conclude],[5] let a man be selected whose faults and offenses are few and whose recommendations for employment [and] [6] merit in his work are great, and whose career and standing are both suitable; he shall be given the commission. Then in his certificate of office [7] set forth fully the name and surname of the sponsor [or sponsors]. If during one term he show ability to manage affairs successfully, give him a special promotion. If he be not successful in his business, [or] have culpable proclivities,[8] even if he be not deprived of his titular office, remove him to a distant, rustic, and lethargic place.

Let the Secretariat and Bureau of Military Affairs prepare the names of all officials, central or local, who have recommended as many as three capable men, and obtain a directive. [Such sponsors] should receive commendation. As to those who have recommended as many as three men who are incapable, [or who] have been punished short of deprivation of their titular office, let there also be a memorial asking a decision. They should be reproved [and] degraded. If there are reasons both pro and con, let them be balanced.

When the fiscal intendancies of the several circuits or the various ordinary and military prefectures have within their jurisdiction matters as yet outside of the normal classifications, or difficult, necessitating selection by the court of officials to take charge on the spot; or when the Finance Commission or Bureau of Judicial Investigation have unfinished financial or legal business involving repeated examinations and reversal of decisions, so that the prefectures and subprefectures are really incapable of unraveling them, and it is necessary to commission an official from the court; [in all such cases] also select and commission a man from the registers.

Civil aides and [lower] prefectural or subprefectural officials who have served for three or more terms [totaling] seven years or more, and military officials who have been in service for ten or more years, if during their career they have been without private offense and have genuine merit, but have been recommended by no one, may state their case through the office to which they belong. The official in charge is ordered to enquire into the question of their abilities. Officials of the executory class will be examined in law and current affairs, three questions on each. Military officials may,[9] if they wish, be examined on border affairs or law and current affairs. If there are any genuinely worthy of selection, send them [respectively] to the Secretariat or Bureau of Military Affairs, where a final decision will be made after a reinvestigation.

If the Bureau of Executory Personnel or the Bureau of the Three Echelons considers that certain executory or military officials are specially free from fault and clearly characterized by accomplishment, and if their writing, dissertations on short subjects, and general capacity for office truly warrant [higher] employment, [such candidates] too may be sent first to the Secretariat or Bureau of Military Affairs for consultation and detailed inspection, [after which they may] receive a special audience. The number of each shall not exceed ten men annually.[10] It is not permissible to fill the number with younger members of influential families.

High quarters must especially refrain from begging special favors for their relatives in violation of the regular procedure, except on occasions in connection with which there are traditional rules of grace: the birthday of the present Emperor, or the time of the Sacrifice to Heaven, or when [the seeker of a favor] has been sent on some service [involving such a custom].

Notes: 1. Day given in *HCP*. 2. Literally, "the magnitude of the six directions and the complexity of the myriad matters." 3. *SS* prefaces this sentence with the words "In the 3rd year [of Ta-chung-hsiang-fu] the system was first fixed that. . . ." *KMPY* prefaces it with the heading "Established quotas for sponsorship." *SS* reads "Han-lin academician and up," but all other sources read "and down." The reading "equality of offense" (*ping t'ung-tsui chü* 並 同 罪 舉) follows *KMPY. SHY* reads "*t'ung chü*," *HCP* "*ping chü*," *TK* "*ping t'ung chü*." The word "*t'ung*" by itself does not fit the context well, and very probably the original text contained the expression "*t'ung-tsui*," thus incorporating the new rule of liability enacted the previous year. *TK* reads "two men each," but all others say "one." 4. *TK* reads "must" (*hsü* 須), but *SHY, HCP,* and *SS* agree on "may" (*hsü* 許). 5. Reading *liao* 了 follows *HCP* and *TK. SHY* reads *yü* 于 . 6. Following *HCP* and *TK.* 7. *Hsüan-ch'ih* 宣 勅 . 8. *Pen fan* 本犯 . 9. *HCP* reads "must," which does not fit context. 10. It does not seem clear whether or not the limit of ten applies also to the above mentioned men who lack sponsors and themselves apply for consideration.

56. *Proclamation of [Ta-chung] hsiang-fu 4th year [1011], 7th month*
     Source: *SHY:*HC,27,12a.
57. *Adopted Proposal of the [High Court of Justice], [1011], 11th month*
     Source: *SHY:*HC,27,12a.

Note: *HCP,* 76, 15b may refer to the same matter. The proposal in *SHY* came from the "legal court" (*fa ssu* 法寺); that in *HCP* from the "legal officials."

58. *Proclamation of [Ta-chung-hsiang-fu] 5th year [1012], 2nd month,*
     [21st day]
     Sources: *SHY:*HC,27,12b; *HCP,*77,7b.
59. *Proclamation of [1012], 6th month, [26th day]*
     Sources: *SHY:*HC,27,12b; *HCP,*78,3b.

60. *Sealed Memorial and Proclamation, [1012], 7th month, [18th day]*
   Sources: *SHY*:HC,27,12b; *HCP*,78,6b.
61. *Proclamation of [1012], 8th month, 22nd day*
   Sources: *SHY*:HC,27,13a; *HCP*, 78, 11a; *SCKY*,3,15b.

Note: *HCP* says 26th day, but *SCKY* agrees with *SHY*. Cf. a case of the 6th month (*HCP*,78,4b).

62. *Proclamation of [Ta-chung-hsiang-fu] 6th year [1013], 4th month*
   Source: *SHY*:HC,27,13a.
63. *Proclamation of [Ta-chung-hsiang-fu] 7th year [1014], 1st month*
   Source: *SHY*:HC,27,13a.
64. *Adopted Proposal of the Secretariat-Chancellery, [1014], 4th month*
   Source: *SHY*:HC,27,13a. *HCP*,82,11a, gives *SHY* as its source and
agrees with the present *SHY* text.
65. *Proclamation of [1014], 12th month, [4th day]*
   Sources: *SHY*:HC,27,13b; *HCP*,83,17a.
66. *Report of the Secretariat and Resulting Action, [Ta-chung-hsiang-fu]*
      8th year [1015], 1st month, 8th day
   Sources: *SHY*:HC,27,13b; *HCP*,84,2a.

Translation: The Executive Censor FENG Cheng has in response to proclamation recommended the Professor of Imperial Sacrifices and Administrator of Kuei-chou, WANG Chuan, and the Assistant Justice of the High Court of Justice and Police Supervisor of the Superior Prefecture of Ho-nan, CHAO Yü.

The Emperor said: These officials who have been recommended should be given a change a little out of the ordinary. He ordered that both should be shifted in office. [WANG] Chuan was given [the commission of] fiscal intendant or assistant. [CHAO] Yü was given the commission of prefectural vice-administrator. The Chief Councilor WANG Tan said: [WANG] Chuan has, first and last, had sixteen men to sponsor him; his [last] shift of office was moreover three years ago. We may truly act in accordance with the Imperial directive. But CHAO Yü has only recently obtained capital rank; [your servant] should like him to receive only a rise in commission. Henceforth in the recommendation of officials, [your servant] wishes that the number of annual merit ratings [1] and career [of the candidate] should be submitted in the report. The Emperor agreed.

Note: 1. *k'ao ti* 考第 .

67. *Report and Request of the Secretariat and Resulting Action, [1015,*
      1st month,] 23rd day
   Sources: *SHY*:HC,27,14a; *HCP*,84,4b.

Note: *HCP* gives as its source *SHY,* and agrees with it except for insertion of the word "without *great* faults."

68. *Proclamation of [1015], intercalary 6th month*
    Source: *SHY:*HC,27,14a.

69. *Proclamation of [1015], 10th month, [12th day]* [1]
    Sources: *SHY:*HC,27,14b; *HCP*,85,17a.

Translation: Let [the Minister of Finance] [1] FENG Cheng [and those below him on the list] [2] each recommend one man among those at present employed as capital or court officials, who have always been free from rapacity or excesses, to fill [the commission] of administrator or vice-administrator of civil or military prefectures in [the Hsi-] ch'uan and Hsia [-hsi circuits]. If after employment [the principal] should offend through personal participation in rapacity, or should pervert the law with cruel punishments and cause unrest, let [both principal and surety be considered to] share the offense equally. If [the principal] fail to act according to his description in the recommendation, let [the surety] also be implicated in the offense. If [the principal] show manifest diligence and accomplishment, wait until the day of his replacement in his post, [at which time] consider a special promotion for him. If during two successive commissions [the principal] act with notable completeness, let the surety as well receive special commendation.

Before this, someone submitted a sealed memorial saying that when the court selected civil aides and [lower] prefectural and subprefectural officials, those who were sponsored by many [3] received capital [rank] offices; the subprefectures in [Hsi-] ch'uan and Hsia [-hsi] often obtained good public servants, while the prefectural administrators and vice-administrators in those circuits were appointed and sent by the Bureau of Administrative Personnel on the basis of seniority, and there were excessively many aged, infirm, and incapable. Hence this order.

Notes: 1. Supplied by *HCP*. 2. Following *HCP*. *SHY* reads *jih-hsia* 日下.
3. *Chung so pao-chü che* 衆所保舉者.

70. *Proclamation of [Ta-chung-hsiang-fu] 9th year [1016], 3rd month, 18th day*
    Sources: *SHY:*HC,27,14b; *HCP*,86,13b.

Translation: The Reigning Dynasty has frequently proclaimed that those in office should each recommend those whom they know, in order to secure capable material to entrust with affairs and responsibilities, but many have selected irresponsibly, leading the search gravely astray. Although those who commit excesses in their recommendations be punished fittingly and self-interest deserves little leniency, We shall now give still another admonition in order that they may conform fully with the common good. In the case of those who have guaranteed officials under the equal implication in offense clause, when the man sponsored has been guilty of offenses such as personal or illegal rapacity and when it comes to the prosecution of the surety, if there are any cases which stop short of attaint and removal from present employment or deserve pardon or modified demotion, let the Bureau of Judicial Investigation set forth the nature of the case and obtain a directive. Consider the relative gravity of the case, whether it merits demotion in official rank or in commission. If one hear that among officials he has heretofore recommended there are greedy and sullied, he may also confess [and escape punishment]. Henceforth let him manifest just recommendation, with ever earnest care selecting the honest and able; he will not again be among those confessing.

71. *Proclamation of [1016, 3rd month], 21st day*
    Sources: *SHY*:HC,27,14b; *HCP*,86,15a.

72. *Adopted Proposal of a Sealed Memorial, [1016], 8th month, 25th day*
    Sources: *SHY*:HC,27,15a; *HCP*,87,17b.

    Note: *HCP* supplies several corrections to present *SHY* version.

73. *Proclamation of [1016, 8th month], 27th day*
    Source: *SHY*:HC,27,15a.

74. *Sealed Memorial [of same date?]*
    Source: *SHY*:HC,27,15b.

75. *Proclamation of [1016], 10th month, 11th day*
    Sources: *SHY*:HC,27,15b; *HCP*,88,11b.

76. *Proclamation of [1016, 10th month], 28th day*
    Sources: *SHY*:HC,27,16a; *HCP*,88,17b.

77. *Proclamation of [1016], 12th month, [11th day]*
    Sources: *SHY*:HC,27,16a; *HCP*,88,11b.

78. *Proclamation of T'ien-hsi 1st year [1017], 4th month, 5th day*
    Source: *SHY*:HC,27,16a.

79. *[Complaint of the Chief Councilor] Hsiang Min-chung and Others, [1017, 4th month], 25th day*
    Sources: *SHY*:HC,27,16a; *HCP*,89,19a.

80. *Memorial of the [(Titular) Assistant Division Chief of the Ministry of Justice, concurrently] Censor of Miscellaneous Affairs, Provisional Associate Supervisor of the Bureau of Executory Personnel, Lü Yi-chien, and Resulting Proclamation, [1017], 5th month, [25th day]*
    Sources: *SHY*:HC,27,16b; *HCP*,89,22b; *CYTC*,II,14,8a; *YYY*,2,2b.

    Note: Each of the above sources supplies additional or divergent details.

81. *Sealed Memorial of [1017], 6th month, and Resulting Proclamation*
    Sources: *SHY*:HC,27,16b; *HCP*,90,4b.

82. *Rejected Proposal of the Bureau of Military Affairs,* [*1017, 6th month*], *28th day*
   Sources: *SHY:*HC,27,17a; *HCP*,90,4b.
83. *Proclamation of* [*T'ien-hsi*] *2nd year* [*1018*], *2nd month, 23rd day*
   Sources: *SHY:*HC,27,17a; *HCP*,91,6a.
84. *Adopted Proposal of the Bureau of the Three Echelons,* [*1018, 2nd month*]
   Sources: *SHY:*HC,27,17a; *HCP*,91,4a.
85. *Proclamation of* [*1018*], *4th month*
   Sources: ˙*SHY:*HC,27,17b; *HCP*,89,19a; 91,10b.

Note: *HCP* enters this under 1017, 4th month, 28th day, but notes that *SHY* places it under the date above given. The second entry in *HCP* appears to be the same text, in response to the same request, and closer to *SHY* in wording; this is dated 1018, 4th month, 13th day.

86. *Proclamation of* [*1018*], *intercalary 4th month,* [*7th day*]
   Sources: *SHY:*HC,27,17b; *HCP*,91,12b.
87. *Adopted Proposal of the Auxiliary Academician of the Bureau of Military Affairs Wang Hsiao,* [*1018*], *10th month*
   Sources: *SHY:*HC,27,17b; *HCP*,92,12a.
87a. *Punishment of a Sponsor,* [*1019*], *5th month, 9th day*
   Sources: *SHY:*CK,64,25a; *HCP*,93,8b.
88. *Adopted Proposal of the Secretariat,* [*1019*], *10th month,* [*4th day*]
   Sources: *SHY:*HC,27,17b; *HCP*,94,8b; *YH*,118,21b; *CYTC*,II,14,8b.

Note: The two latter sources say this was the first use of five sponsors. *CYTC* dates it 1018, 10th month.

89. *Proclamation of* [*T'ien-hsi*] *4th year* [*1020*], *4th month*
   Sources: *SHY:*HC,27,17b; *HCP*,95,9b.
Translation: Henceforth when officials recommend civil aides and [lower] prefectural and subprefectural officials for promotion to capital and court official [rank], when the official recommended is ready for case review let him not wait until replaced in office; it is ordered that the personnel authorities shall review the achievements and faults of his career, communicate them to the Secretariat, and obtain a directive according to rule. In the case of those permitted to be brought to audience, wait until [the time of] the principal's allocation assemblage, and investigate his faults and offenses during his present term. If he has offended through rapacity or excesses, or private offense punishable by forced labor or more, or if the man has been replaced and dropped from office at an abnormal time because of administrative delinquency, wait especially for further directions. In other cases, inform the Secretariat speedily, and let him be appointed to office. For examinations, it is not permitted to wait for two

or three men [to be ready], but [let the associate supervisor of the Bureau of Executory Personnel] [1] give [the principal] his examination in dissertations on short subjects, review his case, and bring him to audience.

Note: 1. Supplied by *HCP*.

90. *Proclamation of [1020], 9th month, [1st day]*
Sources: *SHY*:HC,27,18a; *SHY*:CK,17,6a; *HCP*,96,10a.

90a. *Punishment of the Sponsors of Chu Neng, [1020, 9th month], 14th day*
Sources: *HCP*,96,12a–b; *SHY*:CK,64,26a.

91. *Proposal of the Associate Supervisor of the Bureau of Executory Personnel Liu Yeh and Resulting Proclamation, [T'ien-hsi] 5th year [1021], 5th month, [11th day]*
Sources: *SHY*:HC,27,18b; *HCP*,97,7a.

Note: The *HCP* version includes an important addition.

92. *Proclamation of Ch'ien-hsing 1st year [1022], 6th month*
Sources: *SHY*:HC,27,19a.

93. *Proclamation of [1022], 10th month*
Source: *SHY*:HC,27,19a.

94. *Adopted Proposal of the Secretariat-Chancellery, T'ien-sheng 1st year [1023], 8th month, [11th day]*
Sources: *SHY*:HC,27,19b; *HCP*,101,1b.

94a. *Punishment of Corrupt Officials, [1023], 11th month*
Sources: *HCP*,101,10b; *KMPY*,1023/11.

95. *Instance of Sponsorship and Resulting Proclamation, [1023], 11th month, 13th day*
Sources: *SHY*:HC,27,19b; *HCP*,101,10b.

96. *Adopted Proposal of the Bureau of Military Affairs, [1023, 11th month], 14th day*
Source: *SHY*:HC,27,19b.

96a. *Punishment of Sponsors, [1024, 1st month], 21st day*
Source: *HCP*,102,1b.

97. *Adopted Proposal of the Investigating Censor Li Hung, [T'ien-sheng] 2nd year [1024], 6th month, [22nd day]* [1]
Sources: *SHY*:HC,27,20a; *HCP*,102,10a; *TK*,38,16b; 39,37b; *YH*, 118,21b; *CYTC*,II,14,8b.

Translation: In recent years, when officials recommend civil aides and [lower] prefectural and subprefectural officials, by rule if [sponsors] reach five or more men, and the principal has served through four or more annual merit ratings, he may obtain a case review and be brought to audience. Among [the candidates] there are some who during their term of service have already been recommended by one or two men, but after their re-placement in office there is delay in transfer [to a new post]. They beg the officials employed in the local places to recommend them, or importune officials who have just obtained commissions in local places, to send up memorials [on their behalf]. [Your servant] hopes that henceforth the fiscal intendants, regulators and intendants of exchange, judicial and agricultural intendants, and their respective assistants, and the adminis-trators and vice-administrators of military and ordinary prefectures, and [military officers serving as] *ch'ien-hsia, tu-chien, ch'ung-pan,* and higher, all shall be ordered to recommend civil aides and [lower] prefectural and subprefectural officials under their own jurisdictions. At the capital those with the rank of higher officials of the Secretariat-Chancellery and above all may sponsor. Court officials and those of court rank [2] in the institutes and libraries who have formerly been employed as prefectural administra-tors or vice-administrators may recommend according to regulation. Other court rank officials [2] who have not passed through commissions as ad-ministrator or vice-administrator of ordinary or military prefectures, or higher, are to be excluded as sponsors. The man recommended must be in present employ [as a subordinate].[3] If as sponsors he has just two men who are fiscal intendants, regulators and intendants of exchange, judicial and agricultural intendants, or their assistants, [the recommendation] should be carried through according to rule. If one recommendation has been made, but there is wanting the [recommendation of the] ordinary or military prefectural administrator or vice-administrator of the place he is employed,[4] wait further until two court officials [2] have guaranteed him, and then request a case review. Furthermore, henceforth if [the candidate] has on his record an offense punishable as severely as forced labor, recom-mendation should be disallowed only in cases of rapacity, private offense, excesses, presumption, and stubborn disobedience. In other cases of private offense resulting from administrative delinquencies punishable up to forced labor, if the character of the matter is not grave, let him also be recom-mended. Approved.

Notes: 1. Day supplied by *HCP. YH* agrees on the year, but *CYTC* dates the text 1019, 6th month. 2. A distinction appears to be made here between *ch'ang-ts'an kuan* (here translated as "court official") and *sheng-ch'ao kuan* (here translated as "court rank official"). See above, Chapter V, note 12. 3. Following *YH.* 4. It does not seem clear whether this official was required in addition to both of the intendant spon-sors, or took the place of one of them. *YH,* which condenses the text into a few lines, omits mention of the prefectural heads as sponsors. See above, Chapter X, note 27. *CYTC* comments that this was the origin of three practices: the require-ment of local experience as vice-administrator or higher in order to sponsor, the restriction of candidates to the sponsors' jurisdiction, and the requirement of in-tendants as sponsors. But see Chapters IX and X above.

97a. *Case of the Candidate Li Chih-ts'ai*
Sources: *YHNWC*,6,1a–2a; *SS*,431,32a; *YNLHP*,3,15a.
98. *Proposal of the Judicial Intendant of Fu-chien Circuit, Wang Keng,
and Others, and Resulting Action, [1024], 8th month, [1st day];
Case of the Following Year*
Sources: *SHY:HC*,27,20b; *HCP*,102,15a.

Translation: When officials recommend for office in response to proclamations, although they may see after they have guaranteed [a man] that he
is sullied with greed, because they are not permitted to confess they are
implicated to the extent of removal from office, along with the principal.
There stems from this much stress on routine procedure, to the detriment
of those of honesty and good reputation. Moreover, the laws of sponsorship under liability of equal offense are somewhat severe; we fear that in
the future officials, fearful of punishment, will find it difficult to recommend. This in turn will lead to much neglect of ability in the lower
stations. We hope that the system will be altered.

It was proclaimed that the Bureau of Judicial Investigation, the
Ministry of Justice, and the High Court of Justice should consult on the
details of the matter and report.

Thereupon they concluded and requested that henceforth whenever one
threw aside restraint and became sullied with greed after having been
promoted because of sponsorship, the original sponsor should be allowed to
prepare a true statement and confess. If the facts confessed were found
to be true, dispose of the case according to law, removing the equal
offense of the sponsor. If the facts confessed were false, there should also
be an investigation of the offense [of calumny].[1] Approved.

In [T'ien-sheng] 3rd year [1025], the Senior Lord of Imperial Banquets
and Administrator of Ju-chou, WANG Hsiao, and others, sponsored under
liability of equal offense the Militia-Command Prefecture Staff Supervisor
of that prefecture, CHAN Hsiang. The Bureau of Executory Personnel
reviewed his case and brought him to audience, and he was given by
proclamation the [titular office of] under-secretary in the Left Secretariat
of the Heir Apparent. Thereupon [WANG] Hsiao confessed that [CHAN]
Hsiang had during his term overstepped in an affair. There was a proclamation that the authorities should investigate. They confirmed [the accusa-
tion], whereupon [CHAN Hsiang] was only selected as official of a small
place.

Note: 1. *HCP* summarizes this provision briefly, giving as source the Reign
Chronicle and the annals (of the National History). It mentions that the monograph
(of the National History) says to "remove the implication if [the facts] were *not*
true."

99. *Proclamation of [T'ien-sheng] 3rd year [1025], 9th month, [27th day]*
Sources: *SHY:*HC,27,21a; *HCP,*103,15a.

100. *Proclamation of [T'ien-sheng] 4th year [1026], 6th month, [4th day]*
Sources: *SHY:*HC,27,21a; *HCP,*104,10b.

101. *Proclamation of [1026], 9th month, [13th day], and Resultant Action*
Sources: *SHY:*HC,27,21a; *HCP,*104,21a; 24b.

102. *Proclamation of [1026], 11th month*
Source: *SHY:*HC,27,21a.

103. *Proclamation of [T'ien-sheng] 5th year [1027], 6th month, [23rd day]*
Sources: *SHY:*HC,27,21b; *HCP,*105,8a.

104. *Proclamation of [1027], 7th month, [5th day]*
Sources: *SHY:*HC,27,21b; *HCP,*105,8b.

105. *Proclamation of [1027], 9th month*
Source: *SHY:*HC,27,21b.

106. *Proclamation of [T'ien-sheng] 6th year [1028], 8th month, [22nd day]*
Sources: *SHY:*HC,27,21b; *HCP,*106,17b.

107. *Proclamation of [1028], 12th month*
Source: *SHY:*HC,27,22a.

107a. *Punishment of a Sponsor, [1028, 12th month], 12th day*
Source: *HCP,*106,22a.

107b. *Punishment of the Sponsors of Ts'ao Li-she, 1029*
Sources: *SHY:*CK,64,28b–29a; *HCP,*107,5b; 9b; *KMPY,*1029/1.

107c. *Punishment of Sponsors, [1029, 5th month, 17th day]*
Sources: *SHY:*CK,64,30a–b;*HCP,*108,3a; *SS,*262,13b–14a.

108. *Proclamation of [T'ien-sheng] 7th year [1029], 9th month, [26th day]*
Sources: *SHY:*HC,27,24b; *HCP,*108,10b.

109. *Proclamation of [1029], 10th month, [21st day]* [1]
Sources: *SHY:*HC,27,24b; *HCP,*108,11b; *TK,*38,11a; *YH,*118,20a; *YYY,*5,10a.

Translation: Let court officials who are fiscal intendants of the several circuits, or administrators of ordinary, military, or industrial prefectures, and [military officials of the rank of] imperial warder of the inner hall or higher, [annually] [2] recommend men from among those at present employed as prefectural inspectors [3] and subprefectural registrars and sheriffs, suitable for promotion to the position of subprefect. Regardless of the number of terms [they have served], those formally qualified [must have served through three annual merit ratings; those not formally qualified] [4] must have served through four or more annual merit ratings. They must be honest, diligent, and capable, free from rapacity or private offense. Fiscal intendants are not to be limited in their number of candidates, but administrators of ordinary, military, and industrial prefectures shall each guarantee one man, under liability of equal offense. If they have as yet no man suitable for recommendation, they may continue to examine carefully and make enquiry, and report later. They may not sponsor their relatives. Court officials who have been replaced are excluded from the sponsors. When an official has been recommended by two men, send [his name] to the Bureau of Executory Personnel, which shall move and inscribe him in a place nearby with a vacancy for subprefect. If [the candidate in his new] employment is without offense of rapacity, and any administrative delinquency or private offense is of rather unimportant character; if he is able to settle legal cases without deviation from the law or excesses; and if his method of collecting taxes stops short of pressing and annoying; then the ordinary, superior, military, or industrial prefecture having jurisdiction shall prepare and report the facts of the case.[5] The day the man is replaced he shall be promoted [under such circumstances] to civil aide and again administer a subprefecture. If at the expiration of [a proper number of] annual merit ratings he is as before without offense of rapacity (although he may have an administrative delinquency or private offense of unimportant nature), and if the rest is as above stated, wait until he comes to court, bring him to audience, and specially confer on him a [titular] capital office. [Thereupon, for successive terms he is given dispensation from placement selection. For men recruited through qualification by contribution or transfer from the clerical service and becoming subprefects, the number of annual merit ratings and sponsors is increased in all cases.] [6]

Notes: 1. Day supplied by *HCP*. *YYY*, however, places the action in the intercalary 2nd month, 15th day, of this year. 2. Supplied by *HCP*. 3. *HCP* reads *p'an-kuan* 判官 for *p'an-ssu* 判司 , presumably an error. 4. This passage, found in *HCP* and *YYY*, was apparently dropped by error in *SHY*. 5. *Ch'ing* 請 in *SHY* seems an error. 6. *HCP* adds here the following comment: "Previously, the Bureau of Executory Personnel brought in the executory men for parting audience. Any aged and septuagenarian were made subprefect. The Emperor said to the Chief Councilors that the responsibilities of the subprefect include the people and the altars. The penal administration of the whole locality, severe or lenient, is entirely in his hands. If he is not up to his duty, the damage will not be trifling. Even for a secluded prefecture in a distant place, we should all the more select our men, to manifest the right intentions of the court. If we have this kind, all confused septuagenarians, to oversee the people, there will necessarily come the evils of avarice and futility. At this time, a proposal was submitted requesting the appointment of subprefects through sponsorship, whereupon this proclamation was issued." *HCP* indicates as its source for this passage the *Cheng-yao* 政要 of CHANG T'ang-ying 張唐英 , probably the *Chün-ch'en* 君臣 *cheng-yao* of that author in 40 ch., mentioned in *SS*, 203,15a; *YH*, 49,8b. He lived 1029–1071 (*YNLHP*). *YYY* comments that by the provision of this proclamation the candidate will have passed two terms and six annual merit ratings as subprefectural administrator after recommendation. *TK* and *YH* also mention that under Jen-tsung the service requirement was again raised from four years to six, but give no year. *TK* adds that one year more would be added for men guilty of a private offense.

110. *Adopted Proposal of the Secretariat-Chancellery,* [*1029*], *12th month*
      Sources: *SHY*:HC,27,25a; *YH*,118,21b; *CYTC*,II,14,8a.
111. *Adopted Proposal of the Executive Censor and Provisional Supervisor of the Bureau of Executory Personnel Wang Sui,* [*T'iensheng*] *8th year* [*1030*], *10th month, 28th day* [1]
      Sources: *SHY*:HC,27,25a; *HCP*,109,13a.

Translation: When civil and military officials at the capital recommend civil aides and [lower] prefectural and subprefectural officials for capital office, the memorial forms are often without a seal identification, so that it is difficult to distinguish the genuine from the false. [Your servant] requests that henceforth in recommendations for office the old form of memorial should be used, and it must be sealed. If the place of business lacks a seal, borrow and use a seal from an office that is not legal or financial; then in the margin at the place giving the year and month of the memorial paste a slip of yellow paper stating that the seal of such-and-such place was used. The yellow slip also must have a seal [identification].[2] Then [the memorial] may be deposited at the Palace Postern Office. The thing to be stressed is that at all times there must be validation. Approved.

Notes: 1. *HCP* places this under the 23rd day. 2. Following *HCP*. For *chi* 記 *SHY* reads *ch'i* 訖 .

112. *Proclamation of* [*T'ien-sheng*] *9th year* [*1031*], *2nd month, 23rd day*
      Sources: *SHY*:HC,27,25b; *HCP*,110,3a.
113. *Proclamation of* [*1031*], *10th month, 21st day*
      Sources: *SHY*:HC,27,25b; *HCP*,110,15a.
114. *Proclamation of Ching-yu 1st year* [*1034*], *5th month, 1st day*
      Sources: *SHY*:HC,27,25b; *HCP*,114,14a.
115. *Proclamation of* [*Ching-yu*] *2nd year* [*1035*], *10th month, 18th day*
      Source: *SHY*:HC,27,25b.
115a. *Punishment of a Sponsor*
      Sources: *PHSKTY*,4,76b; *SS*,298,15b; *SSYi*,30,2a.

116. *Proposal of the Supervisor of the Census Office in the Finance Commission, Kuo Chen, and Resulting Proclamation, Pao-yüan 3rd year [1040], 2nd month, 21st day*
Sources: *SHY*:HC,27,26a; *HCP*,126,12a.

117. *Proclamation of K'ang-ting 1st year [1040], 12th month, 23rd day*
Sources: *SHY*:HC,27,26a; *HCP*,129,10b.

Note: *HCP* enters this under 22nd day.

118. *Proclamation of [K'ang-ting] 2nd year [1041], 6th month, 29th day*
Source: *SHY*:HC,27,26b.

Translation: In the recommendation of civil aides and [lower] prefectural and subprefectural officials, [according to the present rule] civil officials of the rank of academician-in-waiting or higher may annually recommend three men; censors of miscellaneous affairs or higher, two men; general censors or lower, one man. Military officials of the rank of regional supervisor or higher [may annually recommend] three men; Palace Postern commandants or higher, two men; commandants of the several offices or lower, one man. Fiscal intendants and assistant intendants, and judicial intendants, as previously are without numerical restriction. For each man the name of only one surety is put. Henceforth, civil officials who are administrators of ordinary or military prefectures, or vice-administrators, from [the lowest] court rank and up; and military officials who are administrators of ordinary or military prefectures, of the rank of imperial warder of the inner hall or higher; all may annually recommend three men. Prefectural judges and staff supervisors of the Superior Prefecture of K'ai-feng, following the rule for prefectural administrators and vice-administrators, annually sponsor three men each from their jurisdictions. At the capital, civil officials of the rank of censor of miscellaneous affairs or higher, and military officials of the rank of regional supervisor or higher, may each annually recommend two men; other court officials at the capital may not recommend for office, but if their forms of recommendation have already reached the Secretariat, they may be carried through nevertheless.

119. *Proclamation of the same month*
Sources: *SHY*:HC,27,27a; *HCP*,132,22a.

Note: *HCP* dates this 28th day, earlier than text 118.

120. *Proclamation of Ch'ing-li 3rd year [1043], 5th month, 22nd day*
Sources: *SHY*:HC,27,27a; *HCP*,141,13b.

Note: *HCP* quotes the *SHY* text verbatim, but dates it 25th day. *HCP* notes that this text does not appear in the Reign Chronicle, but the matter to which the text alludes occurs in a memorial of FAN Chung-yen in *CFTY*. There is, however, no indication whether or not that memorial was approved in full.

120a. *Proposal of Han Ch'i and Fan Chung-yen,* [*1043, 5th month*]
Sources: *HCP*,141,12b–13b; *CFTY*,1,17a; 22a.

120b. *Proposal of Fan Chung-yen and Fu Pi,* [*1043, 9th month*], *3rd day*
Sources: *HCP*,143,1b–4a; 7b–8a; *KMPY*,1043/9; *CFTY*,1,1b.

120c. *Action on Proposal of Fu Pi and Fan Chung-yen,* [*1043, 10th month*], *12th day*
Sources: *HCP*,144,5a–6a; *KMPY*,1043/10.

120d. *Proclamation of* [*1043, 10th month*], *28th day*
Sources: *HCP*,144,8b–9b; *KMPY*,1043/10; *SCKY*,5,13b; *SS*,160,22b; *CFTY*,1,39a.

120e. *Proposal of Policy-Criticism Officials and Resulting Proclamation,* [*1044, 4th month*], *6th day*
Source: *HCP*,148,6a.

120f. *Punishment of a Sponsor,* [*1043, 7th month*], *3rd day*
Sources: *SHY:CK*,64,43a; *HCP*,142,1a–2a; *TTSL*,64,3b; *SS*,294,7a–b; *LPC*,14,3a; *OYWC*,98,7a; 100,6b.

121. *Proclamation of* [*Ch'ing-li*] *4th year* [*1044*], *4th month, 26th day*
Sources: *SHY:HC*,27,27a; *HCP*,148,16a.

122. *Proclamation of* [*1044*], *7th month, 29th day*
Sources: *SHY:HC*,27,27b; *HCP*,151,5b; *SCKY*,6,1b.

Note: *HCP* adds further details. This measure was prompted by a memorial of FAN Chung-yen.

123. *Proclamation of* [*Ch'ing-li*] *5th year* [*1045*], *2nd month*
Sources: *SHY:HC*,27,27b; *HCP*,154,8b.

124. *Proclamation of* [*1045*], *8th month, 23rd day*
Sources: *SHY:HC*,27,28a; *HCP*,157,3b.

125. *Proclamation of* [*1045*], *10th month, 13th day*
Source: *SHY:HC*,27,28a.

126. *Proclamation of* [*Ch'ing-li*] *6th year* [*1046*], *10th month, 22nd day*
Sources: *SHY:HC*,27,28a; *HCP*,159,8a.

127. *Proclamation of* . . . *8th month, 6th day*
Source: *SHY:HC*,27,28b.

Note: The year of this measure is not clear.

127a. *Proclamation of* [*1050, 6th month*], *15th day*
Sources: *HCP*,168,13a; *TK*,38,16b; *KMPY*,1050/6; *YYY*,5,10a; *CKFC*,42,9a.

Note: *CKFC* misprints Yüan-yu for Huang-yu period, but date is otherwise the same. *KMPY* says that quotas were set according to the number of prefectures in a given circuit.

128. *Proposal of the Chief Councilor Wen Yen-po, and Resulting Action,* [*1051, 5th month*], *21st day*

Sources: *SHY*:HC,27,28b; *HCP*,170,13b–14a.

Translation: [1] The Chief Councilor WEN Yen-po and others said: Your servants heard you remark at an audience that the officials at court were addicted to wrangling for preferment. Unless this could be discouraged, no sound usage could be established. If those who quietly and retiringly adhere to principle were rather singled out for appointment, those who wrangled in their restless seeking might in some degree be shamed. [Your servants] venture to note that the [titular] Division Chief in the Ministry of Works and Auxilliary Official of the Institute of History, CHANG Huai, has had no case review for over ten years. The court praises his quiet reticence; he was once specially transferred to the post of fiscal intendant of the Liang-che circuit, and on replacement and return was commissioned administrator of Ying-chou. He has, however, never called attention to himself [when he was entitled to] on grounds of seniority. The [titular] Executive Assistant in the Department of Palace Services, WANG An-shih, was number four on the list of doctors in letters of his year; by old rules at the expiration of one term he should have submitted a sample of his work and sought examination for institute assignment. But [WANG] An-shih for a number of terms has not called attention to himself. Even when the court specially ordered a summons examination for him, he declined because of the poverty and age of his parents. While assignment in the institutes and libraries is the ambition of [most] scholars, [WANG] An-shih quietly preserves his integrity, and it has not been easy for him to get much. The Judicial Investigator of the High Court of Justice, HAN Wei, once was presented for an important post in the Department of Ministries; thereafter, for five or six years he has not been in service. He is a lover of antiquity, thirsty for learning, and satisfied with tranquil retirement. For all, [your servants] ask the special bestowal of a distinguished appointment.

By proclamation there was bestowed on [CHANG] Huai the garb of the third grade. [WANG] An-shih was summoned to court, and special directive was to be obtained after an examination. It was ordered that [HAN] Wei be given an examination in the Bureau of Academicians. Both [WANG] An-shih and [HAN] Wei declined and did not appear.

Note: The translation follows the *HCP* version, which is fuller. *HCP* also supplies some additional notes, not translated.

129. *Proclamation of* [*1051*], *6th* [*month, 16th day*]

Sources: *SHY*:HC,27,28b; *HCP*,170,15b.

Note: Date follows *HCP*. *SHY* reads 6th year. *HCP* supplies other corrections.

130. *Proclamation of [1051], 10th month, [8th day]*
Sources: *SHY*:HC,27,28b; *HCP*,171,8b.

131. *Proclamation of [Huang-yu] 4th year [1052], 8th month, [24th day]*
Sources: *SHY*:HC,27,28b; *HCP*,173,7b.

132. *Proclamation of [1052, 8th month, 27th day]*
Sources: *SHY*:HC,27,28b; *HCP*,173,7b.

133. *Proclamation of [Huang-yu] 5th year [1053], 7th month, 13th day*
Sources: *SHY*:HC,27,29a; *HCP*,175,1a.

Note: *HCP* supplies additional details; it dates the measure 12th day.

134. *Proclamation of [1053], 10th month, 7th day*
Source: *SHY*:HC,27,29a.

135. *Adopted Proposal of the General Censor Wu Shih, Chih-ho 2nd year
[1055], 2nd month, 15th day*
Sources: *SHY*:HC,27,29a; *HCP*,178,4a.

Note: *HCP* places under 7th day.

136. *Proclamation of [1055], 11th month, [8th day]*
Sources: *SHY*:HC,27,29a; *HCP*,181,12a.

136a. *Punishment of Pao Ch'eng as Sponsor, [1055, 12th month], 7th day*
Sources: *SHY*:CK,65,14a; *HCP*,181,14a; *SS*,316,3a; *PHSKTY*, Chuan-
chi, 4b–5b.

137. *Adopted Proposal of the Bureau of Executory Personnel of the
Ministry of Personnel, Chia-yu 1st year [1056], 2nd month, [29th
day]*
Sources: *SHY*:HC,27,29b; *HCP*,182,3b.

138. *Proclamation of [Chia-yu] 2nd year [1057], 5th month*
Sources: *SHY*:HC,27,29b; *HCP*,185,12a.

139. *Proclamation of [1057], 7th month*
Source: *SHY*:HC,27,29b.

140. *Adopted Proposal of the Bureau of Military Affairs, [1057], 9th
month, [12th day]*
Sources: *SHY*:HC,27,29b; *HCP*,186,9b.

141. *Proclamation of [1057], 12th month, [11th day]*
Sources: *SHY*:HC,27,30a; *HCP*,186,14b.

Note: *HCP* adds explanatory material.

142. *Proclamation of [Chia-yu] 4th year [1059], 6th month, 11th day*
Sources: *SHY*:HC,27,30a; *HCP*,189,22a.

143. *Adopted Proposal of the Academician-in-Waiting of the T'ien-chang
Pavilion and Administrator of the Bureau of Policy Criticism,
T'ang Chieh, [1059], 8th month, 2nd day*
Source: *SHY*:HC,27,30a.

144. *Adopted Proposal of the Bureau of Executory Personnel of the Ministry of Personnel, [Chia-yu] 5th year [1060], 8th month, [9th day]*
Sources: *SHY*:HC,27,30b; *HCP*,192,6a.

Note: According to *HCP*, this was not promulgated as an order until 1066, 4th month.

145. *Proclamation of [Chia-yu] 6th year [1061], 8th month*
Source: *SHY*:HC,27,30b.

146. *Proclamation of [Chia-yu] 8th year [1063], 10th month*
Source: *SHY*:HC,27,30b.

147. *Adopted Proposal of the Bureau of Military Affairs, Chih-p'ing 1st year [1064], 2nd month*
Source: *SHY*:HC,28,1b.

148. *Proclamation of [1064], 9th month, 23rd day*
Source: *SHY*:HC,28,2a.

149. *Proclamation of [1064], 10th month, 4th day*
Source: *SHY*:HC,28,2a.

150. *Proposal of the Executive Censor Chia Yen, [Chih-p'ing] 2nd year, 3rd month, 24th day*
Source: *SHY*:HC,28,2b.

151. *Proclamation [in Response to Proposal of Chia Yen], [1065],4th month, 12th day*
Sources: *SHY*:HC,28,2b; *HCP*,204,21a; *TK*,38,16b; *YH*,118,20a–b; *SS*,160,6a.

152. *Proclamation of [Chih-p'ing]3rd year [1066], 4th month, [29th day]*
Sources: *SHY*:HC,28,3b; *HCP*,208,4a–b; *TK*,38,17a; *YH*,118,20b; *SS*,160,6b.

152a. *Proclamation of [1066], 10th month, 13th day*
Sources: *HCP*,208,15b–17a; *TK*,38,17b–18a; *KMPY*,1066/10; *SCSS*, 9,148.

153. *Adopted Proposal of the Associate Supervisor of the Bureau of Executory Personnel of the Ministry of Personnel, [Chih-p'ing] 4th year [1067], 11th month*
Sources: *SHY*:HC,28,4b; *HCP*,208,4b–5b; *TK*,38,17a; *SS*,13,6b; 160,6b.

Note: The date given by *SHY* would place this measure after the death of Ying-tsung. But both *HCP* and *SS*, 13, place it in 1066, 5th month, 11th day, and *SHY* only mentions the accession of Shen-tsung under the following entry. While *HCP* ascribes its version to the *Hui-yao* it is much fuller than that now found in *SHY*.

APPENDIX A

CHRONOLOGICAL OUTLINE

This tabulation is limited to dynasties, reigns, and a few important individuals mentioned elsewhere in this book. Dates following the names of rulers are, unless otherwise stated, those of their reigns. Dates following other persons are those of their lives.

Chou Dynasty (1122?–256 B.C.)
     KUAN Chung (7th century B.C.)
     Confucius (551–479 B.C.)
Han Dynasty (202 B.C.–9 A.D., 25–220 A.D.)
     Emperor Hsiao-wen (180–157 B.C.)
     Emperor Hsiao-wu (141–87 B.C.)
        TUNG Chung-shu
Sui Dynasty (581–618 A.D.)
     Emperor Wen (YANG Chien) (581–604)
T'ang Dynasty (618–907)
     Empress Wu (exercised authority 684–705)
Five Dynasties (907–960)
   North China
   Latter T'ang (923–936)
   Latter Chou (951–960)
   Northern Han (951–979)
   South China
   Southern P'ing (Ching-nan) (907–963)
   Latter Shu (925–965)
   Southern Han (905–971)
   Southern T'ang (937–975)
   Wu and Yüeh (893–978)
Sung Dynasty (960–1279)
     Emperor T'ai-tsu (CHAO K'uang-yin): Born 927, 2nd month, 16th day; proclaimed the Sung establishment 960, 1st month, 5th day; died 976, 10th month, 20th day.
     Emperor T'ai-tsung: Born 939, 10th month, 7th day; acceded 976, 10th month, 21st day; died 997, 3rd month, 29th day.
     Emperor Chen-tsung: Born 968, 12th month, 2nd day; acceded 997, 3rd month, 29th day; died 1022, 2nd month, 19th day.

Emperor Jen-tsung: Born 1010, 4th month, 14th day; acceded 1022, 2nd month, 19th day; died 1063, 3rd month, 29th day.

Emperor Ying-tsung: Born 1032, 1st month, 3rd day; acceded 1063, 4th month, 1st day, died 1067, 1st month, 8th day.

Emperor Shen-tsung: Born 1048, 4th month, 10th day; acceded 1067, 1st month, 8th day; died 1085, 3rd month, 5th day.

Southern Sung (1127–1279)

Yüan Dynasty (Mongol) (1260–1371)

Ming Dynasty (1368–1662)

Ch'ing Dynasty (Manchu) (1644–1911)

APPENDIX B

THE PROTOCOL LIST OF 1038

The following list shows the early Sung titular and honorary offices and assignments according to their priority in rank, beginning with the highest. The exact order of offices was altered from time to time; the order here shown is that fixed by the Palace Postern Office for purposes of protocol in the 8th month of 1038 (cf. *SHY*:YC,3,16b–19b. With minor variations this corresponds to that found in *SS*,168,1a–5a, and there described as "after 960," as distinguished from that "after 1078." The list of 962, *SHY*:YC,3,1a–2a, however, differed in a number of respects.) With a few exceptions, neither commissions nor titles of nobility or prestige, dignities, or other honorific appellations appear in the list. While the order gives both civil and military officials, only those of the latter more frequently mentioned in this book will be included in this appendix. The alphabetical groupings have been added for convenience only.

A

Secretary-general of the Secretariat (chief councilor) *Chung-shu ling* 中書令

Chancellor (chief councilor) *Shih-chung* 侍中

First privy councilor (chief councilor) *T'ung Chung-shu Men-hsia p'ing-chang-shih* 同中書門下平章事

Titular councilor *Shih-hsiang* 使相

Presiding minister *Shang-shu ling* 尚書令

Grand preceptor *T'ai shih* 太師

Grand marshal *T'ai wei* 太尉

Grand tutor *T'ai fu* 太傅

Grand protector *T'ai pao* 太保

Grand instructor *Ssu-t'u* 司徒

Grand master of works *Ssu-k'ung* 司空

B

Commissioner of military affairs *Shu-mi shih* 樞密使

Administrator of the Bureau of Military Affairs *Chih Shu-mi-yüan shih* 知樞密院事

Second privy councilor (assisting civil councilor of state) *Ts'an-chih-cheng-shih* 參知政事

Assistant commissioner of military affairs *Shu-mi fu-shih* 樞密副使

Coadministrator of the Bureau of Military Affairs *T'ung chih Shu-mi-yüan shih* 同知樞密院事

Signatory official of the Bureau of Military Affairs *Ch'ien-shu Shu-mi-yüan shih* 簽書樞密院事

C

Grand preceptor, grand tutor, grand protector of the heir apparent *T'ai-tzu t'ai-shih, t'ai-fu, t'ai-pao* 太子太師太傅太保

Right and left executives of the Department of Ministries *Tso, yu p'u-yeh* 左右僕射

Junior preceptor, junior tutor, junior protector of the heir apparent *T'ai-tzu shao-shih, shao-fu, shao-pao* 太子少師少傅少保

Governor of an ordinary or superior prefecture *Chou, fu mu* 州府牧

Censor-in-chief *Yü-shih ta-fu* 御史大夫

D

Minister of personnel, war, finance, justice, rites, or works *Shang-shu* 尚書
Li, ping, hu, hsing, li, kung 吏兵戶刑禮工

Executives of the Chancellery and Secretariat *Men-hsia, Chung-shu shih-lang* 門下中書侍郎

Regional commandant *Chieh-tu-shih* 節度使

E

Academician of the Wen-ming Hall *Wen-ming-tien hsüeh-shih* 文明殿學士

Senior academician of the Tzu-cheng Hall *Tzu-cheng-tien ta-hsüeh-shih* 資政殿大學士

Finance commissioner *San-ssu-shih* [1] 三司使

Han-lin academician for the transmission of directives *Han-lin hsüeh-shih ch'eng-chih* 翰林學士承旨

Han-lin academician *Han-lin hsüeh-shih* 翰林學士

Academician of the Tzu-cheng Hall *Tzu-cheng-tien hsüeh-shih* 資政殿學士

Academician of the Tuan-ming Hall *Tuan-ming-tien hsüeh-shih* 端明殿學士

Han-lin reader-in-waiting and Han-lin lecturer-in-waiting *Han-lin shih-tu, shih-chiang hsüeh-shih* 翰林侍讀侍講學士

Academician of the Lung-t'u Pavilion *Lung-t'u-ko hsüeh-shih* 龍圖閣學士

Auxiliary academician of the Bureau of Military Affairs *Shu-mi chih hsüeh-shih* 樞密直學士

Auxiliary academician of the Lung-t'u Pavilion *Lung-t'u-ko chih hsüeh-shih* 龍圖閣直學士

F

Left and right general policy advisers *Tso, yu san-ch'i-ch'ang-shih* 左右散騎常侍

Chief councilor of the heir apparent *T'ai-tzu pin-k'o* 太子賓客

Senior lord of Imperial Sacrifices *T'ai-ch'ang ch'ing* 太常卿

Senior lord of the Court of Imperial Family Affairs *Tsung-cheng ch'ing* 宗正卿

Executive censor *Yü-shih chung-ch'eng* 御史中丞

Left and right executive assistants of the Department of Ministries *Tso, yu ch'eng* 左右丞

Vice-minister *Chu hang shih-lang* 諸行侍郎

Deputy regional commandant and supervisor *Chieh-tu-kuan-ch'a liu-hou* 節度觀察留後

G

Reviewing policy adviser *Chi-shih-chung* 給事中

Left and right policy critic-advisers *Tso, yu chien-yi-ta-fu* 左右諫議大夫

Drafting official of the Secretariat *Chung-shu she-jen* 中書舍人

Special drafting official of the Secretariat *Chih-chih-kao* 知制誥

Academician-in-waiting of the Lung-t'u Pavilion *Lung-t'u-ko tai-chih* 龍圖閣待制

---

[1] The exact relation of this office to the two above was variable.

Academician-in-waiting of the T'ien-chang Pavilion *T'ien-chang-ko tai-chih* 天章閣待制

Regional supervisor *Kuan-ch'a shih* 觀察使

H

Director of the Imperial Library *Pi-shu chien* 祕書監

Senior lord of the Imperial Banquets *Kuang-lu ch'ing* 光祿卿

Senior lord of the Imperial Insignia *Wei-wei ch'ing* 衛尉卿

Senior lord of the Imperial Stables *T'ai-p'u ch'ing* 太僕卿

Lord chief justice, High Court of Justice *Ta-li ch'ing* 大理卿

Senior lord of diplomatic reception *Hung-lu ch'ing* 鴻臚卿

Senior lord of agricultural supervision *Ssu-nung ch'ing* 司農卿

Senior lord of the Imperial Treasury *T'ai-fu ch'ing* 太府卿

Director of Education *Kuo-tzu chi-chiu* 國子祭酒

Director of the Department of Palace Services *Tien-chung chien* 殿中監

Director of Imperial Workshops *Shao-fu chien* 少府監

Director of construction *Chiang-tso chien* 將作監

Commandant of the Ching-fu Hall *Ching-fu-tien shih* 景福殿使

Hospitality commandant *K'o-sheng shih* 客省使

Metropolitan prefects of K'ai-feng, Ho-nan, and Ying-t'ien *K'ai-feng, Ho-nan, Ying-t'ien yin* 開封河南應天尹

Superintendent of the household of the heir apparent *T'ai-tzu chan-shih* 太子詹事

Princely tutor *Chu wang fu* 諸王傅

Director of astronomical observations *Ssu-t'ien chien* 司天監

I

Left and right chief secretaries of the heir apparent *T'ai-tzu tso, yu shu tzu* 太子左右庶子

Usher commandant *Yin-chin-shih* 引進使

Regional defense commandant *Fang-yü-shih* 防禦使

Militia commandant *T'uan-lien-shih* 團練使

Assistant finance commissioners in charge of salt and iron, funds and census *San-ssu yen-t'ieh, tu-chih, hu-pu fu-shih* 三司鹽鐵度支戶部副使

J

Junior lords of Imperial Sacrifices and the Court of Imperial Family Affairs *T'ai-ch'ang, tsung-cheng shao-ch'ing* 太常宗正少卿

Vice-director of the Imperial Library *Pi-shu shao-chien* 祕書少監

Junior lords of the seven Courts, of Imperial Banquets, etc. *Kuang-lu teng ch'i ssu shao-ch'ing* 光祿等七寺少卿

Commandant of general comity *Ssu-fang-kuan shih* 四方館使

Vice-director of education *Kuo-tzu ssu-yeh* 國子司業

Vice-director of the Department of Palace Services *Tien-chung shao-chien* 殿中少監

Vice-director of Imperial Workshops *Shao-fu shao-chien* 少府少監

Vice-director of construction *Chiang-tso shao-chien* 將作少監

Metropolitan vice-prefects of K'ai-feng, Ho-nan, and Ying-t'ien *K'ai-feng, Ho-nan, Ying-t'ien shao-yin* 開封河南應天少尹

Vice-superintendent of the household of the heir apparent *T'ai-tzu shao-chan-shih* 太子少詹事

Left and right chief advisers of the heir apparent *T'ai-tzu tso, yu yü te* 太子左右諭德

Master of the palace services to the heir apparent *T'ai-tzu chia-ling* 太子家令

Master of the guards of the heir apparent *T'ai-tzu shuai keng ling* 太子帥更令

Master of the stables of the heir apparent *T'ai-tzu p'u* 太子僕

Prefect of an ordinary prefecture *Chu chou t'zu-shih* 諸州刺史

Superintendent and vice-superintendent of a princely household *Chu wang fu chang-shih, ssu-ma* 諸王府長史司馬

Vice-director of astronomical observations *Ssu-t'ien shao-chien* 司天少監

K

General transmitter of directives in the Bureau of Military Affairs *Shu-mi tu-ch'eng-chih* 樞密都承旨

Commandants of the [East and] West Upper Posterns [*Tung-shang*] *hsi-shang ho-men-shih* 東上 西上閤門使

Transmitter of directives in the Bureau of Military Affairs *Shu-mi ch'eng-chih* 樞密承旨

Assistant general transmitter of directives in the Bureau of Military Affairs *Shu-mi fu tu ch'eng-chih* 樞密副都承旨

L

Chancellery Imperial Recorders *Ch'i-chü lang* 起居郎

Secretariat Imperial Recorders *Ch'i-chü she-jen* 起居舍人

Censor of miscellaneous affairs *Chih-tsa yü-shih* 知雜御史

Office chief and division chief in the Department of Ministries *Chu hang lang-chung* 諸行郎中

Commandants of the several offices, beginning with the commandant of the Imperial Palace *Huang-ch'eng yi-hsia chu ssu shih* 皇城以下諸司使

Assistant transmitter of directives in the Bureau of Military Affairs *Shu-mi-yüan fu-ch'eng-chih* 樞密院副承旨

Assistant transmitters of directives of the several sections of the Bureau of Military Affairs *Shu-mi-yüan chu fang fu-ch'eng-chih* 樞密院諸房副承旨

Palace censor *Tien-chung shih-yü-shih* 殿中侍御史

Left and right policy critics *Tso, yu ssu-chien* 左右司諫

Assistant office and division chiefs in the Department of Ministries *Chu hang yüan-wai-lang* 諸行員外郎

Assistant hospitality, usher, and Palace Postern commandants *K'o-sheng, yin-chin, ho-men fu-shih* 客省引進閤門副使

Left and right policy monitors *Tso, yu cheng-yen* 左右正言

Investigating censor *Chien-ch'a yü-shih* 監察御史

M

Professor of Imperial Sacrifices *T'ai-ch'ang po-shih* 太常博士

Assistant commandants of the several offices, beginning with that of the Imperial Palace *Huang-ch'eng yi-hsia chu ssu fu-shih* 皇城以下諸司副使

Vice-prefect of a secondary superior prefecture *Chu tz'u fu shao-yin* 諸次府少尹

Assistant office chief in a first class government general *Ta-tu-tu-fu ssu-ma* 大都督府司馬

Presenting officials *T'ung-shih she-jen* 通事舍人

Professor of the Directorate of Education *Kuo-tzu po-shih* 國子博士

Professors of the Spring and Autumn Annals, the Record of Rites, the Mao edition of the Odes, the Book of History, the Book of Changes, of the Directorate of Education *Kuo-tzu Ch'un-ch'iu, Li-chi, Mao-shih, Shang-shu, Chou-yi po-shih* 國子春秋禮記毛詩尚書周易博士

Commissioner of waterways *Tu-shui shih-che* 都水使者

Subprefects of K'ai-feng, Hsiang-fu, Ho-nan, Lo-yang, and Sung-ch'eng Subprefectures *K'ai-feng, Hsiang-fu, Ho-nan, Lo-yang, Sung-ch'eng hsien-ling* 開封祥符河南洛陽宋城縣令

N

Executive assistant of the Court of Imperial Sacrifices *T'ai-ch'ang ch'eng* 太常丞

Executive assistant of the Court of Imperial Family Affairs *Tsung-cheng ch'eng* 宗正丞

Executive assistant of the Imperial Library *Pi-shu ch'eng* 祕書丞

Staff authors *Chu-tso lang* 著作郎

Executive assistant of the Department of Palace Services *Tien-chung ch'eng* 殿中丞

Imperial courier of the inner hall *Nei-tien ch'eng-chih* 內殿承制

Chiefs of the Imperial Caterers, Imperial Medical Service, Imperial Wardrobe, Imperial Chambers, Imperial Equerries, and Imperial Sedans in the Department of Palace Services *Tien-chung-sheng shang-shih, shang-yao, shang-yi, shang-she, shang-sheng, shang-lien feng-yü* 殿中省尚食尚藥尚衣尚舍尚乘尚輦奉御

O

Revisory judges of the High Court of Justice *Ta-li cheng* 大理正

Undersecretary of the heir apparent in the Left Secretariat *T'ai-tzu chung-yün* 太子中允

Left and right critic-advisers of the heir apparent *Tso, yu tsan-shan-ta-fu* 左右贊善大夫

Imperial warder of the inner hall *Nei-tien-ch'ung-pan* 內殿崇班

Warder of the Palace Postern *Ho-men chih-hou* 閤門祗侯

Undersecretary of the heir apparent in the Right Secretariat *T'ai-tzu chung-she* 太子中舍

Librarian of the heir apparent *T'ai-tzu hsi-ma* 太子洗馬

Assistant transmitters of directives in the war section, personnel section, finance section, rites section, of the Bureau of Military Affairs *Shu-mi Ping-fang, Li-fang, Hu-fang, Li-fang fu-ch'eng-chih* 樞密兵房吏房戶房禮房副承旨

Princely councilor *Chu-wang yu* 諸王友

Princely adviser *Chu wang-fu tzu-yi ts'an-chün* 諸王府諮議參軍

Chiefs of the spring, summer, central, autumn, and winter agencies of the Directorate of Astronomical Observations *Ssu-t'ien Ch'un-kuan, Hsia-kuan, Chung-kuan, Ch'iu-kuan, Tung-kuan cheng* 司天春官夏官中官秋官冬官正

P

Librarian of the Imperial Library *Pi-shu-lang* [2] 祕書郎

Assistant staff author *Chu-tso tso-lang* 著作佐郎

Assistant justice of the High Court of Justice *Ta-li-ssu ch'eng* 大理寺丞

---

[2] According to a measure of 981, the group of central government officials from here down were classed as "capital officials" (*HCP*,22,1a).

Executive assistants in the courts and directorates *Chu ssu, chien ch'eng* 諸寺監丞

Judicial investigator of the High Court of Justice *Ta-li p'ing-shih* 大理評事

Professors of the National University and School of Literature *T'ai-hsüeh Kuang-wen po-shih* 太學廣文博士

Chief of invocation in the Court of Imperial Sacrifices *T'ai-ch'ang t'ai-chu* 太常太祝

Ritual supervisor *Feng-li-lang* 奉禮郎

Collator of the Imperial Library *Pi-shu-sheng chiao-shu-lang* 祕書省校書郎

Correcting editor of the Imperial Library *Pi-shu-sheng cheng-tzu* 祕書省正字

Q

Registrars of the Censorate and the several courts and directorates *Yü-shih-t'ai, chu ssu, chien chu-pu* 御史臺諸寺監主簿

Teaching assistant of the Directorate of Education *Kuo-tzu chu-chiao* 國子助教

Professors of the School of Literature, the University, the School of the Four Gates, the School of Writing, the School of Mathematics *Kuang-wen, T'ai-hsüeh, Ssu-men, Shu-hsüeh, Suan-hsüeh po-shih* 廣文太學四門書學筭學博士

Teaching assistant of the Law School *Lü-hsüeh chu-chiao* 律學助教

Chief astronomer of the Directorate of Astronomical Observations *Ssu-t'ien ling-t'ai-lang* 司天靈臺郎

Chief computer of the calendar (of the same Directorate) *Pao-chang cheng* 保章正

Chief of the clepsydras (of the same Directorate) *Ch'ieh-hu cheng* 挈壺正

R

Staff supervisors in prefectures under an Imperial deputy capital custodian, in capital prefectures, in regional command prefectures, and in regional supervisory prefectures *Liu-shou, ching-fu, chieh-tu-kuan-ch'a p'an-kuan* [3] 留守京府節度觀察判官

General secretary of a prefecture *Chieh-tu chang-shu-chi* 節度掌書記

Secretary of a prefecture *Kuan-ch'a chih-shih* 觀察支使

Staff supervisors in regional defense and militia command prefectures *Fang-yü t'uan-lien p'an-kuan* 防禦團練判官

Prefectural judges in prefectures under an Imperial deputy capital custodian, in capital prefectures, in regional command prefectures, and in regional supervisory prefectures *Liu-shou, ching-fu, chieh-tu-kuan-ch'a t'ui-kuan* 留守京府節度觀察推官

Staff supervisor in an encampment prefecture *Chün-shih p'an-kuan* 軍事判官

Prefectural judges in regional defense and militia command prefectures, and in encampment prefectures *Fang-yü t'uan-lien chün-shih t'ui-kuan* 防禦團練軍事推官

Staff supervisors in military and industrial prefectures *Chün, chien p'an-kuan* 軍監判官

The associate officials, office chiefs, and assistant office chiefs of the several

---

[3] Officials from here down belong to the executory class.

prefectures *Chu chou pieh-chia chang-shih, ssu-ma* 諸州別駕長史司馬

S

General executive inspector, executive inspector, and police inspector *Ssu-lu, lu-shih ts'an-chün, ssu-li ts'an-chün* 司錄錄事參軍司理參軍

The inspectors of the inspectorates of the prefectures *Chu ts'ao chu ssu ts'an-chün* 諸曹諸司參軍

The police supervisors of the three capital prefectures *San ching fu chün-hsün p'an-kuan* 三京府軍巡判官

Subprefects *Chu hsien-ling* 諸縣令

Assistant subprefects of capital urban subprefectures *Ch'ih hsien-ch'eng* 赤縣丞

Subprefectural registrar and sheriff *Chu hsien chu-pu, wei* 諸縣主簿尉

Inspector of education or teaching assistant in the several prefectures *Chu chou wen-hsüeh ts'an-chün, chu-chiao* 諸州文學參軍助教

BIBLIOGRAPHY

The following list identifies the sources and studies that have contributed to the present book. It is not intended as an exhaustive bibliography. It is divided in two parts. The first and principal list contains works that serve as the basis for statements in this book and which have been cited as sources. The second list contains a smaller number of works which, while they have not been cited, have proven useful as tools of research in the Sung civil service, or have suggested translations of official terms. Dictionaries and other research tools of general application have been excluded. It may be here noted, however, that dates of birth and death in this book, when not otherwise attributed, have been based on *YNLHP*. The *Concordance des Chronologies Néoméniques* of the Reverend Father Pierre HOANG has been used in the conversion of dates. In problems involving avoided characters, the *Li-tai Hui-tzu P'u* of CHANG Wei-hsiang has been consulted.

Notes on the works listed have in most cases been confined to brief comments; further information and references may be found in the places indicated.

A. WORKS CITED

ANTY, *Concours:* Raymond ANTY, *Le Concours: Mode de Recrutement des Fonctions Publiques; Étude de la Jurisprudence du Conseil de l'État* (Paris, 1936).

AYC: HAN Ch'i, *Chung-hsien Han Wei-wang An-yang Chi,* 50 ch. (Chou-chin T'ang ed.). The collected papers of HAN Ch'i (1008–1075).

韓琦　忠獻韓魏王安陽集　晝錦堂

BALÁZS, Beiträge: Stefan BALÁZS, "Beiträge zur Wirtschaftsgeschichte der T'ang-Zeit." *Mitteilungen des Seminars für Orientalische Sprachen* XXXIV, 1–92 (1931); XXXV, 1–73 (1932); XXXVI, 1–62 (1933).

BINGHAM, *Founding:* Woodbridge BINGHAM, *The Founding of the T'ang Dynasty; The Fall of Sui and the Rise of T'ang; A Preliminary Survey* (Baltimore, 1941).

BRUCE, *Masters:* J. Percy BRUCE, *Chu Hsi and His Masters; An Introduction to Chu Hsi and the Sung School of Chinese Philosophy* (London, 1923).

BÜNGER, *Quellen:* Karl BÜNGER: *Quellen zur Rechtsgeschichte der T'ang-Zeit* (Peiping, 1946).

CARTER, *Printing:* T. F. CARTER, *The Invention of Printing in China and Its Spread Westward* (rev. ed., New York, 1931).

CCT: Ch'ao-ting CHI, *Key Economic Areas in Chinese History as Revealed in the Development of Public Works for Water Control* (London, 1936). Presents useful data, though sometimes inaccurate.

CFTY: FAN Chung-yen, *Cheng-fu Tsou-yi,* 2 ch. (In *Ssu-pu Ts'ung-k'an,* 1st coll.) The collected memorials of FAN Chung-yen (989–1052).

范仲淹　政府奏議　四部叢刊

CHANG, *Reform:* Y. Z. CHANG, "China and English Civil Service Reform." *American Historical Review*, XXXXVII, 539–544 (1942).

CH'I, Ch'un-ch'iu: Ssu-ho CHI, "Professor Hung on the Ch'un-ch'iu." *Yenching Journal of Social Studies,* I, 49–71 (1938).

CH'IEN Mu, Hsiang-ch'üan: CH'IEN Mu, "Lun Sung-tai hsiang-ch'üan," *Chung-kuo Wen-hua Yen-chiu Hui-k'an,* II, 145–150 (1942). A discussion of the power of chief councilors of state during the Sung.
錢穆　論宋代相權　中國文化研究彙刊

CHJ:HKP: CHAO Hui-jen, "Sung-shih Ti-li-chih Hu-k'ou Piao." *Yü-kung Pan-yüeh K'an,* II, no. 2, 19–30. A table of population by prefectures and sub-prefectures, based on figures for the later Northern Sung, largely for the period 1102–1106. Persons, families, and averages per unit are given.
趙惠人　宋史地理志戶口表　禹貢半月刊

CHS:NSTM: CH'ÜAN Han-sheng, "Nan-Sung Tao-mi ti Sheng-ch'an yü Yün-hsiao." *Chung-yang Yen-chiu Yüan, Li-shih Yü-yen Yen-chiu So Chi-k'an,* X, 403–431 (1942).　全漢昇　南宋稻米的生產與運銷　中央研究院歷史語言研究所集刊

CHS:PLHY: CH'ÜAN Han-sheng, "Pei-Sung Pien-liang ti Shu Ch'u-ju Huo-yi." *Loc. cit.* VIII, 189–301 (1939).
北宋汴梁的輸出入貿易

CHS:SJYHP: CH'ÜAN Han-sheng, "T'ang Sung Cheng-fu Sui-ju yü Huo-pi Ching-chi ti Kuan-hsi." *Loc. cit.* XX, 189–221 (1948).
唐宋政府歲入與貨幣經濟的關係

CHS:SYSY: CH'ÜAN Han-sheng, "Sung-tai Kuan-li Ssu-ying Shang-yeh." *Loc. cit.* VII, 199–254 (1936).
宋代官吏私營商業

CHS:YCCC: CH'ÜAN Han-sheng, "T'ang Sung Shih-tai Yang-chou Ching-chi Ching-k'uang ti Fan-jung yü Shuai-lo." *Loc. cit.* XI, 149–176 (1943).　唐宋時代揚州經濟景況的繁榮與衰落　These five articles by Dr. CH'ÜAN all cover a wide range of subjects, and it is necessary to read them all, together with his other writings, to find all the data he presents on any single subject. The first is concerned particularly with the distribution of production and consumption during the Southern Sung; the second with the same subject during the Northern Sung, with special reference to K'ai-feng; the third with the development of a money economy as reflected by governmental finance; the fourth with the private business activities of Sung officials; the fifth with the dispersal of Yang-chou's economic activities after the T'ang.

Civil Service Abroad: L. D. WHITE, C. H. BLAND, W. R. SHARP, and F. M. MARX, *Civil Service Abroad; Great Britain, Canada, France, Germany* (London and New York, 1935).

CKFC: SUN Feng-chi, *Chih-kuan Fen-chi,* 50 ch. (In *Ssu-k'u Chen-pen Ts'ung-shu,* Shanghai, 1934–1935). An encyclopedia of governmental institutions, with special emphasis on the early Sung. Offers material supplementing other classified works. Preface dated 1092 (Cf. Kracke, Sung Encyclopedia).
孫逢吉　職官分紀　四庫珍本叢書

CML: CHANG Meng-lun, *Sung-tai Hsing Wang Shih* (Shanghai, 1948). An analysis of the reasons for the early vigor and later weaknesses of the Sung dynasty.
張孟倫　宋代興亡史

CREEL, Confucius: H. G. CREEL, *Confucius, The Man and the Myth* (New York, 1949). A reconstruction of the life of Confucius, based on a critical reëxamination of the sources heretofore accepted.

CS:TTSLC: CH'EN Shu, "Tung-tu Shih-lüeh Chuan-jen Wang Shang Ch'eng Fu Tzu." *Chung-yang Yen-chiu Yüan, Li-shih Yü-yen Yen-chiu So Chi-k'an,* VIII, 129–138 (1939). A study of the authorship of *TTSL.*

陳述　東都事略撰人王賞稱父子

CTK:SHKTYCS: CH'AI Te-keng, "Sung Huan-kuan Ts'an-yü Chün-shih K'ao." *Fu-jen Hsüeh-chih,* X, 181–225 (1941). The military role of Sung eunuchs.

柴德賡　宋宦官參預軍事考　輔仁學誌

CYTC: LI Hsin-ch'uan, *Chien-yen Yi-lai Ch'ao-yeh Tsa-chi,* 40 ch. (Wu-ying-tien ed.). Historical memoranda by a famous Southern Sung historian. The prefaces to the two parts are dated 1202 and 1216. Much on institutions. (Cf. PELLIOT, IX, 434).

李心傳　建炎以來朝野雜記　武英殿

DORN, Prussian Bureaucracy: Walter L. DORN, "The Prussian Bureaucracy in the Eighteenth Century." *Political Science Quarterly,* XLVI, 403–423; XLVII, 75–94 (1931–1932).

DUBS, *History:* PAN Ku, *The History of the Former Han Dynasty, A Critical Translation with Annotations,* by Homer H. DUBS, with the Collaboration of JEN T'ai and P'AN Lo-chi, 2 vols. (Baltimore, 1938, 1944).

FINER, *Theory and Practice:* Herman FINER, *The Theory and Practice of Modern Government* (rev. ed., New York, 1949).

FRANKE, *Bericht:* O. FRANKE, *Der Bericht Wang Ngan-schis von 1058 über Reform des Beamtentums, ein Beitrag zur Beurteilung des Reformators* (Sonderausgabe aus den *Sitzungsberichten der Preussischen Akademie der Wissenschaften, Phil.-Hist. Klasse,* 1932, XIII). The most careful and accurate available translation of the "Myriad Word Memorial" in a Western language.

FRANKE, *Geschichte:* O. FRANKE, *Geschichte des Chinesischen Reiches, eine Darstellung seiner Entstehung, seines Wesens und seiner Entwicklung bis zur neuesten Zeit. IV. Band, der Konfuzianische Staat, II, Krisen und Fremdvölker* (Berlin, 1948). This volume is particularly useful for its treatment of China's neighboring peoples and their relations with the Chinese, to which topics the greater part of its space is devoted. Completed under wartime difficulties, it depends primarily on *SS* as its source on the Sung. It covers the period from 907 to 1368.

FRIEDRICH, *CGD:* Carl J. FRIEDRICH, *Constitutional Government and Democracy, Theory and Practice in Europe and America* (Boston, 1941).

FUNG-BODDE, Rise: FUNG Yu-lan, "The Rise of Neo-Confucianism and Its Borrowings from Buddhism and Taoism," Translated with Notes by Derk BODDE. *Harvard Journal of Asiatic Studies,* VII, 89–125 (1942).

GOODRICH-FENG, Firearms: L. C. GOODRICH and FENG Chia-sheng, "The Early Development of Firearms in China." *Isis,* XXXVI, pt. 2, no. 104, 114–123 (1946). Addendum, *ibid.,* pt. 3–4, nos. 105–106, 250–251.

Han Kuan Yi: YING Shao, *Han Kuan Yi,* 2 ch. (in *Hou Chih-pu-tsu Chai Ts'ung-shu,* 1891 ed.). Information on Han government by a later Han author.

應劭　漢官儀　後知不足齋

HCLY: CHIANG Shao-yü, *Huang-ch'ao Lei-yüan,* 78 ch. (*Sung-fen-shih Ts'ung-k'an* ed., 1911). An encyclopedia of Sung government, consisting of quotations from various sources, which are indicated by annotations. Preface dated 1145. (Cf. *SKTM*,123,4b; *PSL*,58,20b).

江少虞　皇朝類苑　誦芬室叢刊

HCP: LI Tao, *Hsü Tzu-chih-t'ung-chien Ch'ang-pien*, 520 ch. (Chekiang Shu-chü ed., 1881). This and *SHY* are the most valuable sources for the history of the Northern Sung institutions. Completed in 1174, it is in annals form, recording in much detail the events of the years 960–1127. Its material has been drawn from the reign chronicles (shih-lu), the national histories (kuo-shih), the selected documents (hui-yao), and also private works. References and comments are supplied when sources fail to agree or when an item is not confirmed by a source which might be expected to include it; and problems of textual criticism are discussed. Most of the sources quoted are no longer extant, but the close correspondence of texts quoted from the selected documents with those now found in *SHY* suggests that editorial alterations have been confined to a minimum. Items are usually briefer in form than those found in *SHY*, but the exact date is more often indicated. Much of the original work has been lost, but the surviving portions, recopied from the Yung-lo Encyclopedia, have been supplemented by extracts drawn from other early works based on it. (For further information, cf. ROTOURS, *Examens*, 83–84; PELLIOT, IX, 230–231; *SKTM*,47,6b; *PSL*, 20,17b–18b; *CYTC*,I,4,10b–11a.)

李燾　續資治通鑑長編　浙江書局　實錄
國史　會要

HERRMANN: Albert HERRMANN, *Historical and Commercial Atlas of China* (Cambridge, Massachusetts, 1935).

HHHY: Hsü T'ien-lin, *Hsi-Han Hui-yao*, 70 ch. (in *Kuo-hsüeh Chi-pen ts'ung-shu*, Shanghai, 1935). A work completed in 1211, and based on PAN Ku's history (cf. DUBS, *History*), but invaluable for the study of Han institutions because of its analytical arrangement of materials that were originally scattered. (Cf. TENG-BIGGERSTAFF, 139–140).

徐天麟　西漢會要　國學基本

HK:SK: HINO Kaizaburō, "Sōdai no Kiko o Ronjite Kokō Mondai ni Oyobu. (*Shigaku Zasshi*, XXXXVII, no. 1, 83–105). A discussion of the factors causing inaccuracies in the Sung census returns. (Summary by REISCHAUER, *Harvard Journal of Asiatic Studies*, II, 33–35.)

日野開三郎　宋代の詭戸を論じて戸口問題に及ぶ　史學雜誌

HK:*TRD*: HINO Kaizaburō, First section of article "Sō," in *Tōyō Rekishi Daijiten*, V, 289–297 (Tokyo, 1939). Includes a general description of the Sung economy, with useful statistics.

宋　東洋歴史大辭典

Hsiao Ching: *Hsin-k'an Ch'üan-hsiang Ch'eng-chai Hsiao-ching Chih-chieh* (photolithographic facsimile of 1308 ed., Peiping, 1938). An illustrated edition of the *Book of Filial Piety*, with explanations in fourteenth-century colloquial Chinese.

新刊全相成齋孝經直解

HSIEH, *Government*: Pao Chao HSIEH, *The Government of China, 1644–1911* (Baltimore, 1925). A description of Chinese government under Manchu domination.

Hsing-t'ung: Tou Yi, *Hsing-t'ung,* 30 ch. (Chia-yeh t'ang ed., 1921). Originally a private work, this was revised by the author and adopted as the official code of the Sung in 963 (cf. PELLIOT, IX, 130).

竇儀　刑統　嘉業堂

HTK: Ch'in-ting Hsü Wen-hsien-t'ung-k'ao, 250 ch. (*Chiu T'ung Ch'üan-shu* ed., Chekiang Shu-chü, 1882–1896). Officially compiled after 1747 as supplement to *TK* (cf. TENG-BIGGERSTAFF, 134).

欽定續文獻通考　九通全書

HTS: OU-YANG Hsiu, SUNG Ch'i and others, *Hsin T'ang-shu,* 225 ch. (Po-na ed., facsimile of original ed.). The rewritten official history of the T'ang Dynasty, completed in 1060 (cf. ROTOURS, *Examens,* 56–64).

歐陽修　宋祁　新唐書　百衲

JCSP: HUNG Mai, *Jung-chai Sui-pi,* 74 ch. (Hsin-feng Hung Shih ed., 1875). Historical memoranda of a famous Southern Sung scholar (1123–1202). (Cf. *SKTM,*118,6a; *PSL,*56,3b–10a.)

洪邁　容齋隨筆　新豐洪氏

JK:CCSC: JUNG Keng: "Sung-tai Chi-chin Shu-chi Shu-p'ing" (in *Ch'ing-chu Ts'ai Yüan-p'ei Hsien-sheng Liu-shih-wu Sui Lun-wen Chi,* II, 661–687. Peiping, 1935). An annotated list of Sung writings on ancient bronzes, with introductory remarks on the earlier history of Chinese archaeology.

容庚　　宋代吉金書籍述評　　慶祝蔡元培先生六十五歲論文集

KARLGREN, The Authenticity: Bernhard KARLGREN, "On the Authenticity and Nature of the Tso-chuan." *Göteborgs Högskolas Arsskrift,* XXXII, 1–65 (1926).

KENNEDY, *Geständnis:* G. A. KENNEDY, *Die Rolle des Geständnisses im Chinesischen Gesetz* (Berlin, 1939). A study and translation of the provisions concerning confession in the T'ang code.

KKK: Anonymous Ming compiler, *Kao-k'o K'ao* (in *Hsüan-lang T'ang Ts'ung-shu.*) Lists first palace graduates and, for certain periods, the total number of doctoral graduates, from 960 to 1511.

高科考　玄覽堂

KMPY: CH'EN Chün, *Huang-ch'ao Pien-nien Kang-mu Pei-yao,* 30 ch. (photolithographic facsimile of Sung ed. with Ms repairs, Tokyo, 1936). A brief history of the Northern Sung in annals form, on the model of the *T'ung-chien Kang-mu.* Preface dated 1229. While much briefer than *HCP,* this work is useful for its clear subheadings and for its variant accounts of important events. Since the page numbers of this edition are not clear, citations of it are made by year and month. (Cf. *SKTM,*47,9a. The work is sometimes known as the [*Sung*] *Chiu Ch'ao Pien-nien Pei-yao.*)

陳均　皇朝編年綱目備要　（宋）九朝編年備要

KRACKE, Family vs. Merit: E. A. KRACKE, Jr., "Family vs. Merit in Chinese Civil Service Examinations under the Empire." *Harvard Journal of Asiatic Studies,* X, 103–123 (1947).

KRACKE, Sung Encyclopedia: E. A. KRACKE, Jr., "A Sung Encyclopedia and a Case of Mistaken Identity." *Loc. cit.,* VII, 162–165 (1942).

Kuo Yü: Kuo Yü. (*Ssu-pu Ts'ung-k'an* ed.) (Cf. Chapter I, note 14.)

國語

KYH:*CKYSCT:* KAO Yi-han, *Chung-kuo Yü-shih Chih-tu ti Yen-ko* (Shanghai, 1933). A historical sketch of the Chinese Censorate.

高一涵　中國御史制度的沿革

LCHSWC: WANG An-shih, *Lin-ch'uan Hsien-sheng Wen-chi,* 100 ch. (*Ssu-pu Ts'ung-k'an* ed.) The collected papers of WANG An-shih (1021–1086).

王安石　臨川先生文集

LIN, *Gay Genius:* LIN Yutang, *The Gay Genius: The Life and Times of Su Tungpo* (New York, 1947). The biography of SU Shih is illustrated by liberal quotations from his writings.

LPC: TSENG Kung (?), *Lung-p'ing Chi,* 20 ch. (Ch'i Yeh T'ang ed., 1701). A classified book of historical memoranda, containing valuable information on the first five reigns of the Sung. It bears a preface dated 1142, but the authorship was early attributed, on uncertain evidence, to TSENG Kung (1019–1083). (Cf. *SKTM,*50,3a; *TK,*196,14a.)

曾鞏　隆平集　七業堂

LTKS: CH'ENG Chü, *Lin-t'ai Ku-shih* (in *Shih-wan Chüan Lou Ts'ung-shu*). A collection of historical material concerning the Sung state libraries, and the officials attached to them. Dated 1131. (Cf. PELLIOT, IX, 232.)

程俱　麟臺故事　十萬卷樓

Lun Yü: Lun Yü. (in James LEGGE, *The Chinese Classics,* 2nd ed., rev., vol. II. Oxford, 1893). The *Analects of Confucius* (c. 551–479 B.C.).

論語

MASPERO: Henri MASPERO, Review of KATO Shigeru, *Journal Asiatique* CCXII, 171–172 (1928).

MATTINGLY, *ICSR:* Harold MATTINGLY, *The Imperial Civil Service of Rome* (Cambridge, 1910).

Mencius: MENG-tzu. In James LEGGE, *loc. cit. The Works of Mencius* (c. 372–289 B.C.).

孟子

MI:TS: MIYAZAKI Ichisada, "Tokushi Sakki" (in *Shirin,* 21, 1, 124–158). An explanation of the Sung census returns. (Cf. summary by REISCHAUER, *Harvard Journal of Asiatic Studies,* II, 28–29.)

宮崎市定　讀史劄記　史林

MKCKL: HUANG Ch'ung-lan, *Ming Kung-chü K'ao-lüeh,* 2 ch. (in *Tseng-pu Kung-chü K'ao-lüeh.* Rev. ed. of Chin-ling, Wen-ying T'ang, 1879.) Presents tables of data on examinations in the Ming. Preface dated 1803.

黄崇蘭　明貢舉考略　增補貢舉考略
金陵文英堂

NCC:FCCC: NIEH Ch'ung-ch'i, "Sung-tai Fu, Chou, Chün, Chien chih Fen-hsi." *Yen-ching Hsüeh-pao,* XXIX, 1–56 (1941). An analysis of data on the founding and reclassification of Sung prefectures of the four kinds.

聶崇岐　宋代府州軍監之分析　燕京學報

NCC:SLCP: NIEH Ch'ung-ch'i, "Sung-Liao Chiao-p'in K'ao." *Loc. cit.,* XXVII, 1–51 (1940). A study of diplomatic intercourse between the Sung and Khitan courts.

宋遼交聘考

NCC:STCC: NIEH Ch'ung-ch'i, "Sung-tai Chih-chü K'ao-lüeh." *Shih-hsüeh Nien-pao,* I, no. 5, 17–37 (1938). A study of the Sung decree examinations.

宋代制舉考略　史學年報

NCC:SYFS: NIEH Ch'ung-ch'i, "Sung Yi-fa Shu." *Yen-ching Hsüeh-pao,* XXXIII, 195–270 (1947). The evolution of Sung methods of providing local public services.

宋役法述

NCC:TLCKY: NIEH Ch'ung-ch'i, "Sung-shih Ti-li Chih K'ao-yi." (*Yü-kung Pan-yüeh K'an,* I, no. 6, 8–11; no. 8, 8–10; no. 9, 10–14; no. 11, 12–15; no. 12, 6–8; II, no. 1, 4–9; no. 2, 12–16; no. 4, 5–8; no. 5, 27–31; no. 6, 11–12; no. 7, 28–32; no. 9, 21–23; no. 12, 37–40: III, no. 2, 26–28; no. 3, 32–37; no. 5, 41–43.) Corrections to the monograph on geography in *SS.*

宋史地理志考異

NIIDA, *Tōsō Hōritsu:* NIIDA Noboru, *Tōsō Hōritsu Bunsho no Kenkyu* (Tokyo, 1937). A study of T'ang and Sung legal documents, stressing especially the manuscripts of those periods found at Tun-huang.

仁井田陞　唐宋法律文書の研究

NYSSP: SHEN Ping-chen, *Nien-yi Shih Ssu P'u,* 54 ch. (Ch'ing-lai T'ang ed., 1871). Includes four series of tables: one of reign periods in Chinese history, one of titles of nobility and their occurrence in history, one of councilors of state, and one of posthumous appellations. The author lived 1679–1737. (Cf. ROTOURS, *Examens,* 119–120).

沈炳震　廿一史四譜　清來堂

OU, *La Peine:* OU Koei-hing, *La Peine d'après le Code des T'ang* (Shanghai and Tientsin, 1935).

OYWC: OU-YANG Hsiu, *Ou-yang Wen-chung Kung Wen-chi,* 158 ch. (in *Ssu-pu T'sung-k'an*). The collected papers of OU-YANG Hsiu (1007–1072).

歐陽修　歐陽文忠公文集

PELLIOT: Paul PELLIOT, "Notes de Bibliographie Chinoise." *Bullétin de l'École Française d'Extrême-Orient,* II, 315–340 (1902); IX, 123–152; 211–249; 425–469 (1909). The first article of this series is devoted to the contents of the *Ku-yi Ts'ung-shu;* the second to literature on Chinese law; the third (in two parts) to the work of the bibliophile LU Hsin-yüan.

PHSKTY: PAO Ch'eng, *Pao Hsiao-su Kung Tsou-yi,* 10 ch. (Sheng-hsin Ko ed., 1863). The collected memorials of PAO Ch'eng (999–1062).

包拯　包孝肅公奏議　省心閣

PSL: LU Hsin-yüan, *Pi-Sung Lou Ts'ang-shu Chih,* 124 ch. (Shih-wan Chüan Lou ed., 1882). A carefully annotated catalogue of the collection of Lu Hsin-yüan, supplementing the data to be found in *SKTM.* (Cf. TENG-BIGGERSTAFF, 40–41.)

陸心源　皕宋樓藏書志　十萬卷樓

ROTOURS, *Examens:* Robert DES ROTOURS, *Le Traité des Examens, Traduit de la Nouvelle Histoire des T'ang, chap. XLIV, XLV* (Paris, 1932).

ROTOURS, *Fonctionnaires:* Robert DES ROTOURS, *Traité des Fonctionnaires et Traité de l'Armée, Traduits de la Nouvelle Histoire des T'ang (chap. XLVI–L),* 2 vols. (Leyden, 1947–1948). These two monumental works provide full and carefully annotated translations and interpretive outlines of the primary source of information on T'ang governmental structure and civil service practices, as well as military organization. They give in addition a detailed discussion of the sources for T'ang institutional history. Through their comprehensive indices they serve also as dictionaries of T'ang official terminology.

SCKY: Lɪ Ch'ih, *Huang Sung Shih Ch'ao Kang-yao,* 25 ch. (Tung-fang Hsüeh-hui ed., n.d.). A brief account in annals of the Northern Sung and the first reign of the Southern, useful for comparison and for the lists of officials and other data supplied in connection with each reign. Author active 1190–1241. (Cf. PSL,21,7a.)

李埴　皇宋十朝綱要　東方學會

SCSS: Lɪ Yu, *Sung-ch'ao Shih-shih,* 20 ch. (in *Kuo-hsüeh Chi-pen Ts'ung-shu,* Shanghai, 1935). A discussion of Sung government in analytical form, treating the period 960–1125. The author is known to have been active soon after 1111; the material on later years may be from another hand. It offers material lacking in other histories such as *HCP,TTSL,* and *SS;* it served as a source for *HCLY* and apparently *SS.* The original work having been lost, the present incomplete version was reconstituted from the *Yung-lo Encyclopedia.* (Cf. *SKTM,*81,2a.)

李攸　宋朝事實

SCWC: Suɴɢ Ch'i, *Sung Ching-wen Chi,* 65 ch. (Hu-pei Hsien-cheng Yi-shu ed., 1923). The collected papers of Suɴɢ Ch'i (998–1061).

宋祁　宋景文集　湖北先正遺書

Shih Chi: Ssu-ᴍᴀ Ch'ien, *Shih Chi,* 130 ch. (punctuated ed. prepared by Ku Chieh-kang and Hsü Wen-shan, 3 vols., 1936). Ssu-ᴍᴀ Ch'ien lived about 145–90 ʙ.ᴄ.

司馬遷　史記　顧頡剛　徐文珊

SHY: *Sung Hui-yao Chi-kao,* 200 ts'e (Shanghai, 1936).

宋會要輯稿

*SHY:*CJ: Ch'ung-ju section of the above (scholarship and education).

崇儒

*SHY:*CK: Chih-kuan section of the above (organization and operation of the government).

職官

*SHY:*FYi: Fan-yi section of the above (foreign peoples).

蕃夷

*SHY:*FYü: Fang-yü section of the above (geography).

方域

*SHY:*HC: Hsüan-chü section of the above (methods of recruitment, appointment, and promotion in the civil and military services).

選舉

*SHY:*HFa: Hsing-fa section of the above (law, and judicial and penal administration).

刑法

*SHY:*YC: Yi-chih section of the above (forms observed in court audiences and other governmental activities).

儀制

*SHY:*YF: Yü-fu section of the above (uniforms, decorations, and sumptuary regulations). 輿服

This work, the remaining part of the huge collections of selected documents made during the Sung, is one of the two primary sources for the study of Northern Sung institutions, the other being *HCP.* The materials covering the period 960–1043 presumably come from *Ch'ing-li Kuo-ch'ao Hui-yao,* whose compilation was ordered in 1030 and completed in 1044. The materials for 1043–1067 come presumably from the *Yüan-feng Tseng-hsiu Wu Ch'ao Hui-yao,* a continuation of the former work, ordered in 1070 and submitted to the throne in 1081. Together with later collections of selected documents, these two met partial destruction during successive military disasters. The remaining parts were copied into the *Yung-lo Encyclopedia* after 1403, and recopied from that compendium in 1809–1810, before that in turn was entirely scattered. As a result of its history, the present edition of *SHY* shows large gaps and many scribal errors. But the documents it preserves are still very much fuller than in other available sources. As at present arranged, the documents are classified in seventeen sections; the materials bearing on government and civil service are found primarily in the Chih-kuan and Hsüan-chü sections, and to a lesser extent in the other sections mentioned above.

Most of the material in *SHY* consists of proclamations or approved memorials, with occasional insertions of commentary. Many or most of the proclamations as they now appear have been divested of preambles, some of which may be found in other extant works. Inserted in *SHY* there are, on the other hand, occasional quotations from one or another of the national histories, which but for such quotations here or elsewhere are no longer extant. (Cf. *SHYYC;* TENG-BIGGERSTAFF, 142–144; Introd. to *SHY.*)

慶歷國朝會要　元豐增修五朝

SHYYC: T'ANG Chung, *Sung Hui-yao Yen-chiu* (Shanghai, 1932). A study of the history of the *SHY* text. A detailed table of the contents of *SHY,* included as an appendix, is of particular value since the current edition of *SHY* lacks such a table. The chapter divisions of the table differ somewhat from those of the current edition of *SHY.*

湯中　宋會要研究

SJYS: TING Ch'uan-ching, *Sung Jen Yi-shih Hui-pien,* 2 vols. (Shanghai, 1935). Biographical data and anecdotes, not found in the usual sources, about Sung men.

丁傳靖　宋人軼事彙編

SKTM: CHI Yün and others, *Ch'in-ting Ssu-k'u Ch'üan-shu Tsung-mu,* 200 ch. (Ta-tung Shu-chü ed., 1930). The standard source of bibliographic information on Chinese works. Officially compiled, on the basis of the Imperial Library of Ch'ien-lung, and completed 1782. (Cf. TENG-BIGGERSTAFF, 22–26.)

紀昀　欽定四庫全書總目　大東書局

SLCH: YEH Te-hui, *Shu-lin Ch'ing-hua,* 10 ch. (Sao-yeh Shan-fang ed., 1920). Notes by a famous bibliophile, including much on Sung printing.

葉德輝　書林清話　掃葉山房

SLYYP: WANG Ying-ch'en, *Shih-lin Yen-yü Pien,* 10 ch. (in *Ju-hsüeh Ching-wu,* 1924). Critical notes on the *Shih-lin Yen-yü,* a collection of historical memoranda by the noted scholar YEH Meng-te, which latter were completed after 1136. WANG Ying-ch'en lived 1118–1176. (Cf. *SKTM,*121,2a; *PSL,* 57,13b–14b; Preface to *SLYYP.*)

汪應辰　石林燕語辨　儒學警悟　葉夢得

SMKWC: SSU-MA Kuang, *Wen-kuo Wen-cheng Ssu-ma Kung Wen-chi,* 80 ch. (*Ssu-pu Ts'ung-k'an* ed.) The collected papers of SSU-MA Kuang (1019–1086).　司馬光　溫國文正司馬公文集

SOPER, *Experiences:* A. C. SOPER, *Kuo Jo-hsü's Experiences in Painting (T'u-hua chien-wen chih). An Eleventh Century History of Chinese Painting Together with the Chinese Text in Facsimile* (Washington, 1951).

SS: T'o-t'o, OU-YANG Hsüan, and others, *Sung Shih,* 496 ch. (Po-na ed.). The official history of the Sung, completed in 1345. Generally accepted to be one of the poorest of the official standard histories, it is still indispensable because of the biographies to which the major portion is devoted. The monographs on government and civil service recruitment usually follow verbatim the statements found in *TK,* except that those in *SS* are still further abbreviated. In the edition used they retain some value, for purposes of comparison, however, since they present in facsimile the original edition (with occasional lacunae supplied from the edition of 1480): (Cf. *SKTM*,46,4a.)

托托   歐陽玄   宋史

SSYi: LU Hsin-yüan, *Sung Shih Yi,* 40 ch. (Shih-wan Chüan Lou ed.). Biographies of Sung individuals lacking in *SS.* Preface dated 1906.

宋史翼

SSYT: WANG P'i-chih, *Sheng-shui Yen-t'an Lu,* 10 ch. (*Chih-pu-tsu Chai Ts'ung-shu*). Historical memoranda by an author who received his doctorate in 1067. Much of the original has been lost. (Cf. *SKTM*,140,9b; *PSL*,62,12a–13b.)

王闢之   澠水燕談錄   知不足齋

STPCC: SU Shih, *Su Tung-p'o Ch'üan-chi,* 110 ch. (T'ao-chai Shang-shu reproduction of Sung edition). The collected papers of SU Shih (1036–1101).

蘇軾   蘇東坡全集   陶齋尙書

SYCC: WANG Chih-jui, *Sung-Yüan Ching-chi Shih* (Shanghai, 1935). A brief economic history of the Sung and Yüan dynasties.

王志瑞   宋元經濟史

SYKCSL: Sung-Yüan K'o-chü San Lu (Hsü Nai-ch'ang ed., 1923). Annotated lists of doctoral examination graduates in 1148, 1256, and 1333. (Cf. KRACKE, Family vs. Merit, 109 *et passim.*)

宋元科舉三錄   徐乃昌

T'ang-lü Shu-yi: CHANG-SUN Wu-chi and others, *T'ang-lü Shu-yi,* 30 ch. (*Ssu-pu Ts'ung-k'an* ed.). The Code of the T'ang, with commentaries. Completed in 653. (Cf. ROTOURS, *Examens,* 98; PELLIOT, IX, 125.)

長孫無忌   唐律疏議

TC: CHENG Ch'iao, *T'ung Chih,* 200 ch. (*Chiu T'ung Ch'üan-shu* ed., Chekiang Shu-chü, 1882–1896). A history of China, in "standard history" form, covering a period from early historical times through 618 A.D. (or 907 A.D. in the case of the monographic sketches). The author lived 1104–1162. (Cf. ROTOURS, *Examens,* 85–87; TENG-BIGGERSTAFF, 130–131.)

鄭樵   通志

TENG-BIGGERSTAFF: Ssu-yü TENG and Knight BIGGERSTAFF, *An Annotated Bibliography of Selected Chinese Reference Works* (Peiping, 1936).

TENG, Chinese Influence: Ssu-yü TENG, "Chinese Influence on the Western Examination System." *Harvard Journal of Asiatic Studies,* VII, 267–312 (1943).

THY: WANG P'u, *T'ang Hui-yao,* 100 ch. (Kiangsu Shu-chü ed., 1884). Selected documents of the T'ang. Completed in 961; based largely on earlier such works. (Cf. ROTOURS, *Examens,* 92–93; TENG-BIGGERSTAFF, 141–142.)

王溥   唐會要   江蘇書局

TK: MA Tuan-lin, *Wen-hsien T'ung-k'ao,* 348 ch. (*Chiu T'ung Ch'üan-shu,* Chekiang Shu-chü, 1882–1896). An encyclopedia devoted to the history of Chinese institutions, completed before 1319 by an author who was the son of a Sung councilor of state. A primary source on Sung institutions. (Cf. ROTOURS, *Examens,* 87–89; TENG-BIGGERSTAFF, 131–132.)

馬端臨　文獻通考

TOUT, *ECS:* T. F. TOUT, *The English Civil-Service in the Fourteenth Century* (Manchester, 1916).

TSH:*WCK:* TS'AI Shang-hsiang, *Wang Ching-kung Nien-p'u K'ao-lüeh,* 29 ch. (Peiping, 1930). A study of the chronology of WANG An-shih's career. Author's preface dated 1804.

蔡上翔　王荆公年譜考略

TT: TU Yu, *T'ung Tien,* 200 ch. (*Chiu T'ung Ch'üan-shu,* Chekiang Shu-chü, 1882–1896). A study of Chinese institutions down to about 800 A.D., written between 766 and 801. (Cf. ROTOURS, *Examens,* 84–85; TENG-BIGGERSTAFF, 128–130).

杜佐　通典

TTCCSS: CH'EN Yin-k'o, *T'ang-tai Cheng-chih Shih Shu-lun Kao* (Chungking, 1943). A group of significant studies on the government of the T'ang period, leading to certain novel conclusions.

陳寅恪　唐代政治史述論稿

TTHTSL: CH'IEN Jo-shui and others, *T'ai-tsung Huang-ti Shih-lu,* 20 ch. (*Ssu-pu Ts'ung-k'an* ed.). The sole remaining fragment of the series of Sung reign chronicles. The original work, completed in 998, contained 80 ch. The present edition was made by combining two old Mss, one probably dating from the thirteenth century. It covers the period from 983, 6th month, to 986, 2nd month; from 987, 5th month to 988, 9th month; and from 996, 1st month to the end of the reign of T'ai-tsung. It presents many documents at length, in versions differing from those of other sources, and often including interesting preambles not preserved elsewhere.

錢若水　太宗皇帝實錄

TTS:KHCT: TSENG Tzu-sheng, "Sung, Liao, Chin, Yüan ti K'ao-ho Chih-tu Kai-k'uang." *Tung-fang Tsa-chih,* XLI, no. 12, 34–40 (1945). A brief summary of merit rating procedures, the first three and a half pages covering the Sung. The references for this are mostly to *SS,* especially to the reign annals (*pen chi*).

曾資生　宋遼金元的考核制度概況　東方雜誌

TTSL: WANG Shang? and WANG Ch'eng, *Tung-tu Shih-lüeh,* 130 ch. (Sao-yeh Shan-fang ed.). A history of the Northern Sung including annals and biographies, possibly begun by WANG Shang, and completed by his son WANG Ch'eng by 1186. (Cf. *SKTM,*50,4a; CS:TTSLC.)

王賞　王稱·　東都事略

WCWKYS: WANG Su, *Wen-cheng Wang Kung Yi-shih,* 1 ch. (in Po-ku Chai ed. of *Po-ch'uan Hsüeh-hai,* 1921). A biography of WANG Tan (957–1017) by his son.

王素　文正王公遺事　博古齋　百川學海

WILLIAMSON: H. R. WILLIAMSON, *Wang An Shih, A Chinese Statesman and Educationalist of the Sung Dynasty,* 2 vols. (London, 1935–1937). Particularly useful for the many translations from WANG An-shih's writings presented.

WITTFOGEL-FENG: K. A. WITTFOGEL and FENG Chia-sheng, with the assistance of John DE FRANCIS, Esther S. GOLDFRANK, Lea KISSELGOFF, and K. H. MENGES, *History of Chinese Society, Liao (907–1125)* (Philadelphia, 1949). A systematic and comprehensive survey of Khitan institutions.

WITTFOGEL, Public Office: K. A. WITTFOGEL, "Public Office in the Liao and the Chinese Examination System." *Harvard Journal of Asiatic Studies*, X, 13–40 (1947). This article constitutes a part of Section XIV of WITTFOGEL-FENG.

WTHY: WANG P'u, *Wu-tai Hui-yao*, 30 ch. (Fukien Wu-ying Tien ed.). Selected documents of the Five Dynasties period, completed in 961. (Cf. TENG-BIGGERSTAFF, 142.)

王溥　五代會要

WYHC: YANG Yi, *Yang Wen Kung Wu-yi Hsin Chi*, 20 ch. (In *P'u-ch'eng Yi-shu*). The collected papers of YANG Yi (974–1020).

楊億　楊文公武夷新集　浦城遺書

YANG, Chin Economy: Lien-sheng YANG, "Notes on the Economic History of the Chin Dynasty." *Harvard Journal of Asiatic Studies*, IX, 107–185 (1946).

YFCY: WANG Ts'un, *Yüan-feng Chiu-yü Chih*, 10 ch. (FENG Chi-wu ed., 1788). A geographic description of the Sung empire, partly based on earlier works, completed in 1080. Includes a listing of administrative units, and their previous changes of name and classification. (Cf. *SKTM*,68,2b.)

王存　元豐九域志　馮集梧

YH: WANG Ying-lin, *Yü Hai*, 200 ch. (Ch'eng-tu Wang Shih ed.). An encyclopedia designed especially for students planning to take the special examinations for documentary experts. The author, a preëminent scholar, lived 1223–1296. Useful for generalized interpretations of the facts presented; the interpretations concerning sponsorship seem to some extent derived from *CYTC*. (Cf. RÓTOURS, *Examens*, 96–97; PELLIOT, II, 336; TENG-BIGGER-STAFF, 101–102.)

王應麟　玉海　成都王氏

YHNWC: YIN Chu, *Yin Ho-nan Hsien-sheng Wen-chi*, 28 ch. (Shou-cheng Shu-chü ed., 1910). The collected papers of YIN Chu (1001–1046 or 1047).

尹洙　尹河南先生文集　守政書局

YNLHP: CHANG Wei-hsiang, *Yi-nien Lu Hui-pien*, 17 ch. (Hsiao Shuang Ch'i An ed., 1925). A compendium of data on the birth and death dates of some four thousand Chinese historical personages. (Cf. TENG-BIGGERSTAFF, 210; ROTOURS, *Examens*, 122.)

張惟驤　疑年錄彙編　小雙寂庵

YYY: WANG Yung, *Sung-ch'ao Yen-yi Yi-mou Lu*, 5 ch. (in Po-ku Chai ed. of *Po-ch'uan Hsüeh-hai*). A book of historical memoranda treating the period from 960 to about 1060. The author's preface, dated 1227, claims that it uses only material from official sources, rejecting all "romantic tales." Despite its small scale, it contains much valuable material and interesting comment. 王栐　宋朝燕翼詒謀錄

B. OTHER USEFUL WORKS

Édouard BIOT, *Essai sur l'Histoire de l'Instruction Publique en Chine* (Paris, 1847). This book remains even today valuable for the Sung period, being based on *TK* and carefully done, but one must be on guard against occasional mistranslations.

CHAO Yi, *Nien-erh Shih Cha-chi* (ed. of 1800). Cf. ROTOURS, *Examens*, 115.
趙翼　廿二史劄記

CH'IEN Ta-hsin, *Nien-erh Shih K'ao-yi* (ed. of 1894). Cf. ROTOURS, *Examens*, 113.
錢大昕　廿二史考異

CHIN Yü-fu, "Sung-tai Kuan-chih yü Hsing-cheng Chih-tu." *Wen-shih Tsa-chih*, II, no. 4, 3–25 (1942).
金毓黻　宋代官制與行政制度　文史雜誌

E. D. EDWARDS, "Classified Guide to the Thirteen Classes of Chinese Prose." *Bulletin of the School of Oriental Studies*, London, XII, 770–788 (1938).

J. K. FAIRBANK and S. Y. TENG, "On the Types and Uses of Ch'ing Documents." *Harvard Journal of Asiatic Studies*, V, 1–71 (1940).

P. Eugen FEIFEL, transl., *Geschichte der Chinesischen Literatur und ihrer gedanklichen Grundlage, nach Nagasawa Kikuya, Shina Gakujutsu Bungeishi übersetzt* (Peiping, 1945).

C. S. GARDNER, *Chinese Traditional Historiography* (Cambridge, Mass., 1938).

J. R. HIGHTOWER, *Topics in Chinese Literature* (Cambridge, Mass., 1950).

HUNG Yeh, NIEH Ch'ung-ch'i and others, *Jung-chai Sui-pi Wu Chi Tsung-ho Yin-te* (Peiping, 1933). A detailed index to the historical memoranda of one of the greatest Sung scholars (see *JCSP*).
洪業　容齋隨筆五集綜合引得

———, *Ssu-shih-ch'i Chung Sung-tai Chuan-chi Tsung-ho Yin-te* (Peiping, n.d.). This index makes easily available the contents of the principal collections of Sung biographical information.
四十七種宋代傳記綜合引得

TENG Kuang-ming, "Sung Shih Chih-kuan Chih K'ao-cheng." *Chung-yang Yen-chiu Yüan, Li-shih Yü-yen Yen-chiu So Chi-k'an*, X, 529–682 (1943). Critical notes on the monograph on governmental organization and operation in *SS*.
鄧廣銘　宋史職官志考正

TENG Kung-san, "Sung Shih Chih-kuan Chih Chüeh-yüan K'uang-miu." *Wen-shih Tsa-chih*, II, no. 4, 27–38 (1942). A textual study of the same monograph, with particular attention to the problem of its sources.
鄧恭三　宋史職官志抉原匡謬

TENG Ssu-yü, *Chung-kuo K'ao-shih Chih-tu Shih* (Nanking, 1936). A general history of the Chinese civil service examination system. Copies unfortunately rare.
鄧嗣禹　中國考試制度史

Etienne ZI, *Pratique des Examens Littéraires en Chine* (Shanghai, 1894). Deals with the Manchu period.

INDEX

This index includes the major topics and technical terms in Chinese or in translation that appear in the main body of the book, all proper names listed in Appendix A, all official titles in Chinese or translation listed in Appendix B, and all authors and the titles of all older Chinese works listed in the Bibliography. For persons, official titles, and governmental organs mentioned in the main body of the book and in the texts and footnotes, only the more important references are here included.